EXPANDED
THIRD
EDITION

ADVENTURE HANDBOOK

DREW KNOWLES

SANTA
MONICA
PRESS

ROUTE 66

ADVENTURE HANDBOOK

DREW KNOWLES

Published by: Santa Monica Press LLC
P.O. Box 1076
Santa Monica, CA 90406-1076
1-800-784-9553
www.santamonicapress.com
books@santamonicapress.com

SANTA
MONICA
PRESS

Printed in the United States

Santa Monica Press books are available at special quantity discounts when purchased in bulk by corporations, organizations, or groups. Please call our Special Sales department at 1-800-784-9553.

Library of Congress Cataloging-in-Publication Data

Knowles, Drew, 1956-
    Route 66 adventure handbook / by Drew Knowles.
        p. cm.
    Includes bibliographical references and index.
    ISBN 1-59580-012-3
    1. West (U.S.)--Description and travel. 2. United States Highway 66--Guidebooks. 3. West (U.S.)--Tours.   4. Automobile travel--West (U.S.)--Guidebooks.   5. West (U.S.)--History, Local. 6. United States--Description and travel. I. Title.
F595.3.K67 2006
917.8'3404--dc22
                                    2006008373

Cover and interior design by Future Studio

CONTENTS

Over the years, thousands of individuals have tied their futures and livelihoods to Route 66—individuals who made their livings preparing meals, providing motel rooms, or perhaps offering whimsical diversions to the cross-section of America passing by their doors.

To those individuals, this book is gratefully dedicated.

DREW KNOWLES

Hackberry, Arizona.

OPEN

HISTORIC
US
66

Rod's Steak House, Williams, Arizona.

FOREWORD

by David Knudson

Like so many people who have traveled it in recent years, Drew Knowles fell in love with the Mother Road. I don't mean "love" in the popular, overused sense, but a real love and respect for something very dear. Yet, he is not just another enamored router. Far from it. He has spent many years on and off the road digging into every nook and cranny so he could write this important guide.

As Drew takes you down America's most legendary highway, he tempts you with just enough historical details to make you want to search for more. He shares his secrets for finding unmarked stretches so you can become an informed explorer. He challenges you to travel beyond the route itself, so you can enjoy even more of our country's texture.

If you read and use this guide, there is a very good chance you will change your attitude towards motoring. Rather than simply driving to a location, your trip will become the destination. In fact, this attitude is relatively new in our country. When I was growing up, nearly every trip we took was a series of dots and dashes on the map. You dashed from one dot to the next, then bragged about how quickly you got there. The advent of super highways was our dream come true; so were franchise operations because you could always count on them to provide the same service and products no matter the location. This was what we wanted and it was what tourists from other countries came to see. But today, every country in the civilized world has more than its share of these "modern" conveniences.

Enter the "Heritage Tourist." This breed of foreign and domestic tourist is more interested in experiencing the roots of

The neon still burns at Finn's Motel, St. James, Missouri.

America than the rides at its theme parks—and what better way to do that than to travel Route 66, the route to our roots. As it passes by vintage motels, bustling cafés, colorful trading posts, and through picturesque villages, three time zones, dozens of cultures, and numerous geographic and weather changes, the old road is a microcosm of historic roadside America that every age can enjoy.

So it's time to do something different. Pack up the car, put this guide in the glove box, strap that water bag on the front, and get ready for a serious love affair.

DAVID KNUDSON
Executive Director
National Historic Route 66 Federation

INTRODUCTION

by Michael Wallis

I **was fortunate** to grow up in the 1950s within easy striking distance of Route 66. Throughout the heyday of that fabled highway that Steinbeck appropriately dubbed "The Mother Road," my family, like so many others, used the artery of concrete and asphalt to our advantage.

It was a time when just the act of "getting there" was an important part of the vacation experience. We didn't want to be gypped out of a single moment, so we made the drive an indispensable component of the overall trip. There was an assortment of man-made and natural attractions to visit, tourist traps to survive, detours to avoid, and truck stop meals to consume.

Times may have changed, but Route 66—the highway some folks believed dead and gone—is alive and kicking like never before.

The old road (at least a major percentage of it) survived the attempts of five interstate superslabs that tried in vain to take its place. Today's rendition of Route 66 is a grizzled veteran—tried and true—but with the allure and prestige of an aging celebrity. Sometime ago the highway achieved American icon status and not just because of the physical roadbed or all the historical and cultural treasures that litter its shoulders from Chicago to Santa Monica. The road is much more than remarkable examples of commercial archeology, diverse natural and fabricated attractions, and gentle curves tailor-made for a purring Harley or a speedy Corvette.

Most of all, Route 66 is about people. That is what the road has always been about and that is why it remains active and relevant to this day.

It is inspiring to realize that Route 66 truly is America's highway, just as it has been ever since 1926. Other venerable roads, longer or older than Route 66, crisscross the land, but the reality is that none of them measure up to the Mother Road. Not even close. Through the years, this celebrated highway—despite attempts to do away with it—has persevered. Route 66 has become a destination in and of itself.

Although it seems there is something for everyone on Route 66, there are some exceptions. It is not a road for those who like cookie-cutter culture, food in Styrofoam boxes, or sprawling shopping malls filled with indistinguishable people pawing through look-alike merchandise. Even though franchise restaurants, chain stores, and homogenized fast-food joints have invaded the old highway, the true Route 66 crowd does not fully embrace them.

Route 66ers want kitsch that often is so bad it is good. They go for window decals, refrigerator magnets, salt and pepper shakers, and the other kinds of merchandise sold at the best tourist traps. They crave real hash browns, milk shakes, and berry pies made from scratch and on premises. They like nothing but open road ahead of them. They do not mind taking chances.

Since 1990, when the Route 66 resurgence really began, tens of thousands of enthusiasts from around the globe have discovered that this road is not just another American highway. Neither is it a romanticized corridor of nostalgia that only allows people to return to the so-called good old days. True, Route 66 serves as the definitive symbol of certain key segments of the nation's past, but it is also very much part of the present as well as of the future.

Today, people from around the globe continue to take the open road—the free road. I enjoy showing these travelers the distinct layers of history along the highway. Their numbers are growing. I meet with them in diners and curio shops, at Smithsonian lectures, in university classrooms, and all along the old road. Through these many people and their enthusiasm, my sense of pure adventure and my passion for the highway and its people remains strong. The old road has again become an important part of the nation's cultural scene. Route 66 fans range from commercial archeologists, historians, and American culture buffs to motorcycle club members, students, and the RV crowd.

Still, after they have listened to my stories and words of advice, every traveler needs a good guidebook to help show them the way.

Through the years there have been many books published about Route 66, including guidebooks that have helped legions of travelers traverse the Mother Road.

This particular book, so carefully written by Drew Knowles, is unlike any other. Drew's writing is as smooth as a cup of fresh custard and captures the adventure and excitement of traveling the open road.

The *Route 66 Adventure Handbook* exposes a true slice of America—a nation of movement and energy. This book shows us people living in secret corners and hidden towns that can still be found if travelers merely dare to exit the interstate highway. To do that, they have to believe that life begins at the off-ramp. Then, with the windows rolled down and the radio playing, they can open their eyes to the past and, just maybe, discover something of themselves.

It is a journey worth taking.

Enjoy the ride.

MICHAEL WALLIS
Author of *Route 66: The Mother Road*

The author, with camera, Springfield, Illinois.

AUTHOR'S PREFACE

I **wrote this book** because it's exactly what I need to take with me whenever I travel Route 66, and it is my sincere hope that it can be of similar service to you in your own explorations of the Mother Road.

I began driving, exploring, and photographing what remains of U.S. Route 66 back in 1992. Some might call it an obsession, but it's a passion that has stayed with me ever since, with no apparent end.

I live near Fort Worth, Texas, a considerable distance from the nearest portion of the Route, and so the time that I spend on the Mother Road is precious and comes at irregular intervals. Over the years, my knowledge of Route 66 has gradually expanded by exposure to many things: books and periodicals; conversations with people who live, work, or travel extensively on Route 66; documents on the world wide web; and, of course, my own travels, on which I've spent thousands of hours and taken thousands of photographs.

The problem I had, which this volume seeks to solve, is this: each time I get out on the Mother Road, there are many things I'd like to see and experience myself which I might only have heard or read about up to that time. Invariably, while out exploring the Route, there are things which I remember to investigate, but there are others which I simply forget about until after I've returned home. This book solves that problem by putting all of that Route 66 information in one volume which I can easily take along and refer to, so that each Mother Road excursion can be as jam-packed as possible.

My sincere hope is that the *Route 66 Adventure Handbook* will be of similar service to you as you do your own explorations of Route 66, and that those explorations cause you to appreciate America's Main Street as much as I do.

See you on the road!

DREW KNOWLES
Fort Worth, Texas

PS—ABOUT MY 1957 ATLAS

Throughout this book, you will see mention of something I refer to as "my 1957 atlas." It's a 12 × 16-inch paperbound road atlas, published by Rand McNally in 1957, and containing individual road maps for all 50 states (plus Canada and Mexico).

It was in 1956 that President Eisenhower signed the bill which launched what we today call our Interstate Highway System, and which also started the slow decline of the *old* system of interstate highways, of which U.S. 66 was a part. Therefore, my 1957 atlas depicts Route 66 and her sisters at their zenith, just before our nation's road-building energies were diverted to the creation of a decidedly different type of highway.

I obtained my treasured 1957 road atlas at a local antique mall/flea market, and it has been invaluable to me in my quest to explore everything Route 66 has to offer. To peruse its pages is to take a step back in time, and that's been a journey well worth taking.

**Part of the ambience at the Snow Cap
Drive-in, Seligman, Arizona.**

WHAT IS ROUTE 66, ANYWAY?

In the early years of the twentieth century, America was criss-crossed by a collection of disorganized and poor-quality roads (often no more than dirt paths). That was considered adequate when most travel occurred via horse-and-buggy or railroad. However, the development of the automobile—and especially its mass-production in the 1910s—fueled a demand on the part of the American public for more and better roads.

More and better roads did begin to be constructed, but their construction occurred at a local or regional level, and so development was spotty and haphazard. Naming and marking conventions also varied considerably, making cross-country travel confusing at best.

In 1926, the now-familiar numbered federal highway system was launched. This facilitated the marking of highways consistently across state and regional boundaries. Furthermore, in order to qualify for federal funding and inclusion in the new scheme, highways had to meet standards for surface quality and other criteria. In the beginning, the U.S. highways—including Route 66—were established as such simply by posting the well-known black-and-white numbered shields at strategic points along pre-existing roads to act as guides. The roads thus connected then became part of a "route," even though they had not been originally built as such.

Numbers ending in zero, such as 60, were reserved for the major coast-to-coast routes (as they still are in today's interstate system). The highway between Chicago and Los Angeles, considered to be of lesser importance, was designated U.S. 66.

That highway, which we now commonly refer to as Route 66, began its ascension into America's cultural lore when John

Steinbeck made mention of it in his famous 1939 novel, *The Grapes of Wrath*. It was there that he gave it one of its many nicknames, "The Mother Road." The highway received another boost in public awareness when, just after World War II, Bobby Troup penned his popular song "(Get Your Kicks on) Route 66" while driving to California for a shot at a career in show business. At about that same time, Jack Rittenhouse, realizing that the post-war years would mean increased auto travel in America, published his *A Guidebook to Highway 66* (see bibliography).

During the late 1940s, and throughout the 1950s, America became a much more mobile society, and lots of people began to have firsthand experience using Route 66 either on business, fami-

Staunton, Illinois.

ly vacations, or while moving households. It was during those years that Route 66 experienced its most prodigious growth, while simultaneously gaining its reputation for tourist traps such as snake pits, trading posts, and roadside zoos. Countless Americans today still have fond memories of family trips taken along Route 66 while traveling to Disneyland and other Southern California destinations.

Then in the early 1960s, a national television series was produced, called simply *Route 66*. Although the series was seldom filmed on the highway for which it was named, it served to reinforce the highway's place in popular culture, and in fact is indicative of the status the highway had already achieved.

Beginning in the late 1950s, the United States began building a new set of cross-country highways which would change highway travel profoundly. For a variety of reasons, the new highways (which we now refer to as "interstates") were constructed as limited-access freeways, with only a relatively small number of access ramps, and no roadside driveway access whatsoever. This was the death knell for small roadside businesses all over the country, including those flanking Route 66.

The entire length of Route 66 was functionally replaced by a series of interstates paralleling it—in some cases only yards away from the older highway, but in the majority of cases, far enough away to make it next to impossible for the modern motorist to gain access to the multitude of businesses left high and dry.

An adventure on Route 66 is an opportunity to see exactly what those interstate highways cast aside so many years ago.

WHY TRAVEL ROUTE 66?

You're wearing a pair of tight, ill-fitting shoes. Sure, they're stylish, and they look pretty sharp with that suit of clothes you have on, but the fit is not right. They're confining. Furthermore, it's been a long day and you've been in those shoes so long, and become so acclimated to their shortcomings, that you've stopped paying attention to them. You've repressed your pain, and forgotten what it feels like to be barefoot on a soft, cool carpet of green grass.

Now take off those shoes. Right away, good things begin to happen. The blood vessels in your feet begin to open up, allowing an influx of fresh oxygen and nutrients. The pores of your feet open up and bre-e-e-ath for the first time in far too long. Even the rhythm of your own breathing becomes less strained, and your mind is sharpened. You flex your toes with enthusiasm and think: "Aaah, now that's more like it!" And you wonder how you could have put up with your discomfort for so long.

If you've never driven old Route 66, you're in for a similar sensation. And the analogy is far more apt than you might imagine.

For decades now, highway travelers—you included—have been subjected to an onerous set of circumstances which are, by and large, passively accepted. Furthermore, this condition has been accepted for so long that many of us have either forgotten that things weren't always this way, or—even scarier—may never have known anything different ever existed.

That set of ill-fitting restrictions I'm referring to is of course part and parcel of today's Interstate Highway System. Now, before you accuse me of wrongly condemning America's most ambitious peacetime engineering project in its history, hear me out.

Bob's Big Boy, Kingman, Arizona.

Admittedly, the interstates—like the ill-fitting shoes—are not entirely without practical benefits. They are, after all, designed with graceful, high-speed curves, and enable us to travel from point A to point B in minimal time. We accomplish this with greater fuel efficiency, thanks to the ability to move with unvarying speed. And a limited-access highway is safer from the standpoint that there are no driveways for irresponsible motorists to pop out of unexpectedly. These qualities are quite attractive, particularly to the long-distance truckers among us.

But what are those features costing us? That snazzy pair of oxfords does have a few important drawbacks. Did you ever stop to think of what a tremendous misnomer the word "freeway" is? There's not much freedom in interstate travel. Consider that you are shielded and encapsulated against the world at large. Sealed in your fast-moving mobile cocoon, your perception of the world is distorted. You are cut off from sound and smell by your tightly sealed windows. Open the window, and the buffeting and roaring of the air will cut you off from your senses just as effectively. Visually, the interstate corridor offers only the barest glimpse of the surrounding countryside; your visual stimulation is often limited to mile markers, exit signs of uniform appearance, and perhaps a swath of trees to block your view of anything outside the world of the superslab. This isolation is partly due to the enormous amount of land which America's interstates have taken as their own. There are large swaths of acreage on both sides of the interstate, in the medians, and still more locked up in the countless clover leafs, flyovers, and other interstate-grade interchanges. All of that empty acreage contributes to the interstate traveler's isolation from his or her surroundings.

Furthermore, there are restrictions which make it *unlawful* to attempt to squeeze a little more gusto from the experience. There are minimum speeds which must be maintained, preventing you from taking advantage of whatever paltry visual stimuli might actually be available. There are also prohibitions against non-emergency stopping or slowing, and against turning your vehicle around. No wonder it's hard to stay awake.

Ah, but Route 66. Now there's highway travel for you. Kick off your shoes, because the above restrictions do not apply.

On Route 66, there is healthy stimulation for all the senses, and conditions encourage you to take full advantage. Sensory experience is in no way out-of-fashion on the Mother Road. Smell the new-mown hay and the honeysuckle. Hear the clamor of children playing softball in a nearby park, or the tolling of a church bell. Feel the breeze on your face and know that the coolness signals a change in elevation, or even a new climate zone.

Visually, the difference is even more dramatic. There are schools and stores and mountains and crosswalks and downtowns and trains and depots and rivers and billboards and murals and cafés and menus and humanity.

Don't forget: you can pull over and stop at almost any time to savor it a little more. You can even travel Route 66 by bicycle, horseback, or even on foot, so as not to miss a single nuance—don't try doing that on the interstate!

A few words about the concept of efficiency: efficiency is the maximum of one thing with a minimum of another. For example, an efficient automobile is one that goes maximum miles on minimal fuel; and an efficiency apartment is one with maximum amenities in a minimum amount of space. Significantly, the thing which is maximized ought to be something desirable, while the thing which is minimized should be something either undesirable or expensive. I think that the two examples cited above—the auto and the apartment—fulfill this requirement.

One of the knocks against Route 66 which eventually led to its demise was a call for increased efficiency. The interstates are considered efficient because they transport us with a maximum of speed in a minimum of time. That's well and good. But my point is this: the interstates have had some unforeseen and undesirable side effects, because at the same time that they minimized the *amount* of our time in getting to our destination, they also minimized the *quality* of our time on the road by placing us in an experiential vacuum.

That quality of experience is what you'll put back in your life when you kick off those shoes and travel Route 66.

ROUTE
66

THE BOOK OF REVOLUTIONS

The following text was found printed on the back of what appeared to be a very old paper placemat discovered in the glove compartment of an abandoned '58 Buick somewhere in the American Midwest.

n the Beginning, Man yearned to Move. And in this yearning, he did make use of his own limbs, and he left behind the comforts into which he was born, and did venture out further into the World, and did come upon a Continent in which to build a new Society, and it was called America. And Man saw that it was good.

Ere long, Man put to use the beasts of the field—horses, oxen, asses—so as to make his wanderings in the Continent more speedily, and without fear of bunions. And Man spanned America with his settlements even unto the nether ocean. And he saw that it was good.

By and By, the men spaketh among themselves: "Lo, we have spanned the continent, even unto the nether ocean, and our movements are since limited by that Great Water. Let us now harness the power of the anthracite, and of the other substances of the Earth, and make ourselves conveyances which will allow us to move hither and yon at Will, so that we and our descendants need not forsake our Adventurous Spirit."

And Mankind built Horses of Iron, and placed them on Rails, and moved hither and thither over the land with great Speed, and without concern for the travails which had heretofore plagued him in his meanderings. And he saw that it was good.

And lo, at the dawn of the new Century there was a man from the House of Ford. And he looked out over the Continent and saith: "I shall build an Iron Horse for the Common Man, and it shall not require the use of the rails, and Man shall henceforth be freed from the constraints of Schedules and Timetables forever." And he did build the Lizzie, and her numbers did increase, and she had Dominion over the Continent. And Mankind saw that it was very good.

But anon the People began to murmur amongst themselves: "Yea, verily, whereas our horses and other beasts did steppeth easily over stones and other impediments, and our railroads did have the benefit of iron rails, our private chariots suffer mightily from lack of smooth surfaces. Let us build for America a vast system of Good Roads, that we and our chariots be not hindered in our movements to and fro."

And there dwelled in that time in the Land of the Red Earth, a young man from the House of Avery, and he saith: "Let there be a Great Highway which passeth through my Homeland, and which beareth the number Threescore and Six. And that highway shall bind two of the Great Waters, and shall pass from the Home of the Railsplitter, across the Prairie, and on to Eldorado in the West."

And Mankind built the Great Mother Road, and placed the number sixty-six all along her length, and when she was completed, she did span more than eight thousand *thousand* cubits from end to end. And she henceforth brought the People to the Great Cave at Meramec, to the Great Fish of Catoosa, to the Great Stone Trees in the desert, and, yea, even unto the Mecca of Mickey.

And it came to pass that all along her length, from east to west, there sprang up all manner of conveniences to feed, equip, and shelter the multitudes. And the People saw that it was good.

And these are the Generations of Route 66: Avery, Cuthbert, Delgadillo, Hamons, Redmon—their names are legion.

And as the years passed, the snake keepers and the bull-whip purveyors prospered and did multiply across the face of the Continent. And Great Billboards extolled the virtues of all of Man's creations. And it came to pass that after the Great Conflict, the Movements of humanity and their conveyances along the Mother Road were more than the People had prepared her for, and the Route became choked and overburdened, and the People venturing onto the highway did suffer greatly.

Now there were in that time some Men who had visions of another kind of highway—roads unfettered by urban alignments, narrow bridges, unregulated signage, and the other afflictions which began to plague America's travelers. And a new vision came forth: "Why doth we endure these vexations? Let us create new roads, and cast away the old, that we might increase our average Speed, and thereby bring ever-greater blessings to ourselves and our posterity."

As with Man's earlier visions, that Dream, too, began to take concrete form. And there was yet another hue and cry: "Let us furthermore do away with our regional differences, our dialects, and our former ways of life, and let us instead strive for sameness in all of our works—our hamburgers, our tourist accommodations, and all the rest—so that we are all One. So that whithersoever any of us should go, we should always find exactly the same perfection of Speed and Form and Utility that we seek."

And the People *thought* that this was good.

And generations passed, and the multitudes in their Iron Chariots did move ever more swiftly across the Continent through the use of their Grand Roads; and those Roads were marked in the colors of Blue, and Red, and White; and their numbers did increase mightily.

And the Billboards were torn down by popular decree; and the snake keepers and the bullwhip purveyors were forsaken by the fast-moving masses, and they were soon pushed to the brink of extinction. And the Power and reach of Corporate Enterprise did grow and prosper; and the cherished ideal of Uniformity became Reality: sameness and monotony cast a shadow over each and every ramp-side from one end of the Continent to the other. And ere long, what had once seemed ideal did, in the increase thereof, become like unto a Plague.

And certain of the people therefore became restive, and they began to raise a new voice in the land: "What hath our ambition wrought? Our conveyances do move us more swiftly than ever, and yet each journey seemeth an eternity: the miles, they draggeth; the roadside lunches do boreth; and the tiresome monotony putteth us to sleep."

And there were in that time a small number of Adventurers, men and women for whom the blandness of the Interstates was intolerable. And they raised a Voice across the Continent: "Let us travel the back roads of America, Route 66 and her ilk, and let us furthermore sing the praises thereof, that the unenlightened citizenry may again come to know the joys of the Great American Road Trip."

And they rolled down their windows, and did drive their chariots up and down the Mother Road at a leisurely pace, and their senses were filled with the sweetness of Life, and they took great pleasure in re-connecting with the People and Places and History found all along the Roadside.

And they *knew* that this was truly good.

GET THE MOST FROM YOUR ROUTE 66 ADVENTURE

Ask several people what you should bring with you on your Route 66 Adventure, and you'll likely get several different answers. One well-meaning friend might mention such practical travel items as maps, compass, pen or pencil, notebook, camera, and sunglasses. Another person's suggestion might emphasize such things as proper footwear, layers of clothing, and sunblock. Someone else might recommend an ice chest with bottled water and plenty of trail mix. Oh—and don't forget your cell phone and credit cards.

I travel with most of those things, too. But there is one thing which is far more important than all of the above *combined* when it comes to getting the most enjoyment out of your trip on old Route 66. And that one thing is a Spirit of Adventure. I never take a road trip without it.

In a nutshell, I urge you not to plan to take charge of your Route 66 experience too precisely; instead, plan for the Adventure on Route 66 to take charge of you.

As much as possible, I encourage you to simply "go with the flow." Don't set an itinerary which requires you to make it to city "X" by a certain time of a certain day. Keeping to such a schedule will inevitably cause you to hurry through certain portions of your journey, and there's no way of knowing how much you'll miss by doing so.

Move as the spirit moves you; pause and take in the sights and the sounds of your Adventure as they present themselves to you. Your reward will be a trip like no other.

Duarte, California.

Dare to dare. Try new food and drink, meet some strangers, turn down a road just because it looks interesting or because you're curious as to what's there. This is the stuff of which lifelong memories are made.

Things can change rapidly out on Route 66. What you see today might be gone tomorrow or soon after. Keep your camera loaded and be ready to use it liberally. Film and processing expenses are cheap compared to the other costs of your trip, such as food, lodging, and fuel. This is even more true if you shoot digital, since digital storage media is reusable. Don't scrimp, and don't worry about whether the resulting photographs will be worthy of a museum exhibition or not. If you don't consider yourself an artist, then

Even today, old Highway 66 undergoes fits of construction and re-routing.

be a documentarian. Just record what you see that interests you. It's far too easy to think to yourself: "Well, it's been standing there for 50 years now; I'm sure it'll be there for a few more." Sadly, too often this is not the case. Don't fall into that trap. This is a lesson I've learned again and again over the years, both on and off Route 66.

Bring this book with you. Your navigator can read aloud from it as various points in your journey are reached. Even if you elect to skip a certain side trip, the modest background information can enrich your trip in unexpected ways, sometimes by giving you an appreciation of other features of the countryside.

Incidentally, I certainly don't expect you to take in every feature that I've chosen to make mention of in this *Handbook*. Just pick out some of the ones which most tickle your fancy, or which are most compatible with other attractions you intend to visit, and leave the rest for some other time. A continent is not fit for properly exploring in one outing.

Be cognizant of the fact that the information about various features and attractions is not meant to be authoritative. My objective is primarily to whet your appetite for investigation and exploration. If I provide too much detail in this *Handbook*, it may lessen your own desire to find out more on your own. The key is for you to experience things firsthand, not simply to absorb someone else's research.

Similarly, the lists of attractions and trivia associated with various places are not meant to be complete—they constitute more of a random sampling. How could one hope to compile a list of all of the noteworthy events or personalities associated with Chicago, for example? One of the limiting factors I've used is to eliminate some of the more commonly known attractions which are either already familiar to most people or are featured prominently in published visitors' guides to the areas in question.

Another point about things changing rapidly in 66-land: it took years for me to travel all of the route, and things have been changing the whole time. I have witnessed the disappearance and/or destruction of many distinctive features over the years. Do not be surprised if you find that by the time you use this *Handbook* on your own Adventure, not everything will remain as I've described it. Just consider that a part of the Adventure, and let it make the Mother Road that much more precious to you.

A Spirit of Adventure. Please don't waste your time on Route 66 without it.

TOTAL SALE

GALLONS

DESERT·MOUNTAIN
SUPER

Will Pay For Part
Of Your Trip.

PRICE INCLUDES
11¢ TAXES
PER GALLON

Newberry Springs, California.

HOW TO USE THIS HANDBOOK

This handbook is here to fulfill one objective—to help you get the maximum possible enjoyment from your Adventure on Route 66. That's all. With that in mind, here are a few simple suggestions:

Don't keep your head buried—either in this book or in any other. That's why it's not filled with maps, diagrams, and detailed turn-by-turn descriptions that require close scrutiny. Most of the time, you can follow what's left of Route 66 on your own after reading the "How to Find Route 66" section of this book. That way, you won't miss anything due to trying to drive and read at the same time—plus, it's obviously much safer that way!

Keep this book close at hand at all times. What this book *does* have is a wealth of information on nearby attractions, historical background, fun trivia, and side-trip ideas. As you approach a new town or other landmark, have your navigator (if you've got one) read aloud some of the information from that area, so that both of you will know what to be on the lookout for and can make decisions on whether you're "passing through" or want to stop and take in some of the nearby features more fully. If you're traveling alone, you can just pull to the road's shoulder or into a friendly looking driveway and quickly read about the nearby attractions yourself. That's one of the real advantages of Mother Road driving versus interstate driving—on Route 66, it's okay to slow down, pull over, smell the roses, etc.

You're the boss, so customize your trip based on your own passions and interests. Don't slavishly follow anyone's advice, not even mine. This road trip adventure is all about *your* enjoyment, right? That means that after you've briefed yourself on the area you're entering, make some personal decisions about the things that intrigue you the most. For some people, that'll mean making it a point to seek out each and every architectural treasure mentioned in the entire *Handbook*. But your own tastes might run more toward historic sites or natural wonders or trivia or folk art or whatever—there's something for everyone. So spend *your* time doing what *you* enjoy the most. Ignore the rest, or save it for your *next* Route 66 safari.

Immerse yourself. As you travel Route 66, remember that you are surrounded by the remnants of an enormous support system developed for the transcontinental motoring public in the mid-twentieth century. I urge you to make full use of it. That support system included—and *still does* include—motels, cafés, fuel stations, general stores, and roadside attractions of every description. While this book *does not* attempt to offer a list of these support-system establishments—they are, after all, subject to frequent change—you should nevertheless take advantage of them as the need arises. Many of those old Route 66 businesses today have a marginal bottom line, and would sincerely appreciate your patronage. The other support resource I encourage you to make use of is comprised of the local residents and business operators all along the Route. Inquire locally for advice or directions to local attractions, and I know you'll be pleasantly surprised at the helpfulness of the response. There is also a generous listing of visitors' bureaus, chambers of commerce, and other professional groups in the Travelers' Services section of this *Handbook*. Use those agencies to find out even more local information.

Enjoy!

HOW TO FIND ROUTE 66

U.S. 66 no longer officially exists. The emphasis is on the word "officially." The numerical highway designation system adopted in the 1920s was a system in which pre-existing roads were linked together by being given the same number. A traveler could, then, by following signs bearing that number, arrive at any of the destinations on that highway's route, or gain access to any of the other numbered highways which crossed paths with it. When a given route is no longer needed, for whatever reason, the signs can be removed and the route is no longer recognized as such.

But in most cases, the road itself remains. Although it may no longer carry the federal designation, it is unusual for the pavement to actually be removed and the ground returned to nature. Often, the road is re-numbered by the state or county in which it occurs; other times, the older roadway serves duty as an access road to the limited-access thruway which may have

Interior of the partially restored Kiser station in downtown Alanreed, Texas.

brought about its obsolescence.

Officially, Route 66 ceased to exist when the federal highway authorities ordered the signs removed. But keeping in mind that the route was created in 1926 by the installation of signs marking the way, the only thing preventing a traveler from using the old road today is a lack of knowledge on where to find it without the benefit of all those signs at every turn—thousands in all.

This book will not tell you exactly where each and every turn ought to be made in order to drive old Route 66. Other writers have already attempted this. As the old adage goes, "Give a man a fish and he eats for a day; teach a man to fish and he feeds himself for a lifetime." Similarly, my objective here is to share with you, the reader, sufficient basic knowledge to be able to fend for yourself. A significant advantage to this strategy is that this knowledge will apply for

Ann's Chicken Fry House, Oklahoma City, Oklahoma.

years to come, with little or no regard to how local conditions might change over time. Another advantage is that you will begin to see and discover other old routes in your travels which have undergone the same processes of construction, use, upgrade, re-routing, bypassing, and de-certification as Route 66. I think you'll find that some of those other routes, though not as famous as the Mother Road, are also worthy of exploration, and you'll be well equipped to do so.

In the broadest terms, Route 66 ran (or runs) southwestward from Chicago, Illinois to Los Angeles (technically Santa Monica), California. The next thing for you to take note of is which modern-day highways currently carry that same Chicago-to-Los Angeles traffic. Look at a road map of the overall continental United States if you have one. Today's traffic is borne by a huge network of interstate highways. It turns out that Route 66 was replaced by not one, but *five*, modern highways, none of which bears the number 66. The series which supplanted Route 66 is: I-55 from Chicago, Illinois to St. Louis, Missouri; I-44 from St. Louis across the state of Missouri and all the way to Oklahoma City, Oklahoma; I-40 from OKC to Barstow, California; I-15 from Barstow to roughly San Bernardino, California; and I-10 from there to the Pacific coast at Santa Monica. This is the general corridor in which you'll be traveling in order to experience 66.

This brings us to the first rule in learning to fish: be on the lookout for secondary roads which more or less parallel the interstate highways mentioned in the paragraph above. This goes for roads which take us to a destination city—a city formerly on old Highway 66—and not necessarily a road which literally runs alongside the freeway within sight of it. The main narrative section of this book points out most of these Route 66 towns. Your strategy, then, in keeping to the old route, should be to avoid the interstate whenever possible, and move from one town to the next using secondary roadways. In many cases, this is authentic Route 66 pavement.

The second consideration is the simplest and most obvious:

Figure A - Examples of Business Loop sign (green & white) and Historic Route 66 sign (brown & white).

the placement of "Historic Route 66" signs. In the last several years, the eight states along Route 66 have made great strides in getting the old road marked. Unfortunately, there are considerable gaps in sign placement, so that relying solely on them will drive you off course fairly quickly in many cases. However, you'll find that by keeping on the lookout for those friendly brown-and-white signs, you'll more easily keep to the route and be able to enjoy the sights and sounds thereon, without having your nose perpetually buried in a mile-by-mile guide or map. In places where the old road has been buried or otherwise obliterated, and you are forced to use the interstate, quite often the next exit which includes a stretch of Route 66 will have the Historic 66 symbol on the big green exit sign. This enables you to travel a minimum amount of the sleep-inducing superslab before returning to the central theme of your trip.

Very closely related to the foregoing is the third fishing strategy: "business loop" routes. Again, this is helpful when you have been forced to use the interstate for a distance. In many of the larger cities on Route 66, the old route through town will be desig-

At the site of the former Oasis Drive-in, Lexington, Illinois.

nated "Business Loop X," where the X stands for the number of the interstate that supplanted 66. For example, in the city limits of Albuquerque, New Mexico, and Amarillo, Texas, the path of Route 66 is marked with green signs designating it Business Loop I-40. Similarly, in Springfield, Missouri, Route 66 is marked Business Loop I-44. Keep in mind that in cities such as these, the path of Route 66 in most cases changed several times over the years. The alignment marked in this way is typically the last alignment of 66 prior to its demise as an official route. The earlier alignments will go either unmarked, or may bear the brown-and-white "historic" signs. Exploration is the order of the day.

Some of the rest of our fishing tips are a little more subtle, and will draw upon your powers of reasoning and observation a little more. This makes locating a vintage stretch of old 66 all the more satisfying, however.

For reasons of economy and expediency, most routes of any kind are established along the paths of previously existing routes. Just as immigrant trails often followed older trade routes of Indians or trappers, Route 66 and others like her were constructed along right-of-way corridors established earlier by the railroads. Railroad tracks, then, are often an excellent guide to where the earlier alignments through a region are to be found. Given a choice between two alignments which will eventually reach the same destination, in most cases the one physically following the RR tracks more closely is the older route. Over time, as the highway has been widened or otherwise upgraded, the newer alignment tends to be placed farther from the tracks. An instructive example of this can be found along the stretch of Route 66 between Sayre and Erick, Oklahoma. Two lanes of Route 66 were originally constructed just a few yards to the south side of the railroad right-of-way. Later, the highway was

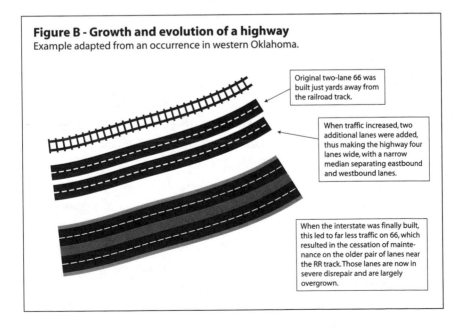

Figure B - Growth and evolution of a highway
Example adapted from an occurrence in western Oklahoma.

Original two-lane 66 was built just yards away from the railroad track.

When traffic increased, two additional lanes were added, thus making the highway four lanes wide, with a narrow median separating eastbound and westbound lanes.

When the interstate was finally built, this led to far less traffic on 66, which resulted in the cessation of maintenance on the older pair of lanes near the RR track. Those lanes are now in severe disrepair and are largely overgrown.

increased to four lanes by the addition of a median and two east-bound lanes further still to the south. Then, when Interstate 40 was constructed, it was placed much farther south. The presence of I-40 resulted in diminished traffic on the older highway, and it was downgraded to two lanes by ceasing maintenance on the oldest two lanes near the railroad track. This is what the visitor sees very clearly today in traveling these several miles in western Oklahoma, and it's one of my favorite features. It's as though one can literally read the historical journal of the highway in this area.

Another tip-off to the location of old Route 66 has to do with some of the ancillary structures associated with it. In more urban areas, this means being observant of buildings—and building remains—which seem to have travelers' needs as their focus. Examples are motels, cafés, and gasoline stations which originate in the era when the old road was in its development (1930s) and growth (1945–55) stages. In small towns which were not crossed by other major highways, this is often simple. In larger cities which may have been hubs for more than one cross-country highway, it becomes more difficult to discern one from another, especially in light of the fact that multiple routes would often follow the same streets for a portion of their journey through town.

In more rural areas, bridges can be excellent indications of a Route 66 alignment. The federal highway system, Route 66 included, was originally formed in the 1920s from pre-existing roads. Shortly thereafter, efforts were undertaken to improve these roads, many of which were not even paved at first. In the late 1920s and throughout the 1930s, many small bridges were constructed during the process of improving the country's network of interstate highways. The bridges built during this period are not only often quite distinctive in design, they also sometimes bear a small plaque or medallion indicating the year of construction. Many of these were projects of the Works Progress Administration, and, in keeping with their dates of origin, exhibit an almost Art Deco appearance. A case

in point is that often there will be
an access road on either side of the
interstate, and you might suspect
that one of these might be old
enough to be Route 66. One of the
clearest indications is the type of
bridges constructed for each of the
two candidates. Often, one of the
two will have bridges which are
easily 50 or more years old, while
the other will have bridges of a
decidedly more modern, less
embellished style. The latter may
have been built at the time of the
interstate's construction for practi-

**A country scene alongside
Route 66 in central Illinois.**

cal reasons, such as access to properties on that side of the freeway.

Somewhat related to the last point about structures to be
found on old 66, another location method has to do with construction methods used in building the highway itself. Road construction in the early- to mid-twentieth century was not as advanced as
in later years, nor were funds as readily available. This is evident in
the fact that the older highways, such as Route 66, appear to follow
the contours of the landscape more closely than more modern
roads. Route 66 tends to rise and fall with the shallow hills and
depressions in its path, and also to curve around prominent geographic features, like mesas. Modern highways, the interstates especially, tend to exhibit considerable modification of the terrain—
blasting of hills and filling of depressions occur more regularly,
while curves tend to be fewer and more gradual than in the case of
the older highways, such as 66.

This results in a very important fact: there are many, many
miles of Route 66 which have been literally cut to pieces by the
interstates. Because the old highway took more turns and curves,

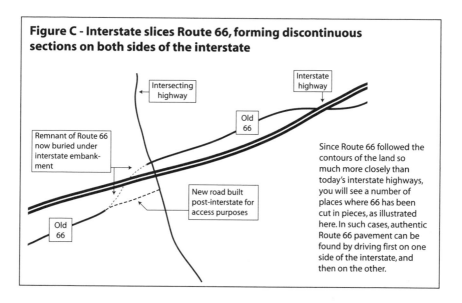

Figure C - Interstate slices Route 66, forming discontinuous sections on both sides of the interstate

Interstate highway

Intersecting highway

Old 66

Remnant of Route 66 now buried under interstate embankment

New road built post-interstate for access purposes

Old 66

Since Route 66 followed the contours of the land so much more closely than today's interstate highways, you will see a number of places where 66 has been cut in pieces, as illustrated here. In such cases, authentic Route 66 pavement can be found by driving first on one side of the interstate, and then on the other.

while the modern interstate is much straighter and more direct, old portions of legitimate Route 66 are often found on both sides of a stretch of interstate highway, having been severed by the straighter cut of modern building methods. So, sometimes you'll need to keep the superslab to your left, and then you might need to cross to the other side and keep it to your right awhile in order to travel authentic Route 66 miles.

Another structural difference you're sure to note in many parts of Route 66 is the use of sectioned concrete rather than the continuous asphalt so prevalent today. This leads to a reassuring *thump, ka-thump, ka-thump* as your tires repeatedly hit the expansion seams in the roadway. You will find some excellent stretches of this type. For me, it evokes a nostalgia for road trips long past.

Finally, one last indication of an old highway alignment. In some cases, when a section of the Mother Road was taken out of service, the pavement was actually taken up and hauled away, leaving a scar in the earth. There are several places between Chicago and Los Angeles where you can see evidence of this. In many cases, even decades later, the grass or other vegetation which re-populates the old roadbed exhibits a different color or texture than that on the undisturbed ground. This can be particularly pronounced in the more arid western portions of the route, where soil breakdown and other changes take place much more slowly than in the east. Keep your eyes peeled for swaths of vegetation that look just a little different than their surroundings, are one to two lanes wide, and alternately approach and diverge from the pavement on which you're driving. These are the ghosts of extinct roadways.

To summarize:

- Be aware of the general direction and next destination town of the highway. Look for older, less-used roads which take you to that next Route 66 town.

- Look for and take advantage of the brown-and-white Historic

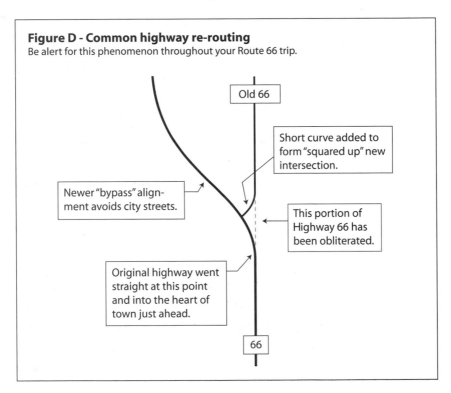

Figure D - Common highway re-routing
Be alert for this phenomenon throughout your Route 66 trip.

Old 66

Short curve added to form "squared up" new intersection.

Newer "bypass" alignment avoids city streets.

This portion of Highway 66 has been obliterated.

Original highway went straight at this point and into the heart of town just ahead.

66

Route 66 signs. These are found not only in rural stretches, but sometimes as a feature of an interstate exit sign.

🌑 In larger cities, be aware that the green Business Loop signs often are used to designate old 66 through town, albeit only the most recent alignment. But also note that following these signs strictly will always return you to the interstate. As you near the interstate after having passed through such a city, be on the lookout for a more authentic route by way of which you could continue without the need to return to the interstate.

🌑 Original stretches of highway are often very close to the shoulder of the railroad tracks in the area. As a general rule, the closer to the railroad, the older the alignment.

🌑 Look for telltale period structures. The prime years of Route 66 occurred prior to the mid-1950s, so look for travel-oriented businesses (or buildings which used to house such businesses) dating from the same era. Other helpful indications include small bridges crossing ravines, especially if constructed in the WPA era.

🌑 Look at the character of the road itself. Older highways such as Route 66 followed the lay of the land, rising and falling with the natural contours, with little or no evidence of large-scale earthmoving. Also, be observant of the road surface itself; a road constructed of poured concrete may be vintage Route 66.

🌑 Finally, look for telltale signs in the local vegetation for evidence of old roadbed that is either severely overgrown or has had the pavement completely removed.

Keep the above recommendations in mind, and in no time at all you'll be ferreting out old alignments of Route 66 like a pro. Now, let's get to it!

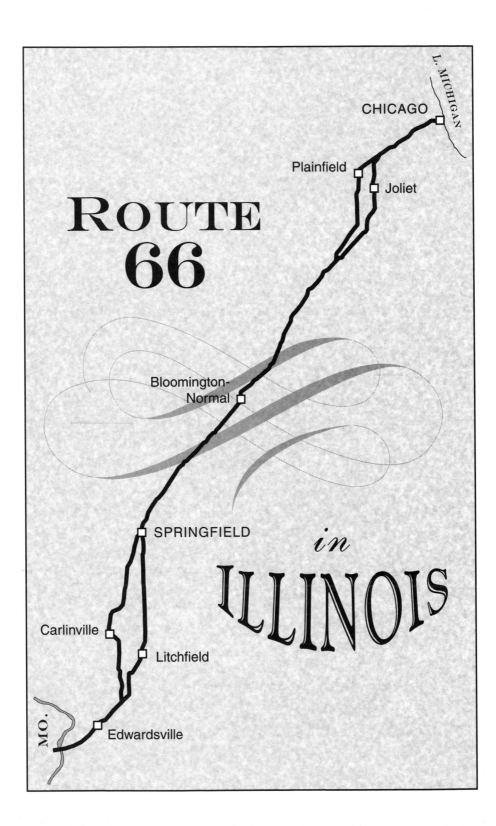

ROUTE 66

L. MICHIGAN

CHICAGO

Plainfield

Joliet

Bloomington-
Normal

SPRINGFIELD

in

ILLINOIS

Carlinville

Litchfield

MO.

Edwardsville

ILLINOIS

Route 66 begins in Illinois, near the shore of Lake
Michigan. Of course, one can just as easily begin a tour of
Route 66 from its western terminus in California, but there
are good reasons not to. Traditionally, the Mother Road runs west-
ward, from Chicago to Santa Monica, just as the United States of
America has always been a westward-moving nation.

The U.S. began as a small grouping of states huddled along
the Atlantic coast. To the west, the future states of Kentucky and
Tennessee were wilderness. Ohio and Indiana were settled by a few
intrepid farmers for the value of their soil. Illinois was at that time
considered The Northwest, and about as far west as any "American"
semblance of civilization existed. Over the generations, more and
more of that West has been tamed, and the outposts of civil society
have moved westward as well.

Traveling Route 66 from east to west, then, you will be following the well-worn path of this country's very development. The
countryside will unfold before you just as it did for the American
people in their conquest of the continent several generations ago,
almost as though you had mastered time travel. You will be richer
for the experience, because you will come away feeling a kinship for
the brave souls who pushed America's boundaries and made her
what she is today.

Inseparable from the story of westward movement is the
availability of water, both as transportation and as sustenance. The
development of Chicago as the outpost of civilization it came to be
was largely due to its being at the far end of a string of lakes and
other navigable watercourses. For many reasons, water sources are
conducive to settlement, while a scarcity of water is a severe hin-
drance to any development. It is no accident, then, that Chicago, St.
Louis, and Los Angeles are the largest cities on Route 66—they are

located at the route's three largest water sources: Lake Michigan, the Mississippi River, and the Pacific Ocean, respectively.

As you move westward on Route 66, the story of water is one which the observant traveler will read all along the way. West of St. Louis, there is a gradual decrease in water availability and a simultaneous decrease in population density. The rivers that Highway 66 encounters are smaller, and the cities which dwell on the banks of those rivers are proportionately smaller as well.

CHICAGO

The famous Chicago fire of 1871, which may or may not have been caused by Mrs. O'Leary's cow, utterly destroyed the city. Afterward, the city made a conscious effort to rebuild using more durable materials and superior building methods so that the new Chicago would stand the ravages of time and nature. More than a century later, the city continues to take pride in its architecture. If you are at all interested in the art and science of architecture, it is worth your while to take advantage of some of the countless tours available. Some of the most well-known tours take place on the water, and launch from either the Chicago River or Lake Michigan. Other tours, which are bus-, air-, trolley-, or bicycle-based, are also available.

Chicago was the scene of the World's Columbian Exposition in 1893, the grounds of which were designed by Frederick Law Olmstead, who also designed New York's Central Park, the campus of Stanford University, and other acclaimed outdoor spaces. It was at the 1893 Exposition that George Washington Gale Ferris introduced the now-familiar Ferris wheel. The original was 250 feet tall, and had 36 cars, each with a capacity of 60 passengers. That original wheel was later moved and used at the 1904 fair in St. Louis. Two lions, which graced the Exposition's Palace of Fine Arts building, have now been made a part of the **Art Institute of Chicago**, where westbound Route 66 begins.

The Exposition of 1893 made some other memorable, or even permanent, imprints. It was there that Cracker Jack was first introduced, later immortalized in the 1908 song "Take Me Out to the Ball Game." Little Egypt, otherwise known as Catherine Devine, scandalized the fair by performing the hoochee-coochee in scanty attire (some say in the nude); the model for Aunt Jemima was a woman named Nancy Green, a cook who advertised food products at the Exposition; and, visitors enjoyed the first-ever public use of electric lighting. The Exposition was also the scene where hot dogs were first served on buns. The vendor, A. L. Feuchtwanger, was handing out white gloves with the sausages so that his customers' hands wouldn't be scalded. To his initial dismay, the gloves were not being returned as he had intended, and so he began substituting bread instead.

Chicago once had a less-than-savory reputation as the home of the underworld. Gangland slayings were for a time not uncommon. The infamous St. Valentine's Day Massacre occurred in 1929 at the **SMC Cartage Company** at 2122 Clark St. That building was demolished shortly after its use as the set for a film based on the event starring Jason Robards and George Segal.

Outlaw John Dillinger was gunned down by law enforcement officials on July 22, 1934, outside the **Biograph Theater** at 2433 N. Lincoln Avenue, where Dillinger had just viewed the gangster film *Manhattan Melodrama*. There is a plaque there to mark the occasion. The leader of the FBI contingent was Melvin Purvis, who committed suicide in 1960 using the same pistol which had been given to him by his fellow officers to commemorate Dillinger's violent end.

Chicago played host in 1933 to the Century of Progress Exposition. It was there that Sally Rand made her splash by riding a white horse to the fair, "attired" more or less as Lady Godiva. Her main act consisted of an essentially nude dance routine which included the strategic use of ostrich feathers. This caused such a sensation that she was able to parlay it into a career which lasted some 30 years.

The 1933 Exposition also brought the first aerial tramway, the first public demonstration of stereophonic sound reproduction, and the debut of Grant Wood's now-famous painting, *American Gothic*. A former student at the Art Institute of Chicago, Wood intended his painting as a sort of spoof of the Holbein style.

Chicago Fire

The Chicago fire of 1871 is a well-known event. What most people don't know is that on the same date in nearby Peshtigo, Wisconsin, there was a "forest fire" that consumed more than a million acres and claimed 1,182 lives. That's more than four times the lives lost in the Chicago fire (250). Over 400 of the dead were buried in mass graves due to the fact that, in many cases, there were not enough survivors left to identify the bodies.

CHICAGO HOME-GROWN

Chicago gave birth to the mail-order catalog business about 100 years ago. This is the home of Sears Roebuck, Montgomery Ward, and Spiegel. Other famous commercial names centered here include Marshall Field, Hertz Rent-A-Car, Wrigley, Yellow Cabs, Kimball Pianos, Schwinn Bicycles, J. L. Kraft, and Oscar Mayer. It was Gustavus Swift, of the meat-packing firm Swift & Company, who made the famous remark that he used every part of the pig but the squeal. The Oscar Mayer wienermobile first appeared here in 1936. Upton Sinclair wrote his classic book, *The Jungle*, about the Chicago stockyards and some of the deplorable conditions therein, which later resulted in the Pure Food & Drug Act of 1906.

In 1896, the zipper was invented here in Chicago by Whitcomb L. Judson, who called it the hookless fastener. The pinball machine was invented here in 1930 by the In & Outdoor Games Company. World-famous Twinkies were invented in nearby Schiller Park by James Dewar, manager of the Continental Baking Company's Hostess Bakery, also in 1930. Chicago was home to Scott, Foresman & Company, publishers of the Dick and Jane readers, beginning in 1909. Brach's Candies originated in Chicago, and in 1977 the heir to the Brach fortune checked out of the Mayo Clinic and was never seen or heard from again—with a fortune estimated at 45 million dollars, she is considered the richest woman ever to have disappeared without a trace.

Ernest Hemingway and Edgar Rice Burroughs grew up in nearby Oak Park. Walt Disney was Chicago-born, but moved to Marceline, Missouri as a young child because the neighborhood here was considered too rough. Chicago was the birthplace of Raymond Chandler, creator of the Philip Marlowe detective character, and known for works such as *The Big Sleep* and *Double Indemnity*. Nat "King" Cole grew up in Chicago after moving here from Montgomery, Alabama as a child. Dick Tracy was created in 1931 for the Chicago *Tribune* by Stephen Gould.

CHICAGO ATTRACTIONS

The **Chicago Historical Society** is the city's oldest cultural institution, having been established in 1856. The museum traces the city's development from outpost through the present day, with a permanent display pertaining to America in the Age of Lincoln. Clark St. at North Ave.

The **Chicago Water Works** is at Pearson St. and Michigan Ave. The water tower was one of the few structures in Chicago to survive the 1871 fire. It now houses a visitor center where you can purchase half-priced, day-of-performance theater tickets. There is also a gallery of photographs by some of Chicago's own native talent.

Dearborn Station, a National Landmark in the Romanesque style, has been converted to a mall and marketplace. 400 S. Dearborn.

The **Charnley-Persky House** is at 1365 N. Astor St. Tours are conducted in this Louis Sullivan-Frank Lloyd Wright-designed Gold Coast building.

Dating from the early 1880s, the **Pullman Historic District** is the country's first planned industrial community. Guided walking tours are available at 11141 S. Cottage Grove Ave. Within the district are the Greenestone Church, the Hotel Florence Museum, and the A. Phillip Randolph Pullman Porter Museum Gallery. The Pullman Porter Museum features an outstanding collection of historical photographs.

The **Near South Side** neighborhood includes the Glessner and Widow Clarke houses, which were constructed immediately after the fire of 1871 and thus stand as two of the oldest buildings in town. Also in this neighborhood is the Illinois Institute of Technology, which has a campus designed by Mies Van Der Rohe, of Bauhaus fame.

The **Prairie Avenue Historic District** (1800 S. Prairie Ave.) includes the Clark House Museum, housed in the oldest residence in the city (1836). The Clark House, designed in Greek Revival, stands at 1827 S. Indiana.

The residences in the 3800 block of **Alta Vista Terrace** are something a little bit peculiar. Each house on one side of the street has a twin (with only minor variations) on the opposite side of the street in exactly the same order. But, since the two series begin at opposite ends of the block, only in the center of the block do the designs directly across from one another match.

The **Chinatown** district has its hub at Wentworth and

Cermack, and even maintains its own chamber of commerce.

Chicago's **Hotel Intercontinental** has its own tape-recorded tours. It started out in 1929 as the Medinah Athletic Club, and its world-class, lavishly decorated swimming pool is where Olympic gold medalist Johnny Weissmuller did some of his training during his years portraying Tarzan on the big screen. 505 N. Michigan Ave.

The **Tribune Tower**, which houses the famous newspaper, was completed in 1925 following a design competition among several distinguished architectural firms. The building includes fragments of some 120 architectural icons from around the world embedded in its walls, including the Reims Cathedral and the Great Wall of China (435 N. Michigan Ave). Right across from Tribune Tower is the world-famous **Wrigley Building**.

Accessible through a subway-like entrance in front of the Tribune building is the **Billy Goat Tavern**, made famous by *Saturday Night Live*'s "cheese-boiga" routine. 430 N. Michigan Ave.

Speaking of eateries, Chicago has myriads of them. But one of the more out-of-the-ordinary ones is the **Weber Grill Restaurant**, at 539 N. State St. All meals are prepared on actual Weber-manufactured grills, much like the one you may have at home. They're fired by charcoal, just like yours, and you can watch your food being prepared in "backyard" fashion. Surrounding the patio is a railing made from Weber grill cooking grates.

The **Chicago Athenaeum** is a museum dedicated to architecture and design. Included are drawings, sketches, models, and furnishings. 6 N. Michigan Ave.

Housed in a landmark structure, the Chicago Cultural Center, is the **Museum of Broadcast Communications**, at 78 E. Washington. Included are thousands of hours of tapes from the glory days of radio, as well as Edgar Bergen's troops: Charlie McCarthy, Effie Klinker, and Mortimer Snerd all reside here.

The **Museum of Contemporary Photography** is the

only museum in the Midwest devoted entirely to photography as an art form. 600 S. Michigan Ave.

The **Museum of Holography**, at 1134 W. Washington Blvd., has over 200 three-dimensional artworks on display, and is the only museum in the United States devoted exclusively to holography as both a science and an art form.

The **Polish Museum of America**, at 984 N. Milwaukee Ave., tells the story of Polish immigration to the new world, Chicago in particular, which is said to be the home of the largest Polish population in the world outside of Warsaw.

The **International Museum of Surgical Science** is housed in a landmark lakeside mansion constructed by one of the heirs to the Diamond Match Company fortune. The museum features more than 10,000 display items, and traces the art and science of surgery from its primitive beginnings to the present day.

Chicago, Illinois.

1524 N. Lake Shore Drive.

The **American Police Center & Museum** at 1717 State St. covers the history of women in law enforcement.

Eli's Cheesecake World is near O'Hare Airport, at 6701 W. Forest Preserve Drive. Eli's makes about 30,000 cheesecakes daily, and there are about 62,000 square feet of bakery, café, gift shop, and visitor center for you to enjoy. There are taste tests, too, of course.

GREATER CHICAGO

Nearby **Oak Park** is the home of the **Frank Lloyd Wright Home and Studio**, at 951 Chicago Avenue. Oak Park features more than 20 of Wright's designs, with tours available.

Oak Park was also the boyhood home of **Ernest Hemingway**. His birthplace is at 339 N. Oak Park Ave., and a museum containing first editions and the author's diary is just a short walk away at 200 N. Oak Park Ave. Visitors are encouraged to begin their tour at the museum.

Within Greater Chicago is **Des Plaines**, home of the first franchised McDonald's restaurant. Their first restaurant, run by the McDonald brothers themselves, was in San Bernardino, California. This was the first one run by Ray Kroc, a former salesman who liked the McDonalds' concept and bought them out. Closed in 1983, it re-opened a couple of years later as the **McDonald's Museum** (400 N. Lee St). Of course, McDonald's is the organization which started the demise of so many mom-and-pop enterprises, and so is actually antithetical to Route 66.

Also in Des Plaines is the home of serial murderer **John Wayne Gacy, Jr.**, at 8213 W. Summerdale Ave., and the **Chicagoland Sports Hall of Fame**, at 1150 N. River Rd.

In the community of **Niles** is a half-size replica of the world-famous **Leaning Tower of Pisa**. It was constructed in the

1930s, and is located on the grounds of the local YMCA at 6300 W. Touhy Avenue.

NEAR CHICAGO

In the community of **Wadsworth**, Illinois, stands a very unusual residence. The **Pyramid House** is notable not for having an outstanding architectural pedigree, like so many Chicago structures, but for being shaped more or less like the Great Pyramids of Giza. It includes a moat, miniature sphinxes, and a 55-foot-tall, 200-ton statue of Ramses II. The house is open by appointment. Take I-94 north to Highway 132, then go east and turn left at Dilley's Road. 708-662-6666.

Wadsworth is also home to Tempel Farms, where you can see world-renowned Lipizzan horses perform. After the performance, check out the collection of antique carriages on the grounds. 17000 Wadsworth Rd.

The **Illinois Railroad Museum** is in nearby **Union**, Illinois, northwest of Chicago. It boasts more than 200 cars and locomotives, including interurbans, trolleys, Els, and a Burlington Zephyr. You can even ride some of these trains. 7000 Olson Rd. On a smaller scale is the **Valley View Model Railroad Museum**, featuring 16 trains operating on eight miles of track. 17108 Highbridge Rd.

The town of **Wheaton** is home to the **Red Grange Museum**. Grange was a star football player at Wheaton High School before going on to greater fame at the University of Illinois and, later, as a member of the National Football League's Chicago Bears.

Also in Wheaton is **Cantigny Park**, home to a pair of museums. Cantigny, named for the first American battle of the First World War, was originally the summer estate of the family that owned the Chicago *Tribune* newspaper, and the **McCormick Museum** is named for the paper's longtime editor, Robert R.

McCormick. The **First Division Military Museum** is dedicated to the history of the First Division, or Big Red One, of which Colonel McCormick was a part.

The town of **St. Charles** is home to an annual **Scarecrow Festival** each fall. Rated one of the top 100 events in North America, the festival features a scarecrow display, carnival, food, and juried craft show. Or check out the **St. Charles History Museum**, at 215 E. Main St.

THE BEGINNING OF ROUTE 66

oute 66 begins in downtown Chicago, by the shore of Lake Michigan. This end of Route 66 presents an immediate challenge, since eastbound and westbound lanes are actually on separate streets. Westbound 66 follows Adams Street, while eastbound 66 is a block to the south, on Jackson. Since you don't want to miss a thing, I suggest you drive on both streets to find as much of the old highway's flavor as possible prior to leaving downtown. Some of that flavor is to be found at **Lou Mitchell's Restaurant**, a downtown Chicago eatery since 1923. It's at 565 W. Jackson (eastbound 66). Westbound travelers can turn left off of Adams at Des Plaines, then turn left again onto Jackson. Don't stop at Lou's if you're on a diet—patrons munch on free Milk Duds while waiting to be seated.

The easternmost end of Adams Street has as its landmark the **Art Institute of Chicago**, where countless American artists have had some of their formal training. The Art Institute, by the way, includes such famous works in its collection as Edward Hopper's *Nighthawks* and Grant Wood's *American Gothic*.

When you're ready to leave Chicago and Lake Michigan, begin your adventure by proceeding west on Adams Street. Like all of the larger cities on Route 66, Chicago itself will not reveal much in the way of that Mother Road feel that you are looking for—at least not when compared with the hundreds of smaller towns ahead of you. Cities like this were plotted out in the days prior to automobile travel, and so you and your car do not feel entirely welcome here.

Westbound Route 66 angles left (southwest) at Ogden Avenue, which is named for Chicago's first mayor, William B. Ogden. He took office in 1837, at the time the city was first incorporated.

On Ogden, you will pass through the communities of Cicero and Berwyn.

CICERO

Here in Cicero once stood a large "muffler man" figure holding a hot dog in front of Bunyon's. In 2003, that figure was removed and relocated to Atlanta, Illinois for more prominent display.

BERWYN

There's not a great deal to differentiate Berwyn—it's suburban Chicago.

For a sample of bizarre artwork, though, check out the **Cermack Plaza Shopping Center**, where Los Angeles artist Dustin Shuler has created "The Spindle." Cermack Plaza looks pretty much like any of the other countless aging strips of retail in greater Chicago, until you notice the stack of several cars impaled on a 40-foot-tall spike in the parking lot. But wait, there's more. There are a number of other oddball pieces of oversized outdoor art scattered nearby, including the "Pinto Pelt," a Ford Pinto flattened against a wall like an animal hide.

LYONS-McCOOK

On what was once Highway 66 in Lyons is the **Hofmann Tower**, a circa-1908 concrete structure built by a local brewer, and which today is home to the **Lyons Historical Museum**. Open only sporadically, it houses several stories of local memorabilia, including a post office and one-room school. Also in Lyons is the **Chicago Portage National Historic Site**, sometimes referred to as "Chicago's Plymouth Rock." 4800 S. Harlem Ave.

A short time after turning onto Joliet Road, you'll be forced to enter I-55. Interstate 55 follows the course of primary 66, which went towards, but ultimately bypassed, the town of Plainfield. For a time, Route 66 split into two separate routes northeast of Plainfield. The rightmost fork was the primary route at the time my 1957 atlas was printed, and went towards the city of Plainfield. The left fork was designated ALT 66, and headed south toward Joliet. Even at this early date, Route 66 was being realigned in such a way as to bypass most cities and their associated traffic. ALT 66 at this time passed directly through towns such as Joliet, Elwood, Wilmington, and Braidwood. At the same time, the map shows the primary route passing near, but not through, Plainfield and other towns, much as I-55 does today. The two alignments later converged again just southwest of the town of Gardner.

Both Plainfield and Joliet were on the Lincoln Highway (U.S. 30), an east-west artery which passed through here. So whichever path you take (and I recommend you explore both), it is here that you cross one of many routes of significance on your way west on 66. The Lincoln Highway was established in 1915, and was the first American transcontinental highway conceived with automobile travel in mind. Later, in the 1920s, when such interstate routes were designated with numbers, the Lincoln Highway officially became U.S. 30, but lovers of history still refer to it more commonly by its original name.

PLAINFIELD

If you enjoy hot rods and custom cars, Plainfield has them. This is the home of **Midwest Hot Rods**. They can either work with what you've got, or you can tour their inventory.

The **Plainfield Historical Society** is at 217 E. Main St., with Indian artifacts, school memorabilia, and other exhibits.

ROMEOVILLE

Formerly Romeo, without the -ville. That was considered pretty cute back when Juliet was just a few miles down the pike. But when Juliet changed her name to Joliet, somehow the magic in the marriage was gone.

Keep an eye out for the **White Fence Farm**, a sort of grand catering enterprise right beside the highway. There was a very large fiberglass chicken on a flatbed truck parked outside the first time I passed through here.

Romeoville also offers exhibits on what life was like for early fur trappers who first came to the region. Check out **Isle de la Cache**, at 501 E. Romeo Rd., a cultural history museum. Fishing, picnicking, and boating are also here to enjoy.

Between Romeoville and Joliet is the **Stateville State Prison**. The grounds cover a huge, well-manicured expanse, and when you first glimpse it you'll be excused for thinking you've come upon a university campus of some prestige.

JOLIET

Once nicknamed the City of Spires due to its many houses of worship (some 122 at one time), Joliet has in recent years taken a liking to gaming, and is now very much a center for casino gam-

Joliet, Illinois.

bling. Even the local **Joliet Prison** has what might be called spires, though.

In the world of fiction, Joliet Prison gave John Belushi's character his nickname, Joliet Jake, in the movie *The Blues Brothers*. You can drive by Joliet Prison and take a look at its depressing walls at 1125 Collins Street. The first prisoners were received here in 1858.

In 1940, the **Dairy Queen** ice cream chain was established, with the first store being in Joliet. The now-familiar confection was actually first offered to the public two years earlier in a special "taste trial" in nearby Kankakee.

Joliet is in the middle of the **Illinois & Michigan Canal National Heritage Corridor** development. This is the name for the nation's first Linear Park, which connects some 40 communities along the waterway which linked Lake Michigan with the Illinois River, and so is considered instrumental in the development of Greater Chicago-land. There is a related museum in the nearby town of Lockport.

Popularly known as the Jewel of Joliet, the **Rialto Square Theater** at 102 N. Chicago St. is a restored 1926 vaudeville theater

**The Rialto is a truly luxurious theater,
sometimes called the "Jewel of Joliet."**

on the National Register. It contains the largest hand-cut chandelier in the U.S. (tours are available). The inner lobby area was fashioned after the Hall of Mirrors at the Palace of Versailles.

Take a free tour of blast furnace ruins at **Joliet Iron Works Historic Site**. Make reservations at 815-727-8700.

Explore Joliet history at the **Joliet Area Historical Museum**, where you can walk through a life-size replica of the construction of the Illinois & Michigan Canal. It's located at 200-204 N. Ottawa Street, in a former Methodist church building. There is also a **Route 66 Welcome Center** adjacent to the museum.

In the South East Neighborhood Historical District is the

Jacob Henry Mansion, an 1873 40-room manor house decorated in lavish style. The house is especially well turned-out at Christmastime. At 20 S. Eastern Avenue, in what was once called "Silk Stocking Row."

Joliet, Illinois, was once a center for the steel industry.

ELWOOD

This is a very small community just south of Joliet. Is this where the inspiration came for the name of the other Blues Brother, Joliet Jake's brother Elwood?

WILMINGTON

Wilmington has been nicknamed the Island City due to the fact that the Kankakee River runs through town, forming an island home for a pair of city parks: North and South Island Parks.

Wilmington is known among Route 66 fans as the home of the **Gemini Giant**. He's one of those giant figures, formerly a muffler man, that used to populate American highways in the 1950s and '60s. This one has been decked out like an astronaut (I guess) and stands in front of the Launching Pad Drive-In restaurant at 801 E. Baltimore St. The shape of his helmet is a bit unusual, perhaps a nod to the Coneheads of *Saturday Night Live*.

Fans of architectural curiosities might want to check out the octagonal house, the **Schutten-Aldrich House**, at 600 Water Street. It dates from 1856.

Muffler Men

Once plentiful across the American landscape, the Gemini Giant at Wilmington is a notable example of what are commonly referred to as "muffler men." Over 20 feet in height, they proliferated in the late '50s-early '60s as roadside icons for automotive muffler shops. Early on, some owners of these figures "personalized" them by customizing the clothing or even the facial features according to whim. As in the case of the Gemini Giant, in later years the oversized muffler held in the figure's hands was often replaced by something else—in this case, a model rocket.

FURTHER AFIELD

Southeast of Wilmington is the city of **Kankakee**. The name comes from the Pottawatomi language, and means "beautiful river." Kankakee is home to the **Kankakee River State Park**, consisting of over 2,700 acres strung out along 11 miles of the river. The town takes its water seriously, with canoe rentals, an annual fishing derby, and the Kankakee River Valley Regatta each Labor Day.

Also in Kankakee is the **Kankakee Historical Society Museum**, home to a collection of plaster studies by native son George Gray Barnard and housed in an 1855 Italianate building at Eighth Ave. and Water St. The **Bradley House** was designed in 1901 by Frank Lloyd Wright, and is considered the first of many in his famous Prairie Style. Harrison St. at the river.

West of Kankakee is **Hillside**, whose cemetery contains the graves of Al Capone and Jack Ruby. Mount Carmel Cemetery, 1400 S. Wolf Rd.

BRAIDWOOD-GODLEY

Through these neighboring towns, there are two versions of old 66 (Washington St. and Front St.) separated by a set of railroad tracks right in between.

Route 66 slices through the southeast corner of Braidwood. Look for the Art Deco ceramic-tile station. There is an annual cruise held here each August sponsored by the 1950s-flavored Polk-A-Dot Drive-In restaurant.

Godley is right on the Will County-Grundy County line.

BRACEVILLE

According to my atlas, the town of Braceville was just west (perhaps a half-mile or so) of Highway 66 in 1957. Today, it sits in a narrow no-man's-land between old 66 and I-55 just to the west.

GARDNER

The Riviera Roadhouse was built in 1928 and features a surprise in the backyard. There you'll find what was originally a horse-drawn streetcar, later pressed into use as a diner, and now a restored piece of Americana. Stories abound that Al Capone frequented the Riviera, which started featuring frog's legs on the menu as early as the 1930s.

Gardner has a sort of "bypass" loop which skirts the town and is easy to follow, but I recommend you enter town on Washington St. and meander through downtown, just as old 66 once did. The town of Gardner features a two-cell jailhouse dating from 1905.

DWIGHT

In 1940, Eleanor Jarman was serving a 199-year sentence at the women's prison, now called Dwight Correctional Center, for her involvement in several hold-ups. On the eighth of August, the "Blond Tigress" escaped, never to be seen or heard from again.

Downtown at the old **Keeley Institute** (now Fox Development Center) are five Tiffany-style windows, each of them portraying one of the five senses. Next door is the **First National Bank**,

This former car dealership now houses a pizza restaurant in Dwight, Illinois.

Dwight, Illinois.

designed by none other than Frank Lloyd Wright. Nearby is an impressive Romanesque railroad depot listed on the National Register and now housing the **Dwight Historical Society Museum**. The **Bank of Dwight** dates from 1855 and features a mural in the interior by Viennese artist Oskar Gross. Also notable is the windmill on the library grounds, which dates from 1896.

Each September, Dwight hosts a basset hound parade called the "Waddle," which benefits Basset Rescue, an organization specializing in finding homes for neglected or abused dogs.

ODELL-CAYUGA

When I first passed through Odell in 1998, the old fuel station here was sagging and dilapidated. But thanks to the efforts of donors and volunteers, the station has since been restored for your enjoyment.

 Between Cayuga and Pontiac is a recently restored barn bearing a Meramec Caverns advertisement. For years now, it has been unlawful to create "new" advertising barns, due to some people's opinions about Highway Beautification. Existing barns such as this one are "grandfathered" under the law, and so can remain and in some cases be restored. However, as they age and are removed, whether by natural or man-made forces, they cannot be replaced. Thus their number continues to diminish year after year.

Just north of Pontiac on Pontiac Rd. is the **Old Log Cabin**

This old service station was sagging and neglected when I first passed through this part of Route 66. Since then, it has been faithfully restored by dedicated volunteers. Odell, Illinois.

Inn. This is the place which has gained some renown for not giving up when the highway was re-aligned and they found that the new Route 66 was at their back door. The owners simply re-oriented the place and barely missed a beat. The older roadway can be seen behind the present orientation, near the railroad tracks, as befits an early highway alignment.

PONTIAC

At the state prison here in Pontiac, inmates manufactured Route 66 shields to meet public demand following the highway's decommission in Illinois in 1977.

The **Route 66 Association of Illinois Hall of Fame & Museum** was established here in 2004 in the old firehouse at 110 Howard St.

The **Catherine V. Yost Museum & Arts Center**, 298 W. Water Street, is a Queen Anne-style home from the late 1800s containing most of the Yost family possessions.

The **Jones House**, a gothic revival brick house built in 1858, is located at 314 E. Madison Street.

CHENOA

Chenoa is home to the **Matthew T. Scott Home** at 227 N. First Street. This was the home of Matthew T. and his wife Julia Green Scott, Julia being one of the founders of the Daughters of the

Chenoa, Illinois.

American Revolution. Organized in 1890 and chartered by Congress in 1896, membership in the DAR is limited to direct lineal descendants of soldiers or others of the Revolutionary period who aided the cause of independence. Applicants must have reached the age of 18 years and be deemed "personally acceptable" by the society.

LEXINGTON

Lexington has an old neon sign announcing your arrival. On the north side of Lexington, Route 66 fans have created a sort of **"Memory Lane"** exhibit, with a stretch of old 66 roadway set aside and enhanced with period billboards and even a Burma Shave sign. If you'd like to get out of your car while in Lexington, try Koch's

A long-retired stretch of Route 66 in Lexington, Illinois, is now the town's Memory Lane.

Lexington, Illinois still has a vintage neon sign pointing the way to the downtown business district.

Depot, an antique store whose main building is an old railroad depot relocated to the downtown business district. This depot is a little different than most in that it is a two-story affair. The Koch family used to run the Lexington Café, which operated right on 66 for years.

The **Patton Cabin** is a log structure, parts of which date from 1829. It was used as an official polling place as early as 1831. Originally located about a mile and a half to the southeast, the cabin was reassembled in the Lexington Pool Park (off N. Cherry St.) in 1969.

TOWANDA

There's a former gasoline station here at Towanda which has an exaggerated sloping roof over the pump islands. At the time of my first trip through here, it was serving duty as a night club. Each subsequent time I see it, it appears to be serving a different purpose.

In recent years, a walking-biking path has been set up beside

Towanda, Illinois.

the newer bypass alignment of 66 in this area.

I've seen an old postcard picturing something called the Asian Arts Gift Shop here in Towanda. It consisted of Polynesian-style huts elevated above the ground on piers.

BLOOMINGTON-NORMAL

When two towns have to coexist this closely (they share the same Main Street), it's natural for a rivalry to develop. Normal is home to Illinois State University, and Bloomington has Illinois Wesleyan College.

Bloomington seems to be able to claim more famous sons. These include Adlai Stevenson, whose home is at 901 N. McLean;

the fictional Colonel Henry Blake, from *M*A*S*H*; author and publisher Elbert Hubbard, who perished on the *Lusitania*; and Pawnee Bill, a.k.a. Gordon W. Lillie, who produced Wild West shows in the first decade of the 1900s, similar to the shows Buffalo Bill became famous for. Bloomington is also the birthplace of the Republican Party, which was organized here at a convention in 1856.

NORMAL ATTRACTIONS

Normal is the home to everything you'd ever want to know about Illinois basketball. The **Illinois Basketball Coaches Association Hall of Fame** is at 8 Traders Circle.

Check out the Art Deco-influenced **Normal Theater**, which first opened its doors in 1937. It's on the National Register and has been fully restored to its original beauty. 209 W. North St.

Bloomington, Illinois.

Normal also has a one-room 1899 schoolhouse you can tour. The **Eyestone School** is at the corner of College Avenue and Adelaide Street.

BLOOMINGTON ATTRACTIONS

Bloomington is home to **Beer Nuts**, at 103 N. Robinson Street. Invented in the 1930s and originally called "Virginia Redskins," Beer Nuts were a rousing success from the word "go." You can't actually see them made here, but you can visit the gift shop and see a video about them.

Bloomington also gave birth to the **Nestle-Beich Candy Company**, known for producing chocolate for fund-raising institutions. Ask for a tour at 101 S. Lumber St.

Also in Bloomington is the **David Davis Mansion State Historic Site**. The home, named Clover Lawn, is a 20-room Italianate villa at 1000 E. Monroe St. The home was built in 1872 for U.S. Supreme Court Justice David Davis. Decorated by his wife, Sarah, the home contains original furnishings and stencil-work. It also has features which were quite luxurious at the time, such as indoor plumbing and a central heating system. You are urged to allow at least 90 minutes to tour this masterpiece.

David Davis Mansion, Bloomington, Illinois.

The **McLean County Museum of History** is at 200 N. Main Street in the former courthouse, which was constructed from 1901 to 1903. The museum includes a "hands on"

area where visitors can experience such age-old tasks as beating a rug and pushing a steel plow.

The **Prairie Aviation Museum** includes a meticulously restored DC-3, a collection of Ozark Airlines memorabilia, and also offers pilot training and passenger flights. At 2929 E. Empire St., at the Central Illinois Regional Airport.

SHIRLEY

At Shirley we have the **Funk Prairie Home** and the **Funk Gem Rock & Mineral Museum**. The home was originally built in 1863–64, and includes the first electric kitchen island (added a bit later, of course). The mineral museum is a collection of gemstones, fossils, and petrified wood accumulated by Lafayette Funk II, one of the county's most illustrious citizens of his time, and located on the same 27-acre property. 10875 Prairie Home Lane, east of town.

A subtle indication that cross-country travel did not always involve automobiles. Shirley, Illinois.

FUNKS GROVE

Just off the highway at Funks Grove, Illinois, is this retired railroad depot.

A few miles past Shirley, look for a right-hand turn that takes you into the forgotten community of Funks Grove. There you'll see a tiny old railroad depot and the remains of a small country store. The Funk family has been tapping trees and making what they call "sirup" for well over 100 years. Stop in and pick some up.

McLEAN

One of two towns by this name on Route 66 (the other being in Texas), the Illinois McLean is home to a restored railroad depot, as well as the **Dixie Truckers' Home**, a truck stop which dates from

Restored railroad depot across from the Dixie Truckers Home, McLean, Illinois.

1928. Personally, I think the Dixie made a mistake when they replaced their sign a few years ago. The old one had much more character.

ATLANTA

At the town center of Atlanta, check out the distinctive **Atlanta**

Public Library, which has been converted to a museum. It's eight-sided, and it has a clock tower standing beside it which came from a nearby school building. The library is on the National Register, and is located at 100 Race St.

Atlanta was fortunate enough recently to host a sort of **mural**-making festival. You'll see a number of buildings throughout the town which have had artwork added to their sides. This project was spearheaded in 2003 by a group of signmakers calling themselves LetterHeads.

On Arch St., between Race and Vine Sts., look for the giant **"muffler man,"** who was moved here from Bunyon's in Cicero.

The town also boasts of a circa-1900 **J. H. Hawes grain elevator**, which is "standing on its original site" and is further described as a "skyscraper of the prairie." 301 SW Second St.

Atlanta was at one time called Xenia.

LAWNDALE

Just a very small community beside Route 66 where the highway crosses Kickapoo Creek.

LINCOLN

This is said to be the only town named for Abraham Lincoln while he was still alive, and on hearing of this plan, he is attributed with the remark that he never knew of anything named Lincoln that amounted to much. He was personally involved in drawing up the legal papers establishing the town, and he actually practiced some law here in the 1850s.

While in Lincoln, look for **The Mill** restaurant on Stringer Avenue. The Mill dates from the early days of the route, and features a lighted, revolving, Dutch-style windmill.

Lincoln, Illinois.

Reconstructed in 1953 on the site of the original is a *replica* courthouse at the **Postville Courthouse State Historic Site** (914 Fifth St.). The original, constructed in 1840, was frequented by Abraham Lincoln during his years of practicing law in the area. In

1848, however, the county seat was moved to Mount Pulaski, and a new courthouse was erected there. The old Postville Courthouse was acquired in 1929 by Henry Ford, who dismantled it and reassembled it at his Greenfield Village complex in Dearborn, Michigan. Incidentally, Greenfield Village is of interest, having more than 200 historic buildings of all sorts spread over an 81-acre tract.

The **Heritage In Flight Museum**, a building that once housed German prisoners-of-war, is now a museum filled with aircraft and other artifacts dating to World War I. At the Logan County Airport.

Check out the downtown monument depicting a life-sized, ear-to-ear watermelon slice, commemorating the day in 1853 when

This old sign is an indication that you are on old Route 66. Lincoln, Illinois.

the future president christened his namesake community with melon juice. The monument was erected in 1964 through the combined efforts of the local Kiwanis, Rotary, and Lions clubs.

FURTHER AFIELD

Southeast of Lincoln (or due east of Springfield if you prefer) is the city of **Decatur**. It was in Decatur that the Lincoln family first settled after coming to the state from Indiana. Here stands the courthouse where the young man first earned a reputation as a trial lawyer, and there is a memorial statue marking where he gave his first political speech. Decatur was also the original home of the Chicago Bears football team.

The **Macon County Museum Complex** is at 5580 N. Fork Rd. Local history is exhibited, including a train depot, print shop, and a log courthouse dating from 1830, in which Lincoln is said to have tried some cases.

The **James Millikin Homestead** is at 125 N. Pine Street. The home was built in 1876 in an ornate and rather gothic style, which contrasts sharply with the Frank Lloyd Wright-inspired designs with which it is surrounded. The home has been fully restored and is listed on the National Register. Open weekends.

The **Scovill Park Complex** includes a zoo, children's museum, visitor's center, oriental gardens, and the **Hieronymous Mueller Museum**. The Muellers, a family of German immigrants, played a significant role as inventors in both the nineteenth and twentieth centuries. They either invented or improved such things as plumbing fixtures, roller skates, soda fountains, auto parts, and munitions. 61 S. Country Club Rd.

Birk's Museum is on the Millikin University campus, and contains more than a thousand pieces of porcelain, china, and glassware, some of it dating to the fifteenth century. 1184 W. Main.

BROADWELL

A short time ago, there were only quiet remains of the once-bustling **Pig Hip Restaurant & Motel** here at Broadwell. Recently, though, the old place has been turned into a museum. Stretch your legs awhile by paying a visit to this Route 66 roadside stop, which was established in 1937. You can even peruse the register that owner Ernie Edwards used to record the hundreds of marriage ceremonies he performed as Justice of the Peace during the 1950s. Hours vary, so call ahead at 217-732-2337.

Pig Hip Motel, Broadwell, Illinois.

After passing through and exploring Williamsville, you'll be forced to enter the interstate for a short distance; exit again at the I-55 business loop in order to pass through the town of Sherman. Soon, you'll be entering Springfield via Peoria Rd./N. Ninth.

SPRINGFIELD

The Illinois state capital was moved here from Vandalia in 1857 by a group which included Abraham Lincoln. Today, Springfield is still the center of the Lincoln universe, as well as being nearly the exact geographic center of the state (the precise center being about 28 miles northeast, in Logan County).

Springfield boasts more Lincoln sites than any other city, not at all surprising

Springfield, Illinois.

when you consider that the man lived and worked here for many years before departing to pursue the presidency. Several of these Lincoln sites can be taken in rather conveniently via the Springfield Trolley Tours.

SPRINGFIELD ATTRACTIONS

"The only home Mr. Lincoln ever owned" is at Eighth and Jackson Streets. Tour tickets for the home are free at the **Lincoln Home Visitors' Center** at 426 S. Seventh. Lincoln's law office (the **Lincoln-Herndon Law Office**) is at Sixth and Adams Streets. The railroad depot here in Springfield is where he gave his eloquent departure speech before leaving permanently to assume the

Lincoln family mausoleum, Oak Ridge Cemetery, Springfield, Illinois.

presidency. And, the Lincoln family tomb is at **Oak Ridge Cemetery** (north of downtown on Walnut St.). There, you can walk the solemn halls of the mausoleum and rub the nose of his bronze likeness for luck, as many before you have. The Oak Ridge Cemetery even includes a souvenir kiosk where you can indulge your lust for more Lincoln memorabilia.

For Route 66 followers, the hands-down centerpiece of Springfield is the **Cozy Dog Drive-In** at 2935 So. Sixth St. Ed Waldmire, who established a small chain of restaurants here, invented the corn dog while serving military duty at Amarillo, Texas (also on Highway 66). After the war, he started serving his invention—which he originally wanted to call the "Crusty Cur"—in his home of Springfield. Today, the Cozy Dog location on Route 66 is still open, and still run by the Waldmire family.

Route 66 devotees will also want to stop at **Shea's Gas Station Museum** and at **Big Boys' Toys**, both of which satisfy the urge to pore over restored gas pumps and other petroliana. Peoria Road.

The **Illinois State Military Museum** salutes the Illinois National Guard through exhibits of uniforms, equipment, weapon-

Part of the collection at Bill Shea's, Springfield, Illinois.

ry, and photographs housed in a Civilian Conservation Corps structure. By far, the most notable item in the museum's collection is the wooden leg worn by General Santa Anna. The story goes that the general and a small group of his men were having a lunch of roasted chicken when an Illinois detachment surprised them. The general had just time enough to mount his horse and escape, but was forced to leave behind his artificial leg and the remains of the chicken. Fortunately for him, he had a spare one just like it elsewhere—the leg, that is. 301 N. MacArthur Blvd.

In front of the Illinois Exhibits building at the state fairgrounds is a 30-foot-tall statue of a clean-shaven Abraham Lincoln, entitled **The Rail Splitter**. It was created in 1968 by Carl W. Rinnus, a Springfield native.

The **Old State Capitol State Historic Site** is where President Lincoln delivered his famous "house divided" speech, and where he lay in state following his assassination in 1865. It was also the scene of the 1858 Lincoln-Douglas debates. Fifth at Adams.

The **Abraham Lincoln Presidential Library and Museum** (recently expanded) is at Jefferson and Sixth Streets, and includes thousands of documents (including the Gettysburg Address) plus numerous artifacts.

The **Dana-Thomas House**, at 301 E. Lawrence Ave., is a 1902 Frank Lloyd Wright-designed home with most of the original furnishings, including art glass. It is considered one of his earliest experiments in what was later to become famous as his Prairie Style. On October 8th each year, citizens turn out to celebrate the birthday of the lady of the house, socialite Susan Lawrence Dana, with an open house, live music, etc.

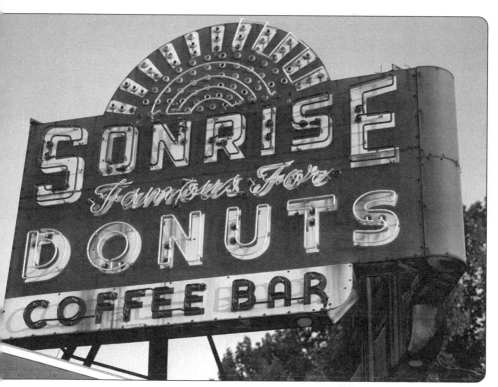

Springfield, Illinois.

Edwards Place, built in 1853, was once the center of Springfield's social and political life. Today it provides the visitor with an interesting tour and a gallery filled with contemporary art. 700 N. Fourth St.

The **Executive Mansion** is the nation's third-oldest continuously occupied governor's residence. Many rooms are open to public viewing, including the state dining room, library, ballroom, and the Lincoln bedroom. 410 E. Jackson St.

The **Vachel Lindsay Home** is the birthplace of the native Springfield artist and poet, who resided here until his death—by suicide—in 1931. Located across the street from the governor's mansion, at 603 S. Fifth St.

The **Oliver P. Parks Telephone Museum** houses a collection assembled by a long-time Ma Bell employee. At last count, there were 117 phones on display here, including such classics as wooden wall-mounted phones, candlestick models, early coin phones, and even a switchboard. 529 S. Seventh St.

The **Museum of Funeral Customs** is located at the entrance to Oak Ridge Cemetery. Exhibits include a 1920s embalming room, horse-drawn hearses, a mock 1870 home funeral, examples of post-mortem photography, and a full-size reproduction of President Lincoln's casket. 1440 Monument Ave.

The **Thomas Rees Memorial Carillon** has 67 bronze bells and is distinguished by the fact that you can actually view the bells and playing mechanism. The largest bell, a G-flat, weighs in at about 15,000 pounds. Rees was publisher of the *State Journal-Register* newspaper and bequeathed the funds upon his death to the construction of this amazing instrument, which was completed in 1962. Regular concerts are given Sunday afternoons. Western edge of Washington Park.

The interior of the **Lawrence Memorial Library** was designed by Frank Lloyd Wright, and has been restored to its original luster at 101 E. Laurel St.

In the fall, you can take in the **Springfield Air Rendezvous Air Show**, an event featuring civilian and military aircraft performing aerobatic maneuvers at the Capital Airport (on J. David Jones Parkway).

The **Route 66 Drive-In Theater** shows two features nightly (in season) beginning at dusk. The theater is on the south side of town, at 1700 Recreation Drive. The theater is actually part of a larger recreational complex called **Knight's Action Park**, which includes a water slide, driving range, picnic areas, pedal boats, and more.

Not getting enough exercise? Then walk or bicycle the **Lost Bridge Trail**, a five-mile-long trail reaching from Springfield's east side to the town of Rochester. The trail follows an old Baltimore & Ohio Railroad line and takes you to a small commercial section in Rochester. And once in Rochester, there is a connecting trail (one mile) to a community park with water fountains, restrooms, and other facilities.

Back on 66: Leaving Springfield, you get a real treat—two distinct Route 66 alignments are here to enjoy. The more modern route takes you south out of town along the I-55 corridor, through Divernon and Litchfield. This was the course of the highway during most of its years of existence. However, there is an older alignment, passing through Auburn, Carlinville, and Gillespie—today bearing the number 4—which carried traffic in the 1920s. In fact, this road predated Route 66 and was a major thoroughfare in the area years earlier. Because of the relatively early realignment (early 1930s), this older highway does not have much surviving road architecture. However, it is certainly worth driving, as it is easier to imagine yourself in an Illinois long gone. If you follow Highway 4, keep alert for a section of very old brick-paved roadway, just over a mile long, north of Auburn.

GLENARM

A nearby park features a restored covered bridge and shady picnic grounds.

Just before reaching Divernon, you'll come across the Highway 104 junction. Inside the Truckers' Homestead Restaurant is a tribute to gunspinning, that artful sleight-of-hand seen so often in older Western movies. You'll also want to keep your eyes peeled for an oversized covered wagon, called the "Railsplitter," with a giant Abraham Lincoln in the driver's seat.

Near Glenarm, Illinois, is a small park which includes this covered bridge.,

DIVERNON

Divernon has a nice quiet little town square, which features a few vintage advertising murals on some of the buildings.

FARMERSVILLE-WAGGONER

Both of these communities are just off to the right-hand side of the highway. Look for the remains of Art's Motel and for the Our Lady of the Highway shrine.

Farmersville, Illinois.

LITCHFIELD

The **Sky View Drive-In Theater** has been in continual operation since 1951 right on 66 on the outskirts of town.

A longtime Route 66 stopping-place is the **Ariston Café**, which has been in business in its present location since 1935. The first restaurant was established in Carlinville in 1924. When Route 66 was re-routed, the family started up anew in

The Ariston Café has been serving locals and travelers alike since the 1930s. Litchfield, Illinois.

Litchfield—across from the current location—in 1931, only to move one last time in 1935.

The **Litchfield Library**, dating from 1904, was one of many around the country endowed by the Carnegie Foundation. The library is in

This sign is all that is left of a gasoline station which served travelers just across the street from the Ariston Café.

The 66 Motel Court is just down the street from a working drive-in theater in Litchfield, Illinois.

the 400 block of N. State St, and is known for its extensive genealogical department.

FURTHER AFIELD

Northwest of Litchfield is the town of **Carlinville**, which was on the older alignment of Route 66 (now Highway 4), and home to some points of interest. The first is the **Million-Dollar White Elephant Courthouse** (Macoupin County Courthouse), at 200 E. Main Street. It is said to have cost more than 10 times its original estimate, taking more than two years to build and 40 years to pay for. It has some rather overwrought features, such as iron doors—some weighing in at over a ton—and interior trim made of either iron or stone. It was at one time the largest courthouse in the United States. The courthouse project also included a new jailhouse, and it, too, has some interesting features, such as leftover cannonballs (this was just after the Civil War) embedded in the walls as an additional escape prevention measure.

Downtown Carlinville also features the **Loomis House**, a former 50-room hotel which was designed by the same architect as the nearby courthouse and jail (above). The Loomis has been pre-served and today contains a number of local businesses.

More on the pragmatic side is Carlinville's **Standard Addition**, a housing subdivision comprised of one of the largest aggregates of Sears Roebuck catalog homes to be found anywhere— more than a 100 of them. This fact has led to the publication of a number of books and documentaries in recent years.

The **Macoupin County Historical Museum** is in the 1883 Anderson Mansion, and also has a schoolhouse, church, and blacksmith shop on the property. 920 W. Breckenridge St.

There is a small stone marker in front of the **United Methodist Church** in Carlinville marking the spot where Abraham Lincoln delivered a speech in 1858 while campaigning for a Senate seat against Stephen A. Douglas. At the Corner of Broad and E. First Sts.

MT. OLIVE

Route 66 street sign near Mt. Olive, Illinois.

Be sure to stop and see the **Russell Soulsby Shell Station**, a restored jewel originally constructed in the 1920s. The town's cemetery includes the gravesite of **Mother Jones** (Mary Harris), the famous mining activist and labor organizer of the same era, who died in 1930.

STAUNTON

In 1923, Staunton High School was defeated by Gillespie High in football by a score of 233-0.

Staunton is home to **Henry's Rabbit Ranch**, with a sign that spoofs the billboard at the Jackrabbit Trading Post many miles to the west in Arizona. Look for the Campbell's "Humpin' to Please" truck trailer.

LIVINGSTON

Just a tad off 66 according to both 1946 and 1957 maps of the region, Livingston nevertheless probably was close enough to have offered some travelers' services.

HAMEL

Keep an eye out for the **St. Paul Lutheran Church**, with its blue neon cross. Scotty's Roadhouse started serving highway travelers here beginning in 1930.

This tile mosaic adorns the side of a pharmacy in downtown Edwardsville, Illinois.

EDWARDSVILLE

The unassuming town of Edwardsville was the scene of some social experimentation in the late 1800s. **LeClaire Village** was a test community founded by

Former tourist accommodations in Edwardsville, Illinois.

industrialist N. O. Nelson on the principles of profit sharing and Britain's cooperative movement, and survived as such into the early years of the twentieth century. In the 1930s, it was annexed by the city of Edwardsville, and is now listed as an official Historic District.

What's left of the **Bel-Air Drive-In Theater** is here. The screen is gone; only the marquee remains. Also be on the lookout for the **Luna Café**, an authentic roadhouse that predates Route 66.

The **Madison County Historical Museum and Library** is housed in an 1836 home with period furnishings, historical costumes, and other exhibits (715 N. Main St.). Also in Edwardsville is **Bilbrey Farms**, with an exotic animal zoo featuring zebras, llamas, and miniature horses. There is also a bed and breakfast on the grounds. 8724 Pin Oak Rd.

FURTHER AFIELD

Directly south of Edwardsville, via Highway 159, is the city of **Collinsville**. Called the Horseradish Capital of the World, the town holds a horseradish festival each spring, with horseradish-eating contests, cook-offs, and a horseradish toss competition.

Collinsville is also the home of the **World's Largest Ketchup Bottle**, at the old Brooks Foods plant. Actually built as a water tower, the bottle is about 70 feet tall and stands atop a 100-foot base. Brooks left town over 20 years ago, but the bottle replica, constructed in 1949, remains. Local legend states that red-headed offspring may result when pregnant women pass too closely. 800 S. Morrison Ave.

Just west of Collinsville is **Cahokia Mounds State Historic Site**. Here are the ruins of a prehistoric city, inhabited from about A.D. 700 to 1400, and which covered nearly six square miles. There are several mounds, the largest of which is called Monk's Mound, which is approximately 100 feet tall. There are also remains of a sort of wooden stockade, which has been nicknamed Woodhenge, due to its astronomical similarity to the world-famous Stonehenge. Partial reconstruction of the site allows for dramatic effects at the time of the equinoxes. Cahokia is considered the largest prehistoric society on this continent north of Mexico.

Further west lies the town center of Cahokia. The **Cahokia Courthouse**, originally constructed as a residence about 1740, was completely disassembled in 1901 and displayed at the 1904 World's Fair across the river in St. Louis. It was then sold at auction and relocated to Chicago, where it was reassembled and stood for many years. In the 1930s, it was reacquired by the citizens of Cahokia, and reassembled in 1939 on its original foundation with the aid of historic photographs. At First and Elm Sts. Nearby is the historic **Jarrot Mansion**, completed about 1810 and formerly the home of one of Cahokia's most prominent citizens. 124 E. First St.

MITCHELL

According to my 1946 map of Illinois, Route 66 split at the town of Mitchell, with City 66 veering southwest toward Nameoki, Granite City, Madison, and Venice, subsequently crossing the river into the central city of St. Louis. The simple "66" designation belonged to what is now Highway 270, which bypassed urban St. Louis in favor of a beltway route. This is the favored route today, which in the old days crossed the Mississippi via the Chain of Rocks Bridge.

Granite City was once known as Six Mile, due to its distance from the Mississippi River. The **Old Six Mile Museum** is housed in the Emmert-Zippel mansion dating from the 1830s. 3729 Maryville Rd.

FURTHER AFIELD

Lovers of petroliana may want to take a side trip to **Roxana**, Illinois, less than 10 miles north of Mitchell. There you'll find the **Wood River Refinery Museum** (formerly the Shell History Museum) in what was formerly part of a still-operating refinery on State Highway 111. The complex dates from 1918 when it was operated by Shell Oil Company; after some 80 years, ownership passed to Phillips Petroleum. In addition to the usual pumps, globes, and advertising examples, the museum has on display a number of authentic vehicles, such as an oil tanker and a fire truck, both of which actually saw service at the refinery.

The Illinois prairie is now behind you. Just ahead is the mighty Mississippi. And beyond that, you and Route 66 will get much better acquainted.

This motel still stands just east of the Chain-of-Rocks Bridge, where
Route 66 used to cross the Mississippi River from Illinois into Missouri.

MISSOURI

L ong before there were roads in the modern sense, there were river-roads. Look at any map of any country and you'll be reminded that the older, more established cities—if not on a coastline—were founded on the banks of rivers, whose currents and near-frictionless surfaces made for quicker and more economical transportation than did the available land-based modes of trans-

A resident alongside Missouri's stretch of Route 66 obviously still appreciates the Mother Road's heritage.

ST. LOUIS

ILL.

port. Yet while rivers have been conducive to transportation and settlement, they have at the same time presented barriers to movement where bridges have been few and far between. And so arises their age-old role as natural borders.

The Mississippi is just such a barrier-road, fostering settlement and commerce while at the same time creating a natural pause in America's relentless westward movement. As you cross the Mississippi River, you pass over one of the North American continent's most vital arteries, one which served to nourish and sustain generations of mankind long before the invention of asphalt and the proliferation of the internal combustion engine. What is more, you leave behind the older and more established portion of the American experience, passing both physically and spiritually into one of America's most important chapters: Westward Expansion.

Missouri—first at St. Louis, later at Independence—was long the staging ground for that westward impulse. Situated at the threshold of an enormous, uncharted wilderness, this was the last bastion of civilization and the last chance to prepare and outfit for the rigorous journey that lay ahead. As Chicago is the starting point for Route 66, so Missouri is the starting place for the famous migratory trails of history that made settlement of the West a reality: the Overland, the Oregon, and the Santa Fe Trails all had their origins here on a Missouri riverbank. And, under the sponsorship of President Thomas Jefferson, a corps led by Meriwether Lewis and William Clark set out from here on their Voyage of Discovery in 1804, eventually finding their way to the Oregon coast.

As for U.S. Highway 66, its crossing of the Mississippi River into the Show-Me State occurred at several places over the years. Today, you will likely want to avoid the older alignments, which crossed the river directly into the central part of St. Louis.

Unfortunately, these alignments of the highway pass through sections of the city in which one does not always feel safe. For that reason, and also because urban alignments tend to fragment over time and be very hard to follow, you are better advised to approach St. Louis via the "bypass" route, which used to take the traveler across the **Chain-of-Rocks Bridge**.

Today, the Chain-of-Rocks is closed to auto traffic, but it has been turned into a recreational attraction (open weekends from June through October). The bridge is just south of Highway 270 and Riverview Blvd., and is touted as "the world's largest bicycle and pedestrian bridge." Earlier in its history, there was a popular park named Riverview which sat at the base of the Chain-of-Rocks Bridge on the Missouri side of the river. There, St. Louisans gathered for picnics, skating, swimming, and softball. **Riverfront Trail** now connects the bridge with the **Gateway Arch** to the south. Up on the bluff overlooking the bridge and the site of the old park, there used to be a fairly elaborate amusement park, called **Fun Fair Park**. Fun Fair Park and its sundry attractions failed to survive the competition from Six Flags St. Louis, which opened in the early 1970s just to the west near Eureka.

Opened to traffic from 1929 until the late 1960s, the former toll bridge with the distinctive bend in the middle was used in the filming of 1981's *Escape from New York*. It is here that Adrienne Barbeau's character meets her demise, while Kurt Russell makes his own escape.

Today's Mother-Roader crosses the Mississippi just a little north of the Chain-of-Rocks Bridge, on Highway 270. This modern-day loop highway has replaced the old route for several miles along here. Exit 270 at Highway 67 and go south to follow the route of 66 as it skirted the city in the old days. Continue south on 67 until meeting up with the city alignment of 66 at Watson Rd., now numbered 366, near the community of Kirkwood. Turn to the east here in order to take in some of what St. Louis has to offer, before continuing your 66 odyssey west.

ST. LOUIS

The city of St. Louis attained what many consider to be its high-water mark in the first decade of the twentieth century. In 1904, the city hosted the World's Fair and the Summer Olympic Games. The Fair was timed to coincide with the centennial of the Louisiana Purchase. The following year, St. Louis had the dubious distinction of being the city with the first recorded auto theft. At the end of the twentieth century, St. Louis was the fastest-shrinking major city in the U.S., declin-

West side of St. Louis, Missouri.

ing by more than 12 percent in population during the 1990s.

The 1904 World's Fair (or St. Louis Exposition) enjoyed a number of distinctions, its having played a role in the evolution of ice cream, hamburgers, and iced tea. It was there that ice cream was first served in cones when a Syrian immigrant named Ernest Hamwi came to the rescue of an ice cream vendor who'd run out of serving dishes. By the end of the fair, it was reported that several vendors were selling ice cream in folded waffles.

That same Fair was also the scene of the mass introduction of the hamburger on a bun, a development which had originated just a little earlier in New Haven, Connecticut. And, an Englishman named Richard Blechyden, tea concessionaire, determined that the weather was simply too hot for his tea to sell well. His solution was to ice it down, thus creating the decidedly un-English iced tea.

The 1904 Fair was held at **Forest Park**, the nation's largest urban park at over 1,300 acres, which still is very much a part of present-day St. Louis. Forest Park contains the St. Louis Zoological Park, the St. Louis Art Museum, and the Missouri History Museum. There are also some giant turtle sculptures on the south side of the park. Judy Garland starred in the 1944 musical *Meet Me in St. Louis*, which portrayed the year the world came to visit this city (the title song, "Meet Me in St. Louis, Louis" actually dates from the year of the Exposition). It was during the filming of that movie that Judy Garland became romantically involved with her future husband, Vicente Minelli.

The St. Louis Exposition was also the scene of something a little less savory to today's more sophisticated sensibilities. Organizers had paid to have African Pygmies, including one Ota Benga, imported to be placed on display in their "University of Man" exhibit, more a carnival sideshow than a serious anthropological exhibit. Along with the pygmies were members of several North American indigenous tribes, all purported to be on display "in their natural habitat." The most famous example was Geronimo, the Apache warrior, who was billed as a "Human Tiger," and whom Benga befriended. What is more astounding is that some time after the St. Louis Exposition, Benga was taken to New York and placed in a cage at the Bronx Zoo monkey house with a parrot and an orang-utan. Public pressure eventually forced his release, but he never found peace here in America, and finally took his own life in 1916.

Charles Lindbergh's famous airplane, the *Spirit of St. Louis*, was so named because his backers for the trans-oceanic flight consisted of the St. Louis *Globe-Democrat* newspaper and a group of local businessmen who wanted to promote their city as a center of aviation. Lindbergh had earlier approached the American Tobacco Company with the idea of naming the craft for their Lucky Strike Cigarettes (he was already named "Lucky Lindy" by that time), but the company refused to back the venture. There is a replica of the *Spirit of St. Louis* at the **Missouri History Museum** (Forest Park, Lindell at DeBaliviere). This replica was manufactured by the same firm that made the original, and it was used in the Jimmy Stewart movie, *The Spirit of St. Louis*.

In 1907, St. Louis became the home of the first gasoline station chain, the American Gasoline Company.

Betty Grable, pin-up girl par excellence during World War II, was from St. Louis and lived at the Forest Park Hotel. Vincent Price graduated from St. Louis's Country Day School. Miles Davis and Chuck Berry were both born here. And another St. Louis native, the moody T. S. Eliot, won the Nobel Prize for Literature in 1948, and then well after his death one of his lighter works, *Old Possum's Book of Practical Cats*, inspired the Broadway musical *CATS*. You will be amazed at the number of St. Louisans who have made it big in the world and have been inducted into the city's **Walk of Fame** on Delmar Avenue (see Attractions, below). In 1915, the city of St. Louis also gave birth to the Junior Chamber of Commerce, or JayCees.

Here in St. Louis, there's a Route 66 institution still going strong which you simply must pay a visit to: **Ted Drewes Frozen Custard**, at 6726 Chippewa. The building itself is an important landmark, but the crucial thing is that here is a business that still believes in the older values of quality product and personal service. They've never "sold out" for a fast buck, and their adoring public appreciates it. Their list of mouth-watering toppings is printed right on the side of the building to stoke your anticipation. Stop by some morning before opening time and watch the people begin to flock in from all over. In no time at all, the place will be mobbed, and it happens vir-

Ted Drewes' Frozen Custard is still a popular stop for both roadies
and St. Louisans, as it has been since the days of Route 66.

tually every day. Stop by and find out why for yourself. And check to
see if there's still a mannequin in one of the upstairs windows.

Before leaving St. Louis and hitting the road once again,
consider going down to the riverfront area that the Highway 270
alignment avoided on your way in. The **Jefferson Expansion
Memorial** (at 11 N. 4th St.) includes the **Gateway Arch** and **the
Museum of Western Expansion** at its foot. Eero Saarinen's
famous 630-foot archway aptly symbolizes the area's role as gateway
to the West. The arch contains a pair of elevator-trams which swiv-
el as they ascend to the top, sort of like a ferris-wheel car, constitut-
ing a feat of engineering in and of themselves. There is a terrific

panoramic view from the top of the arch, and there is also a film, *Monument to the Dream*, which details its construction (the arch was completed in 1965). The adjacent museum, which is as large as a football field, presents information about the Louisiana Purchase and the Jefferson-sponsored Lewis and Clark expedition. William Clark's grave is in the **Bellefontaine Cemetery** in North St. Louis.

Just a couple of blocks away from the arch is the **Old Courthouse**. This building originates from 1839, and was the site of the early trials of the Dred Scott case, which was ultimately decided by the United States Supreme Court in 1857.

Elsewhere downtown, the old **Union Station** railroad depot has been nicely converted to a luxury hotel and eclectic shopping venue. One of the shops specializes in railroad memorabilia, and includes more stick pins featuring railroad logos than any other place I've seen.

ST. LOUIS ATTRACTIONS

At 6504 Delmar is the **Blueberry Hill Café**. You can spend considerable time here just admiring the great memorabilia on display, including posters, album covers, and vintage toys, but the more mainstream reason to come is for the extraordinary burgers. The Blueberry Hill also plays host to the largest annual dart tournament in the United States, with approximately 500 entrants each year.

Also on Delmar Avenue, just down the street from the Blueberry Hill, is an indoor arcade where the clock from the city's demolished **Route 66 Drive-In Theater** is on display. At 6605 Delmar is **Fitz's American Grill and Bottling Works**, where you can enjoy your meal and watch Fitz's Root Beer being bottled at the same time. The equipment dates from the 1940s and is visible from the main dining area.

In the 6200 through 6600 blocks of Delmar is the **St. Louis Walk of Fame**. There are stars embedded in the sidewalk on both sides of the street honoring nearly a hundred men and women who have a St. Louis connection, and who have made an impact on the world at large. They run the gamut from Yogi Berra and Josephine Baker, to William Burroughs and Virginia Mayo.

St. Louis's **City Museum** is located in the heart of the loft and garment district, and is more offbeat than its name would imply. It is housed in the International Arts Complex, which was formerly the home of the International Shoe and Rand Shoe companies, two of the leading shoe manufacturing firms of yesteryear. Included among the exhibits is the Tiny Trailer of Tragedy, once owned by Elvis and Priscilla Presley, as well as the world's largest pair of underpants. The museum has also added a rooftop water park. 701 N. 15th St.

Formerly on display at the City Museum, but since relocated to the Brown Shoe Company headquarters, is the **Shoe of Shoes**. It consists of hundreds—perhaps thousands—of cast-metal life-size shoes welded together in the shape of one enormous woman's pump. This city used to be so well-known for its shoes that at one time wags used to say of St. Louis: "First in shoes, first in booze, and last in the American League." Of course, that was when the St. Louis Browns were still playing America's pastime. At Maryland Ave. and Topton Way in the suburb of Clayton (west St. Louis).

Faust Park includes an 1820s estate home, historical village, and a restored Dentzel carousel. 15185 Olive Blvd.

The **Civilian Conservation Corps Museum** preserves the memory of the New Deal organization responsible for many depression-era public works. 16 Hancock Ave.

Anheuser-Busch Brewery, the world's largest, has tours, beer tastings, and brewing demonstrations (1127 Pestalozzi St.). And don't forget the world-famous Clydesdales.

Calvary Cemetery covers more than 400 acres and includes the gravesites of such notables as playwright Tennessee Williams, General William Tecumseh Sherman, and Dred Scott.

There is also a large crucifix marking the location of a mass grave. At the time of the cemetery's establishment, earlier burials of Native Americans were collected and reinterred at that spot (5239 W. Florissant Ave.). Adjacent to Calvary is **Bellefontaine Cemetery**, where explorer William Clark is buried.

The **Ulysses S. Grant Historic Site** (7400 Grant St.) was the Grant family residence from 1854 to 1858, known as White Haven. Adjacent to it, at 10501 Gravois, is **Grant's Farm**, a ranch with free-roaming animals, an 1856 log cabin, breeding Clydesdales, and a fence made from Civil War rifle barrels. The property was purchased by the Busch family (brewers) in 1903.

The **International Bowling Hall of Fame & Museum** includes an alley with hand-set pins, vintage equipment, and memorabilia from the great stars of the game. At 111 Stadium Plaza (across from Busch Stadium). Recently added is the **Cardinals Hall of Fame** under the same roof.

Canine lovers won't want to miss the **American Kennel Club Museum of the Dog**. The hall of fame section includes tributes to Lassie and Toto; the gallery also includes works by William Wegman. 1721 S. Mason Rd.

Jasper's Antique Radio Museum has over 10,000 radios in its collection, making it the largest in the world. The owner, Jasper Giardina, has the stated goal of finding, repairing, and restoring any radio that he crosses paths with. You'll see everything from fully-restored examples to basket cases fresh from the attic, and everything in between. Many are for sale. 2022 Cherokee Street.

The **Eugene Field House & Toy Museum** is at 634 S. Broadway. Besides being a prominent attorney, Mr. Field was known as the Children's Poet, as well as Father of the Personal Newspaper Column. His former home now features antique and collectible toys.

The **St. Louis Car Museum** has more than 150 legendary vehicles on display. 1575 Woodson Rd.

At 801 N. Second St. is the **National Video Game and**

Coin-Op Museum, featuring an unusual array of exhibits from pinball to Donkey Kong and beyond.

Take a tour of the **Samuel Cupples House** on the grounds of St. Louis University. The 42-room mansion was built in 1888 and features gargoyles, ornate stonework, and 22 fireplaces. It also boasts Tiffany glasswork and other decorative arts dating from the fifteenth century onward. On the third floor is a special exhibit, the Turshin Fine Arts Glass Collection of American and European Art Glass. 3673 West Pine Mall.

Also open for tours is the **Scott Joplin House State Historic Site**, at 2658 Delmar. Here Joplin and his wife kept a modest flat circa 1902. There is a music room with an operating player piano, so that visitors can experience ragtime piano first-hand, much as Joplin himself composed and played it. West of Jefferson Avenue.

The **Cherokee-Lemp Historic District** is a southside neighborhood with two nineteenth-century mansions (the Lemp and the DeMenil) as well as the **Lemp Brewery**, which was once the largest in the world. Bounded by the streets of Cherokee, Lemp, and DeMenil.

Here's an unusual attraction: the **Dental Health Theater**. Dental "instructors" combine education and entertainment using a set of 16 three-foot-tall fiberglass teeth. The teeth light up from within as each is described, and you'll be shown exactly the right technique for brushing—using a really large toothbrush, of course. Admission is free; the theater is located at 727 N. First St.

FURTHER AFIELD

Just northwest of St. Louis is the city of **St. Charles**. There is a visitors' bureau at 230 W. Main.

St. Charles is where Lewis and Clark began their long journey of discovery after camping here in the spring of 1804. You can see the departure point for the Lewis & Clark National Historic Trail at the **Lewis & Clark Center**, at 701 Riverside Drive. Replicas of the vessels used in the voyage can be seen at **Frontier Park**. Oddly enough, it was also here at St. Charles that the first concrete in our Interstate Highway system was poured in the 1950s. That was part of what is now I-70.

A restored 1909 riverboat, the **Goldenrod Show-Boat**, reportedly inspired the motion picture *Showboat*. It presents dinner theater and docks at 1000 Riverside Drive.

The **Miniature World Museum**, 132 N. Main St., St. Charles, has 2,000 models, 135 dioramas, and many exhibits you simply must see to believe. Also called the International Modeler's Hall of Fame, the museum fills over 8,000 square feet with models and dioramas of every description. Reflecting some of the bias in model kits themselves, wartime themes are heavily represented, including exhibits on Pearl Harbor, the Persian Gulf War, and military field artillery and uniforms. The museum itself is housed in a building in the heart of the downtown historic district, the cornerstone of which was laid in 1860.

St. Charles is also home to the Missouri Wing of the **Commemorative Air Force**. The CAF is dedicated to preserving WWII-era aircraft in flying condition as "a tribute to the men and women who built, serviced, and flew them in the defense of democracy." This is the same organization formerly called the Confederate Air Force; the name was changed for the sake of political correctness, but of course they never had anything to do with the War Between the States anyway. Stop in and browse the collection of vintage warplanes on Thursdays and Saturdays.

Also in the St. Charles historic district, at 200-216 Main, is the **First Missouri State Capitol Historic Site**. This Federal-style row home is where the territorial government of 1821–26 met in order to reorganize into a state system of government. Sessions were held here until the new capitol building in Jefferson City was made ready in October of 1826. Included are legislative chambers, two residences, a dry goods store, and a carpentry shop, all of which have been restored to period appearance.

If you've still got some time to spend in St. Charles, there's the **Shrine of St. Rose Phillippine Duchesne** at 619 N. Second Street, site of the first free school west of the Mississippi River. It was established in 1818 by Missouri's only saint, who was canonized in 1988.

Heading back out on our tour of Route 66, the next stop is a suburb to the southwest known as Kirkwood.

KIRKWOOD

Kirkwood, while once a distinct community, has been more or less absorbed by its sprawling neighbor, St. Louis. There is a very nicely restored railroad station in the old Kirkwood business district. The downtown business district in general has also undergone some nice work to make a pleasant, pedestrian-friendly area.

There is a **Frank Lloyd Wright** residence—one of only five Wright-designed structures in the entire state of Missouri—at 120 N. Ballas in the Sugar Creek area of Kirkwood (just off Dougherty Ferry Road). Tours are available, but must be arranged in advance at 314-822-8359. Built in the 1950s, the house is particularly notable in that it is virtually 100 percent authentic, right down to the original furnishings.

Kirkwood is also home to the **Museum of Transportation**, at 3015 Barrett Station Road, not far from the junction of 270 and Dougherty Ferry Road. The museum has an automobile pavilion, as well as several tracks of locomotives and other railroad stock for you to tour and enjoy. The autos include a 1963 Chrysler Turbine and a custom-built aluminum car made in 1960 and used in the Bobby Darin movie *Too Cool Blues*. Among the railroad exhibits are the last steam locomotive to operate in Missouri, a wooden caboose, a complete passenger train, a tank car, and the "Big Boy," the world's largest-ever steam locomotive. Also on display are a tow boat and a C-47 military transport which flew in the Second World War. But most important to Route 66 fans is the fact that the museum now has the facade from one of the **Coral Court Motel** units on exhibit inside. The Coral Court was a very special example of highway architecture from the heyday of postwar travel, and it stood not far from here until "redevelopment" took it in 1995. Thankfully, a small part of it has been preserved for your enjoyment. Built in 1941 from glazed hollow brick and glass block in the Streamline Moderne style, the Coral Court, even when new, was evocative of another time. Legend has it that bank robbers once stashed loot in the hollow walls of one or more units, of which the Coral Court once boasted more than 70.

The original gates to the Coral Court still stand on old 66 (Watson Rd.) where Oak Knoll Manor, the development which sealed the motel's fate, now sits.

TIMES BEACH

This was a planned community which was established about 1925, just on the eve of the birth of the Federal Highway System. Lots were sold or given away by the *St. Louis Star-Times* newspaper as part of a promotion, hence the name. What happened at Times Beach, however, shouldn't happen to anyone. Residents were forced to evacuate decades later when it was determined that the ground on which the community sat had been contaminated with dioxins, which had been present in the materials used to spray on the roads for dust control. This evacuation occurred in 1982. Fortunately, the site has been the object of cleanup efforts for years now, and has since been turned into the **Missouri Route 66 State Park**, with trails, picnic areas, and river access. The visitor center also includes

Route 66 exhibits, and is housed in a vintage roadhouse building. Exit 266 from I-44.

EUREKA

West of Eureka is **Six Flags St. Louis**, one of those large-scale theme parks which adds immeasurably to the traffic in this area. South of I-44 at exit 264 in Eureka is the **Black Madonna Shrine and Grottoes**. Built by a Franciscan brother by hand, the grottoes are "dedicated to the Black Madonna, Our Lady of Czestochowa, Queen of Peace and Mercy." These ornamental works of faith have become known far and wide. 100 St. Joseph's Rd.

ALLENTON-PACIFIC

Somewhere in this vicinity is the **Al-Pac Motel** (Allenton-Pacific) and **Pacific 66 Liquors**. About a mile east of Pacific is the **Red Cedar Inn**, a café and former hotel that first started serving travelers on this stretch of road around 1934. West of Pacific is the **Missouri Botanical Garden Arboretum and Nature Preserve**.

Red Cedar Inn, Pacific, Missouri.

GRAY SUMMIT

This town is best known for its association with Ralston-Purina.

Just north of Gray Summit, on County Road MM, is **Purina**

Farms. This compound holds canine events through most of the year, which include agility trials, herding competitions, all breed shows, and racing. One of my personal favorites is the Jack Russell Fun Days, sponsored by the Missouri Earth Dog Club. These dogs are incredibly enthusiastic about racing around, rooting things out of holes in the ground, and just all-around cavorting. Aside from being fun for pets and owners alike, many of the events presented at Purina Farms are educational as well. There are workshops in dog-obedience training, for example. You can also learn how to milk a cow or operate a simulated pet-food manufacturing machine.

Also very near Gray Summit is the **Shaw Arboretum**, where prairie flora and fauna are preserved and a visitor center and several miles of hiking trails await.

VILLA RIDGE

At Villa Ridge is the **Diamonds Restaurant**—the new one, circa 1969. The Diamonds was once billed as the world's largest restaurant. Not far away is the Gardenway Motel, a colonial-style motel that probably graced the front of many a postcard in its prime. Notice the glass-block detailing in the roadside sign. A little further

Longtime truck stop on old 66 in Villa Ridge, Missouri.

to the west is the Tri-County Truck Stop, which is actually on the site of the old Diamonds, which burned in the 1940s.

West of the Tri-County is the Sunset Motel, which has a unique sunburst-style sign. On one of my earlier trips through here, the Sunset appeared to be serving duty as an apartment house.

ST. CLAIR

This town was formerly known as Traveler's Repose, but it's said the townsfolk grew tired of being thought of as a cemetery. There used to be a motel here with an eye-catching sign, the Arch Motel, overlooking the superslab. For many years, St. Clair was the home of Ozark Rock Curios, a purveyor of interesting geological specimens to Route 66 tourists.

The **St. Clair Historical Museum** contains 23 exhibits, including Indian artifacts, mining-related items, and a Victorian parlor, doctor's office, and general store. 280 Hibbard Street.

Between St. Clair and Stanton, if you follow the road paralleling the railroad track on the south side of I-44, you'll be taken on an old alignment of the highway through **Anaconda**. The town is about midway between St. Clair and Stanton, and was named Morrellton when my 1946 road map was printed. By the time of my '57 atlas, the town had been completely bypassed by the new alignment, and it bore the current name of Anaconda.

Closed motel, east of St. Clair, Missouri.

Alongside the highway just east of Stanton formerly stood the Ozark Court Motel, which had a distinctive sign featuring a prancing deer.

STANTON

This community is best known as the gateway to the **Meramec Caverns** to the south.

You'll want to stop in for a look at the **Antique Toy Museum**, near I-44 exit 230. There are thousands of first-rate antique and collectible toy cars, trucks, tractors, trains, etc., as well as dolls, doll houses, and doll furniture. There are even a few full-size antique trucks on the premises for the really big boys in the family (including one nicknamed the Big Mack Attack).

This distinctive motel sign near Stanton, Missouri, is now gone.

A neighbor to the toy museum is the **Jesse James Museum**, a true roadside attraction. The central focus of this museum is that Jesse James didn't really die of a gunshot wound in 1881 as the authorities have been telling us all these years—he actually lived to a ripe old age under another name and died in 1952! There are even wax figures of the conspirators in this diabolical plot to mislead the public. The museum staff will enthusiastically heap evidence upon you of their version of Jesse's life, such as a list of physical traits (scars, etc.) shared by the original Jesse and the mystery man who survived until well into the Route 66 era. I can also tell you that there is another museum dedicated to this same theory in the small town of Hico, Texas. As of this writing, there is a project afoot to put all of these theories to a DNA test by exhuming Jesse's mother in Lincoln County, New Mexico.

FURTHER AFIELD

Just a few miles south and east of Route 66, via Highway W, is one of the route's most widely known attractions, **Meramec Caverns**. In fact, a trip to Meramec Caverns is more a required pilgrimage than a side trip for anyone traveling the Mother Road. That's largely because clever marketing made this cave a part of almost any trip down 66.

Lester Dill opened Meramec Caverns commercially in 1935, and managed successfully to portray his caverns as a former hideout of Jesse James, even though the evidence for this is fairly thin. Secondly, he paid to have the sides and roofs of barns all over the country painted with his colorful "logo" so that motorists far and wide were made aware of Meramec Caverns. The barns dotted the countryside not just along Route 66, the highway that takes you there, but on roadsides all over the Midwest (some estimates place the number at around 350). Thirdly, each visitor to Meramec Caverns became an advertisement for the attraction. That's because the Dill clan pioneered the bumper sticker. Youngsters were paid to ensure that each vehicle in their parking lot left with a Meramec Caverns tag tied to their rear bumper. The combination of these strategies made Meramec Caverns not just one of the best-known caves in the country, but one of the most-recognized attractions of any kind whatsoever.

Inside, in addition to the usual underground formations, there is a neon sign proclaiming "Jesse James Hideout," and nearby is Loot Rock, where facsimiles of Jesse and his gang divide the spoils of their latest heist. Also included is a moonshiners' cave. The tour climaxes with a light show, which projects the Stars & Stripes onto a structure called the Stage Curtain—the largest such formation in the world—while Kate Smith belts out "God Bless America."

Adjacent facilities include a motel, campground, gift shop, restaurant, and canoe rentals (with shuttle service).

Note on barn painting: well-informed roadies will know of an attraction near Lookout Mountain, Georgia, which began painting barns back in 1936. Those barns, once numbering about 900, covered 19 states with the See Rock City motif. About 80 of those barns remain according to recent count, and Rock City itself is still going strong.

Very near Meramec Caverns, as the crow flies, is the much lesser-known **Fisher's Cave**, on the grounds of Meramec State Park. However, you'll need to approach it via Highway 185 from a junction just east of Sullivan. Visitors use handheld lanterns to explore these caves during a 90-minute tour on paved walkways. This cave is said to have been in use since the 1860s, when then-governor Thomas Fletcher organized a celebration there. 2800 S. Hwy 185.

Meramec and Fisher are just the first of several caves which will be in striking distance of Route 66 as we sweep through Missouri. For spelunkers (cave lovers), Missouri is a paradise. At last count, there were more than 5,400 *registered* caves in the state.

SULLIVAN

The last time I passed through here, there was a **muffler man** figure, decked out as a lumberjack, by the side of the road as part of a trampoline display. Not only did he help sell trampolines, but he had also been victimized by someone doing some target practice with a bow and arrow. The poor fellow had a number of arrow shafts sticking out of his anatomy. I've been told that the lumberjack has since been removed.

Just east of the town of Bourbon, the highway passes a huge barn sporting a stone silo.

BOURBON

The main street through town is named Old Hwy 66. The town slogan: Make Our Bourbon Your Bourbon.

FURTHER AFIELD

Former "muffler man," latter-day interstate sentry.

Between Bourbon and Cuba, spelunkers can take exit 214 (Highway H) to **Onondaga Cave**, a National Natural Landmark, known for its wide variety of formations. Take advantage of the guided tours of the underground river, or simply enjoy the camping and picnicking areas and the nearby hiking trails. Close by is the neighboring **Cathedral Cave**.

About two-thirds of the way from Bourbon to Cuba, right where the railroad track sidles up close to the south side of I-44 and just east of exit 210, is what remains of a town called

Hofflins. A full-fledged town in the 1940s, my 1957 atlas chose to omit it completely. That atlas shows U.S. 66 in this vicinity already as a four-lane divided highway. That highway growth nearly on its doorstep—along with the concomitant traffic—likely made Hofflins unlivable for its residents. Today, very little remains.

After Hofflins, old 66 wanders away from the interstate and towards the town of Cuba.

CUBA

According to the 1990 U.S. population census, the mean population center of the United States was just northwest of Cuba, Missouri. As of the 2000 census, it's near Edgar Springs, Missouri, which is about 20 miles south of Rolla. That shift was expected, inasmuch as the population center has been shifting to the south and west ever since we've been conducting censuses (1790).

The most important feature of Cuba to a Route 66 traveler is the **Wagon Wheel Motel**, which is not only still in operation, but looks every bit as tidy and inviting as the day it opened for business. If you haven't stayed in a good old-fashioned mom-and-pop motel yet on this trip, this is an excellent place to do so. If you'll be moving on, then just stay around long enough to snap a few photos and appreciate the one-of-a-kind sign, with its neon-trimmed wagon wheel suspended over the road. Cuba these days is also home to several outdoor murals.

Business is not what it used to be in Cuba, Missouri.

The Cuba-to-St. James stretch of Route 66 takes you through the Rosati wine country. Years ago, this area was sprinkled with vendors offering grapes from small roadside stands. Today, the old highway takes you through the towns of Fanning and Rosati, and there are several operating wineries in the vicinity. Established in 1933—the year prohibition was repealed—the **Rosati Winery** offers tours which include a look at its subterranean wine cellars.

ST. JAMES

Finn's Motel caters to travelers here, not far from the St. James Winery. The town was established in 1859 under the name of Scioto.

FURTHER AFIELD

About eight miles southeast of St. James via Missouri State Highway 8 is **Maramec Spring Park** [sic]. Maramec Spring proper is a National Natural Landmark, and it exudes some 96 million gallons of water each day from the base of a bluff. This spring used to provide the power for the Maramec Iron Works, established circa 1857, the ruins of which can still be seen within the park.

As you exit the vicinity of St. James and continue your southwesterly trek across Missouri, you are leaving the Big Prairie section of the state and climbing atop the Ozark plateau. You will begin to see a change in the topology as you encounter exposed rock outcroppings more and more. The hilly Ozark region, which extends into northwestern Arkansas, is well-known as moonshine territory and home to the Hatfields and McCoys.

DILLON

South of I-44, Dillon had already been bypassed by 1957 in favor of a faster, four-lane alignment in the corridor now occupied by the interstate. On the opposite (north) side of the interstate, on the frontage road, is **Route 66 Motors**. At the time I visited, they had an impressive array of signs on display outside, making an excellent photo-op. Also outside were gasoline pumps, a power boat, and sundry vehicles in various stages of neglect or restoration.

NORTHWYE

This village did not appear on my 1946 map, but evidently the U.S. 63/66 junction location spurred growth. By 1957, it was plotted by the cartographers. Now it's home to **Memoryville, USA**, an antique auto museum and gift shop, which also features a working automobile restoration workshop where you can see works in progress. Displays include a fully restored 1938 Nash owned by radio personality Paul Harvey.

ROLLA

Named after the North Carolina capital—but spelled more phonetically, based upon a southern drawl—Rolla has a surprisingly active downtown, with the **Ritz and Uptown Theaters**, **Lambiel Jewelers**, and **Alex's Pizza** keeping things going. It doesn't hurt that it's a college town.

ROLLA ATTRACTIONS

The U.S. Geological Survey's **Mid-Continent Mapping Center**, at 1400 Independence Rd., performs research and production func-

Rolla, Missouri.

tions for the USGS and its cartographic products, be they conventional maps or modern-day digital systems. There is a water resource division providing information about the region's—yep, you guessed it—water resources.

The University of Missouri at Rolla (UMR) offers a number of points of interest. The **Mineral Museum** is at 125 Nutt Hall, and features mineral displays from the 1904 St. Louis World's Fair, as well as objects donated by friends and alumni of the university.

Elsewhere on the university campus is a half-sized replica of **Stonehenge**, carved by the college's high-pressure water lab. The builders (carvers?) claim that theirs is the only replica (of the four that exist) which can accurately be used for timekeeping. UMR also has an **experimental limestone mine**, which was created in 1921 and can be toured.

The **Dillon House** is a log structure which served as the area's first courthouse circa 1857. The logs used are 18 feet in length. Third and Main.

The **Totem Pole Trading Post** was moved to the west side of Rolla about 30 years ago from its original location near Clementine. The carved totem pole which used to adorn the roof of the old trading post is now on display indoors at the present location.

Leaving Rolla, you are heading into the heart of the Ozark country. Keep an eye out for some curbed sections of the highway as you leave town headed west.

The Rolla-to-Springfield portion of Route 66 here in Missouri roughly follows the infamous **Cherokee Trail of Tears**. There were a number of variants on the route of the forced march from Georgia to Oklahoma, and the Northern Route went through this very corridor, circuitous as it may seem. It began in 1838, when a combination of congressional maneuvering, along with some wholesale trickery, led to the expulsion of the Cherokee people from their homes in Georgia. That year, U.S. troops under the command of General Winfield Scott began rounding up men, women, and children and herding them hundreds of miles across the country. As implied by the name, many perished along the way.

In recognition of this fact, someone has paid tribute by building a **stone gateway** to his property, over which hangs a sign proclaiming simply "Trail of Tears." The work that went into this tribute is nothing short of astounding: there is the arched gateway, several walls, circular wheel-like formations, more arches, and things resembling obelisks, all constructed of thousands of stones piled upon one another. Keep on the alert as you pass through the area near Arlington.

DOOLITTLE

The town was named for air-racer and World War II hero **Jimmy Doolittle** of Alameda, California. Doolittle set a world speed record in 1932; then in 1942 he led the famous attack on Tokyo and other cities using B-25s launched from the aircraft carrier U.S.S. *Hornet*. That raid, coming as it did only a few months after Pearl Harbor, was a tremendous boost to American morale. Doolittle also served in Italy, Germany, and North Africa during the war.

West of the I-44 exit 176 is something you really should stop and see. **John's Modern Cabins** was a tourist abode made up of a set of small cabins. For the time that they were erected—early 1950s—these were rather primitive accommodations, as evidenced by the remains of an outhouse in the rear. Somewhat ironically, in the midst of this rather rustic encampment, a neon sign glowed in "modern" welcome. A stone's throw from the cabins is **Vernelle's Motel**, which has a vacant convenience store of the vintage variety out front.

ARLINGTON

On the bank of the Little Piney River, the town of Arlington has been effectively cut off from highway traffic, and you might assume that this was a result of the replacement of U.S. 66 by Interstate 44. However, if you read Jack Rittenhouse's 1946 account of his passage through here, you learn that Arlington had already been cut off by that time due to earlier construction. He went on to state that the area was rumored to be earmarked for the development of a resort. More than 50 years later, Arlington is a very sleepy place indeed.

Onyx Mountain Caverns is just to the west of the highway between Powellville and Clementine, and appears as King Cave on some earlier maps.

**Close-up of sign and cabin at John's Modern Cabins,
near Arlington, Missouri.**

CLEMENTINE

Rittenhouse stated that Clementine was "hardly a town," and it does not appear (nor does Powellville) on 1946 or 1957 maps of the

One man's tribute to the Cherokee Trail of Tears, near Arlington, Missouri.

region. At one time, this section was characterized by its plentiful basket vendors arrayed beside the highway.

After Clementine, you will need to take Highway Z in order to pass through the village of Devil's Elbow.

DEVIL'S ELBOW

The ominous name of Devil's Elbow comes not from any highway hazard, but rather from the fact that there is a severe bend in the Big Piney River here, which caused problems for those whose livelihoods depended on the transport of goods up and down the waterway. There is a 1920s-era bridge which crosses the river, and which carried Route 66 traffic in the highway's early years. However, the narrow bridge and twisting road were considered a real problem during the war years when military material began being transported back and forth, and so the highway was re-routed for a straighter course.

Allman's Market (now Sheldon's) also serves as the post office for the village of Devil's Elbow, Missouri.

The Munger Moss Sandwich Shop plied its trade here at the town of Devil's Elbow (at the location of the current **Elbow Inn**), but during the highway's re-alignment in the 1940s both the town and the restaurant were unceremoniously cut off, and so the proprietors moved to Lebanon and established the Munger Moss Motel.

There is a combination post office and general store in Devil's Elbow which has changed its name over the years from Miller's to Allman's to Sheldon's, but otherwise it has looked very much the same for decades.

FURTHER AFIELD

After Devil's Elbow and just before you reach the city of Waynesville, there is a turnoff for **Fort Leonard Wood** at Spur 44. General Leonard Wood was quite an accomplished officer, and well deserving of having an army post named after him. After the outbreak of the Spanish-American War in 1898, then-Colonel Wood and his friend Theodore Roosevelt recruited the 1st Volunteer Cavalry—the famous Rough Riders—of which Wood was the commanding officer. Meritorious conduct at the battles of Las Guasimas and San Juan Hill gained Wood promotion to brigadier general. After the war, Wood served as military governor of Cuba from 1899–1902, during which time he oversaw improvements in sanitation, education, and law enforcement. He also served as governor over the Phillippines from 1921 to 1927. General Wood even ran for the Republican presidential nomination in 1920, narrowly losing that bid to Warren G. Harding.

There is a group of **museums** at Fort Leonard Wood, among them exhibits honoring the army's Engineer Corps, Chemical Corps, and Military Police Corps. There is also information about General Wood's life and career, and an area set up as a replica of Fort Leonard Wood as it appeared during the 1940s.

WAYNESVILLE

The town is named for the revolutionary war hero, "Mad" Anthony Wayne. Located as it is just northwest of Fort Leonard Wood, Waynesville was the chief recreational center for troops training here during the war years. During that time, the streets were lined with bars, cafés, and other businesses which tended to attract young GIs. This was very much in evidence immediately following the war when our friend Jack Rittenhouse came through here.

While downtown, look for the Tinkle Bar, and also the glassed-in storefront with classic cars on display inside.

WAYNESVILLE ATTRACTIONS

At 106 Lynn Street is the **Old Stagecoach Stop**, a two-story station which also saw duty as a Civil War hospital and as a hotel during its 140-year history. On the National Register.

Keep on the lookout for **Frog Rock** jutting out of a hillside near the town square. Locals decided the rock outcropping looked a lot like a frog, so it's been painted very nicely now to *really* look like a frog.

BUCKHORN-HAZELGREEN

Historic 66 crosses I-44 (at exit 153) here at Buckhorn. Buckhorn was named for the **Buckhorn Tavern**, a former stagecoach stop on the old Wire Road, which displayed a set of antlers. Just east of the Highway 133 junction is an area called Gascozark. That name was coined by a developer in the 1920s, and is a hybrid derived from Ozark and Gasconade (for the nearby river).

LEBANON

Lebanon is home to the **Munger Moss Motel**, which has a huge red porcelain-and-neon sign out front manufactured just a little up the road by a firm named Springfield Neon. If you'll be staying the night in the

The Munger Moss Motel is a place every Mother Roader should plan to stay the night sometime. Lebanon, Missouri.

Lebanon area, I highly recommend you do so here at the Munger Moss. The owners really care about Route 66 and roadies like you and me. The lobby is also a combination gift shop and vintage toy display.

Not far from the Munger Moss is **Wrink's Market**. Unfortunately, Glenn "Wrink" Wrinkle passed away in 2005. Wrink started operating the market in 1950, and kept it open until only a few weeks before his death 55 years later.

LEBANON ATTRACTIONS

Opened in 2004, the LaClede County Library houses a great **Route 66 Museum** run by the Lebanon/LaClede County Route 66 Society (915 S. Jefferson). The old LaClede County Jail is on the National Register. 262 N. Adams.

The **International Stave Company** (a.k.a. Barrels of Fun) is a barrel manufactory with "thru the window" tours of the operation available at any time. The gift store has wines and whiskies packaged in barrels made right on the premises. Immediately adjacent is a shop where you can buy walnut bowls and other woodcraft items.

Ballhagen's Puzzle Source, at 25211 Garden Crest Rd., is a must-stop for serious puzzle lovers. There are literally thousands in stock, and you can see a couple hundred completed jigsaw puzzles on display, including one which covers 24 square feet and is composed of more than 7,000 pieces.

Hall-Moore Stuff (get it?) is a place full of junk and collectibles between interstate exits 130 and 135 (a couple of miles east of town).

FURTHER AFIELD

North of Lebanon (about 25 miles) via Highway 5 is **Camdenton**.

A nearby park, **Ha Ha Tonka State Park**, includes the remains of a nearly 100-year-old European-style **castle**. In 1905, a Kansas City businessman named Robert Snyder began construction of a three-story stone castle on 2,500 acres of land that he had acquired for its natural beauty. He intended to create a retreat that would rival any in the world, and he spared no expense in its creation, hiring the most qualified artisans and obtaining the best materials available. Tragically, he died suddenly in 1906, and the unfinished project was taken over by his sons. The property eventually included the castle, an 80-foot water tower, stables, and several greenhouses. In later years the family came upon hard times and was forced to lease the property to someone who operated it as a hotel. In 1942, more tragedy struck when a spark from a fireplace spread rapidly and gutted both the main house and the stable. Those ruins now stand stark and haunting atop a 250-foot bluff overlooking the Lake of the Ozarks.

The state of Missouri purchased the estate in 1978 and opened it to the public as a state park. The park's beautiful natural features confirm Mr. Snyder's good taste in obtaining the property. Today, park visitors can enjoy sinkholes, caves, a natural bridge, springs, and of course the famous ruins via some 15 miles of trails. The trails run the gamut from paved, "accessible" paths and boardwalks to strenuous, rocky climbs suitable for overnight backpacking. Some of the caves here—much as with others throughout Missouri— are said to have been used as hideouts by criminals during the 1830s. The Ha Ha Tonka (Laughing Water) visitor center features a relief map of this wondrous area carved from a block of stone.

PHILLIPSBURG

According to a 1946 oil company road map of Missouri, the towns of Conway, Sampson, and Niangua were all Route 66 towns strung out between Phillipsburg and Marshfield. By 1957, however, a new

**Pair of Meramec advertising barns.
Phillipsburg, Missouri.**

four-lane alignment had been constructed which bypassed all of these towns by a few miles and occupied the present-day I-44 roadbed through the region. Also, by 1957 the village of Sampson was no longer deemed worthy of mention at all. These towns are still there, but you'll have to make a greater effort if you intend to see them.

MARSHFIELD-HOLMAN-STRAFFORD

Marshfield is the hometown of **Edwin Hubble**, creator of the space-based telescope of the same name known for its customized corrective lens. The town has a one-quarter sized replica of the telescope occupying the courthouse lawn.

East of Strafford, near the small hamlet of Holman, is **Exotic Animal Paradise**, one of those zoological parks which you drive through in your car (9½ miles) and view hundreds of animals in captivity, some of which may not even know it is they, and not you, who are in the lockup. Denizens of this paradise include bison, llamas, and zedonks (zebra-donkey hybrids). Unlike most zoological parks of one kind or another, you are not forbidden to feed the animals here. In fact, there is animal feed for sale, so that you can toss some out of your car to entice the animals to approach more closely. There are also paddle boats and a petting zoo.

SPRINGFIELD

Established in 1825 when pioneer John Polk Campbell carved his initials in a tree near the confluence of four springs, and soon thereafter known as the Queen of the Ozarks, Springfield won't disappoint the Route 66 traveler. There are multiple Route 66 alignments, so exploration is strongly encouraged. The best-known versions enter Springfield on Kearney Street, turn south on Glenstone, and then head west again after turning onto either Chestnut or St.

The Rest Haven Motel in Springfield, Missouri, sports an enormous neon sign in excellent condition.

Louis, which will take you through the heart of downtown. There are still a number of classic motels and other vintage businesses all along this corridor to excite your senses. Among them are the **Rest Haven**, **Rancho**, **Skyline**, and **Rail Haven**, to name only a few.

Springfield has a special distinction. It was here in 1947 that Red Chaney opened the first hamburger stand with a drive-thru window—Red's Giant Hamburg. Red eventually retired, and his landmark was demolished in 1997, with more than a few nostalgic souls turning out for the occasion. There had been a song written about the place in 1982 called "Red's" and recorded by The Morells. A photo of Red's place even appeared on the album cover.

Another business originating here in Springfield was Campbell's 66 Express, the trucking firm which used Snortin' Norton, the "Humpin' to Please" camel, as its trademark.

The **Steak 'n' Shake** restaurant chain still has a sizable presence in Missouri, and in Springfield in particular there are a number of the earlier examples still extant. Their famous directive to Take Home a Sack (modified to Takhomasak) has been echoed many times over by famous burger chains nationwide: White Castle's "Buy 'em by the Sack"; White Tower's "Buy a Bag Full"; and Krystal's "Take Along a Sack Full" all encourage us to indulge the same impulse.

As you pass through town on what is now College Street, be on the lookout for a small embankment beside the road adorned with mosaic-style artwork.

This gem graces downtown Springfield, Missouri.

Ed Galloway

Nathan Ed Galloway was born in Stone County near Springfield, Missouri in 1880, and from a very young age he showed a talent and propensity for wood carving.

He joined the U.S. Army and served in the Spanish-American War in 1898 and was then assigned to duty in the Phillippines. While there, he came into contact with creatures such as crocodiles and other reptiles which would inspire some of his later art.

After leaving the Army, Galloway returned to Springfield and pursued his wood carving. He specialized in household objects such as coat and smoking stands, which he covered with intricate carvings of animals and other figures. He also fashioned many large-scale items from tree trunks; these, too, were often decorated with human and animal figures. Galloway planned to be an exhibitor at the Panama-Pacific

International Exposition in San Francisco taking place in 1915. Tragically, there was a fire at his studio which destroyed most of his work.

Ed managed to salvage a few pieces, including what is known as his "Lion in a Cage," and began making his way west toward California for the exposition. It is said that he had been temporarily waylaid in Tulsa, Oklahoma, when his work was seen and admired by Charles Page. Page was a business-man and philanthropist who had established a home for orphaned children in nearby Sand Springs. He offered Galloway a job teaching woodworking to the boys at the Sand Springs Home. Ed Galloway remained at Sand Springs in that capacity for the next 20-plus years.

In 1936–37, Ed and his wife, Villie, moved to several acres near Foyil, Oklahoma (Villie was from the Bushyhead area) and began the chapter of his life for which he is best-known. Ed began building a stone residence on the property (completed 1937) and a collection of large Native American-inspired structures. The largest of those structures is a 90-foot-tall totem pole which took him 11 years to complete (1948).

Galloway also constructed his "Fiddle House," an 11-sided building created expressly to house the growing collec-tion of fiddles which he was carving during this time. That collection is said to have exceeded 300.

Ed Galloway seems to have been speaking to Mother Road lovers such as you and me when he said: "All my life, I did the best I knew. I built these things by the side of the road to be a friend to you."

Ed Galloway died of cancer on November 11, 1962 (Veteran's Day). His Foyil property was donated by his family in 1989 to the Rogers County Historical Society, which main-tains the present-day Totem Pole Park.

SPRINGFIELD ATTRACTIONS

The town is widely known as the home of **Bass Pro Shops Outdoor World**, a veritable theme park of a retail experience for the outdoor set. There's a 140,000-gallon game fish aquarium and a four-story waterfall. If that's not enough, check out the stuffed and mounted bears, the antique fishing gear, and the wildlife art gallery.

The **PFI Western Store**, at U.S. 65 and Battlefield Rd., has over 10,000 pairs of boots, a 16-screen video wall, and a working radio station.

The **American National Fish and Wildlife Museum** opened in 2001 at 500 W. Sunshine Street.

The **Typewriter Toss** is held each April on Secretaries Day, just in case you thought that was a "holiday" you could live without. From a height of 50 feet, the typewriters are thrown at a bull's-eye.

The **Frisco Museum** is said to be the only facility devoted exclusively to Frisco Railway, Pullman, and Railway Express Agency memorabilia (over 2,000 items). 543 E. Commercial St.

If pioneer history interests you, check out the **Gray-Campbell Farmstead**. Centered around the oldest house in Springfield (ca. 1856), exhibits include a log kitchen, two-crib barn, family cemetery, and Civil War-era artifacts. There are costumed docents on hand to explain the history of the place. 2400 S. Scenic, in Nathanael Greene Park.

Also at Nathanael Greene Park is the **Japanese Stroll Garden**, with over seven acres of lakes, winding paths, and other traditional features of Japanese-style gardens.

The Dickerson Park Zoo has on display a wood carving—entitled "Lion in a Cage"—created by folk artist Ed Galloway for the 1904 St. Louis Exposition. Ed's true claim to fame is Totem Pole Park near Foyil, Oklahoma, which you'll have a chance to visit further west. The zoo is at 3043 N. Fort Ave.

At the **Missouri Sports Hall of Fame**, you'll become acquainted with some of the great names that have called the Show-

Me State home base: Stan Musial, Whitey Herzog, and Bob Gibson, to name only a few. There's even a cage where visitors can stand behind home plate while 100-mph fastballs come blazing in from the mound. 3861 E. Stan Musial Dr.

The **Springfield Art Museum**, 1111 E. Brookside, is the city's oldest cultural institution, featuring eight galleries.

Military memorabilia abounds at the **Air and Military Museum of the Ozarks**, including restored aircraft, a variety of military vehicles, dioramas, and flight simulators. 2305 E. Kearney.

Civil War buffs will want to visit **General Sweeney's Museum**. An official site of the Civil War Trust, it's the only museum to focus on the trans-Mississippi portion of the conflict, and it houses more than 5,000 wartime artifacts. 5228 S. State Hwy ZZ.

In the town square is a **plaque** commemorating the shootout which occurred here between Wild Bill Hickok and Dave Tutt as a result of an argument over a poker game.

FURTHER AFIELD

Just northwest of Springfield you'll find **Fantastic Caverns**. Acclaimed as America's Only Drive-Thru Cave, the tour takes visitors along the path of an underground river in Jeeps while the guides extol the considerable virtues of protecting the environment by powering the tour vehicles with propane. Furthermore, the cave was once owned by the Klu Klux Klan, who held meetings in one of the caverns here.

In contrast to the above, due north of Springfield via Highway H is **Crystal Cave**. Here, the operators have endeavored to provide a cave experience in a more natural state. There are no vehicles; instead, visitors clamber about on narrow paths and must negotiate tight spaces. Unusual features include Rainbow Falls, the Cathedral, fossil crinoids, and numerous Indian symbols.

About 10 miles southwest of Springfield is **Wilson's Creek**

National Battlefield, where the first Union general to die in combat during the Civil War, Nathaniel Lyon, lost his life on August 10, 1861. There are structures which have been restored to their 1861 condition, and films and maps are on display in the museum.

The town of **Marionville**, also southwest of Springfield, has a reputation for **albino squirrels**. Keep your camera ready.

To the south of Springfield, via U.S. 65, is the town of **Branson**, Missouri. Though considered by many people of sound mind to be a tad overblown, Branson does have at least one redeeming feature—the **Branson Scenic Railway**, a restored Ozark Zephyr, plies the area and hearkens to the passenger service glory days of the 1940s and '50s.

To the northwest of Branson via Highway 76 is a semi-Christian theme park called **Silver Dollar City**. The park sprang up due to the presence of nearby **Marvel Cave**, a subterranean attraction in the area since 1950. The theme park was officially established in 1960, and then received some additional notoriety when a few episodes of the *Beverly Hillbillies* television series were filmed there in 1967.

Head out of Springfield on the Chestnut Expressway, which is Historic 66.

PLANO

Somewhere in this vicinity is an extremely vine-covered building of masonry construction just a few feet from the edge of the highway. The interior is completely gutted and roofless. Inside many small trees grow, reaching for the windows and the sky.

If you have a detailed map of this region, you can see that Route 66 (present-day Hwy 266 from here to Paris Springs, and Highway 96 from Spencer to northeast of Carthage) was plotted as nearly a straight line over the next 40 miles or so.

HALLTOWN

Established in 1833 and later named for a merchant named George Hall, the town is known for its antique shops, the largest of which is the Whitehall Mercantile. Amazingly, Jack Rittenhouse characterizes Halltown by making mention of antique shops way back in 1946.

Coming up is one of my favorite stretches of old Route 66. Ahead of you now is a string of very small towns between here and Carthage. This section of the highway was bypassed and the main traffic flow diverted elsewhere many years ago. Hwy 166, which passed through Republic, Mt. Vernon, and Sarcoxie to the south, began to bear more of the traffic in the mid-1950s. The result is that towns such as **Albatross** and **Phelps** had their lifelines pulled from them, and they became almost frozen in time. It is very similar to the Seligman-to-Topock segment in Arizona, in that the old highway remained the only road through the affected communities, and yet the flow of traffic had been halted by completion of the newer alignment several miles away.

As you pass through this section, I urge you to slow down considerably. Take your time through the communities of **Paris Springs**, **Spencer**, **Heatonville**, and the aforementioned Albatross and Phelps. You will see the ruins of convenience stores, tourist courts, and other structures, many of which look as though the owners left suddenly and never returned. You will also see some structures which have been re-assigned to new uses, such as a set of tourist cabins now being used as storage sheds.

RESCUE-PLEW-AVILLA-MAXWELL

Between Rescue and Plew is a turnoff (YY north) to Red Oak. This reference will be more meaningful later when you encounter Red Oak II near Carthage.

RED OAK II

You won't find it depicted on a road map, but here it is anyway, northeast of Carthage. Red Oak II is a village (Red Oak) which was brought over from its original location more than 20 miles away and installed here, presumably to attract nostalgia-minded Mother Road travelers. It features a multitude of vintage structures, including a blacksmith shop, general store, restored Phillips 66 station, and several residences, both occupied and otherwise.

CARTHAGE

The famed Carthage marble is quarried here, and more than a few Carthaginians have made their living in the field. There is a home tour which begins and ends at the courthouse in the square (pick up a brochure at the chamber of commerce) and which takes you on a drive to see several homes of Carthage's most prominent citizens, all constructed between 1870 and 1910, many of which were built by stone quarry and mine owners.

The **Jasper County Courthouse** itself was constructed in 1894–95. There is a mural inside depicting the history of the area, painted by a local artist. The courthouse also features a wrought-iron cage-style elevator which is still in operation. Take a stroll around the town square, which is lined with buildings dating from as early as the 1870s.

Marlin Perkins, longtime host of the popular television series *Wild Kingdom*, grew up in Carthage, and there is a statue of him standing in the town's Central Park. Belle Starr also grew up here, in her father's hotel downtown, prior to the Civil War.

For a reminder of authentic Route 66, the **Boots Motel** is hard to beat. It's at 107 S. Garrison; you'll see it just as you make the left turn from Central onto Garrison. There used to be a Boots Drive-In & Gift Shop in town also. According to a local tourism brochure, Clark Gable once stayed at the Boots in room number 6.

Further west on 66, on the outskirts of town, is the 1940s-era **66 Drive-In Theater**. This theater was restored in 1998, re-opening exactly 49 years after its original grand opening in September '49.

CARTHAGE ATTRACTIONS

The **Battle of Carthage Civil War Museum** is at 205 Grant. A mural, prints, historic relics, and souvenirs memorialize the battle and its participants. The Battle of Carthage was fought early in the war (1861) and was a victory for the Confederates, setting an early tone for the hostilities. The **Battle of Carthage State Historic Site** is also nearby (east of River on E. Chestnut Road).

Historic Phelps House, 1146 S. Grand Avenue, is a restored Victorian mansion (ca. 1895) offering tours. Some of the furniture and fixtures here are the originals. It has 10 fireplaces, each with different-colored tile, and a hand-operated elevator serving four floors. The house is built of local stone.

Local history is the focus at the **Powers Museum**, which has rotating exhibits on a variety of themes. Located at 1617 W. Oak St. (historic 66), the museum is on the former site of Taylor Tourist Park, later known as the Park Motor Court & Cafe. In 2005, the museum instituted what it calls its "Traveling Classroom Trunks" program for educators. The theme of one of these trunks is Jasper County highways, including Route 66 and other early auto trails.

The city of Carthage hosts an annual **Maple Leaf Festival** in October.

One of Carthage's most-visited attractions is the **Precious Moments Chapel**. To get there, take Highway 71 south and then HH west; then turn south on Chapel Rd. Recently added is an exhibit on the late Diana, Princess of Wales.

CARTERVILLE

According to Rittenhouse, Carterville in 1946 was already a virtual ghost town, with "boarded-up stores, empty buildings, and general air of desolation." Furthermore, it offered no facilities for motorists. My 1957 atlas, however, still affords it the status of a viable highway community.

There is a short stretch of vintage 66 which connects Carterville with nearby Webb City.

WEBB CITY

Webb City is well worth some exploration. Named for a local farmer, John Webb, who discovered lead in the area, the town's fortunes were tied to mining in earlier days. There seems to be an identity crisis of sorts in Webb City: the water tower is emblazoned "City of Flags," while a sign at the nearby park proclaims "Zinc City." I haven't found anyone who can explain the "flags" moniker.

Webb City has a very large neon arrow which points in the direction of its business district, which is slightly off the highway. Adjacent to the business district are some very nice older homes which are worth a walking tour. There are also some murals—one on the side of **Bruner Pharmacy** and another in **Webb City Bank**. At Ball and MacArthur Streets is a 105mm howitzer from World War II named Jeannie.

There is also a small park (**King Jack Park**) which features a large sculpture of a miner or prospector with pick in hand. The park also features a tiny train depot, which was moved there after having functioned as part of the interurban commuting system which was shut down in the 1930s. Overlooking King Jack Park is an enormous pair of praying hands, a sculpture created by 20-year-old Jack Dawson in 1974.

JOPLIN

Downtown Joplin features **Wilder's Fine Foods**, which has a wonderful old neon sign. Joplin is also the hometown of actor Dennis Weaver.

Exhibits at the **Dorothea Hoover Historical Museum** recall the Joplin of the 1870s, with antique dolls, a miniature animated circus, and a replica of a nineteenth-century tavern. At Schifferdecker Ave. at Fourth St., Schifferdecker Park. Also at Schifferdecker Park is the **Joplin Historical and Mineral Museum**. The park is on the western outskirts of the city.

The **Thomas Hart Benton mural**, called *Joplin at the Turn of the Century, 1896–1906*, is the last signed large-scale work by this Missourian. There are also sketches documenting the mural's progress.

Richardson's Candy House occupies the 60-year-old Rock Tavern building and still does things the old-fashioned way. Watch hand-dipped chocolates and divinity being made. Somehow I'm reminded of an *I Love Lucy* episode . . . . 454 Redings Mill Rd. (Hwy 86 S.).

FURTHER AFIELD

The **George Washington Carver National Monument** is southeast of Joplin, and about 2.5 miles southwest of the town of Diamond on County Road V—his birthplace. Carver was born into slavery, but through hard work became the director of agricultural research at the Tuskegee Institute. There, his experimentation led to the development of more than 400 new products made from peanuts, cotton, and soybeans.

Highway 66 leaves Joplin heading due west, and it's only a few miles to the Kansas border. The **State Line Bar & Grill** is there to remind you that you are passing into the Sunflower State.

KANSAS

Kansas has a reputation, at least among some of us, as epito-
mizing the safety and security of home. The impressions we
form at an early age are slow to change, and many of us in
twentieth-century America have grown up with a picture of Kansas
heavily influenced by the classic 1939 film, *The Wizard of Oz*. There,
Kansas was portrayed first as dull, then as a secure place to return

to, but always—fundamentally—as Home. Perhaps this impression is reinforced by the fact that Kansas is so centrally located within the contiguous 48 states. The state of Kansas seems to be officially satisfied with this image, having adopted "Home, Home on the Range" as its state song.

Even beyond that, stereotypes have a way of persisting. Someone who's never set foot in Kansas will tell you with great certainty that Kansas is very flat, monotonous country, with nothing but wheat fields for mile after mile after mile.

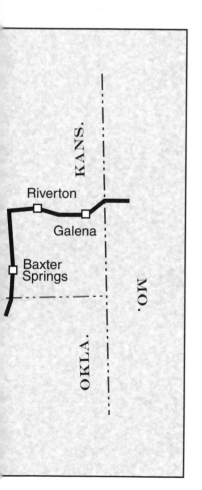

But in fact, Kansas is a place well worth getting to know. It's more diverse than most people realize, and it's far less a Home than it is a Crossroads. Numerous legendary trails traversed the state of Kansas en route to more remote objectives, such as California or Oregon, while others, like the Chisholm Trail, were laid out with Kansas as their destination.

A complete inventory of the historic tracks crisscrossing the state would be difficult to compile, but the list would have to include the Oregon Trail, which took settlers to the Oregon Territory by way of Topeka; the California-Overland Trail, which followed the same route during its passage through Kansas; the Santa Fe Trail, a trade route to the ancient capital passing through the longest dimension of the state and exiting near Elkhart; the Pony Express Route, along which mail was carried between Missouri and California; and the Chisholm Trail, the path of countless cattle and cowboys between the ranches of south Texas and the railheads at Abilene, Kansas.

Other trails in Kansas are less known, but served their purposes in their own time: the Parallel Road, the Ellsworth Trail, and the Pawnee Trail. And there have yet been others, including U.S. Route 66. Highway 66 was one of many such paths which touched Kansas only in order to reach someplace else.

Route 66—like so many of us—never gave Kansas a chance, never got to know her well. The path of Route 66 took barely a nibble from the southeast corner of the state—a mere 13 miles of road in a land of 82,000 square miles, 52 million acres, and 2.6 million people. To appreciate Kansas from so meager a sample is to emulate the blind man who tried to envision the elephant by touching only its tail.

The Kansas that you see from Route 66 isn't a lot like the stereotype you expect. No amber waves of grain shifting in the breeze here. Southeast Kansas is mining country, and mining districts are not often candidates for scenic postcard views. This is a different kind of bountiful earth, one that yields its rewards grudgingly, and one that does not find its way easily into glossy tour guides.

But that's not to say this portion of Kansas is any less proud of what it is. Route 66 paid its respects here and departed; the people of Kansas have gotten used to the idea and have moved on with their lives.

As you head westward into Kansas, past the State Line Bar & Grill, the first stop in the Sunflower State is Galena.

GALENA

Formerly two distinct towns, Galena and Empire, Galena annexed the other in 1911. The town is named for lead-bearing ore, which is plentiful in the area. Surprisingly to this traveler, Galena is a very

This retired M. K. T. Railroad depot now serves as the local history museum in Galena, Kansas.

Many of the buildings in Galena, Kansas, show signs of having been covered in advertising at one time.

popular name for American towns. At least 21 other states have—or have had—a town so named.

Downtown Galena has a number of buildings that have old advertising murals painted on the sides which are becoming visible again due to weathering. There is also an old gasoline station with a locomotive parked next to it on a downtown corner.

Also in Galena is the **Route 66 Howard "Pappy" Litch**

Park, named for a local citizen and historian. The park contains one of the original 1952 Will Rogers Highway plaques—this one was brought from a site at the Missouri-Kansas border—and is located on a plot of land formerly occupied by a Federal Highway weigh station.

The old Katy railroad depot, which is right on Highway 66 (319 W. 7th St.), now houses the **Galena Mining & Historical Museum**. Pappy Litch, for whom the park (above) was named, was one of the major forces in establishing this museum.

For a very short side trip, you can take Kansas Highway 26 south two miles from downtown Galena to **Schermerhorn Park**, in an area of the state called the Kansas Ozarks. There, you'll find a

Sign in downtown Galena, Kansas.

great-looking, WPA-constructed building and stone terraces from the 1930s. Formerly a boy scout meeting place, the structure has recently been transformed into a Nature Center. Also in the park is a cave—Schermerhorn Cave—which, like Meramec Cavern in Missouri, is reputed to have been a hiding place of outlaw Jesse James.

West of Galena en route to Riverton, you'll cross the Spring River. Covering several acres on the bank of the river at one time was the Spring River Inn, a neon sign for which was still standing when I last passed through. The Spring River Inn started life as a private residence shortly after 1900, but then served stints as part of a country club, yacht club, and finally a restaurant before falling victim to a fire in the 1990s.

RIVERTON

This is truly the center of Route 66 in Kansas. The **Eisler Brothers Store** (ca. 1925) is the de facto headquarters of the Kansas Route 66 Association, and serves not only as a general store, but also carries a

This bridge just outside Riverton, Kansas, was restored in 1994.

wide array of roadie paraphernalia intended just for adventurers like you and me.

Just to the west of town (on old 66/Beasley Rd.) is a restored arched bridge, sometimes referred to as the **Rainbow Bridge**, with a commemorative marker. Continue on Beasley, then curve left onto SE 50th St. toward Baxter Springs.

FURTHER AFIELD

Northwest of Riverton is the town of **Columbus**. There is a **clock tower** featuring a 1919 Seth Thomas movement still in operation. The clock was built using public donations as a memorial to servicemen of the First World War (at that time known as the Great War). 101 W. Maple Ave.

The nearby **Columbus Museum** (100 S. Tennessee Ave.) includes memorabilia from Merle Evans, a hometown boy who for 50 years was a bandleader with the Ringling Brothers circus. Also at the museum is a giant ball of string which was featured on the *I've Got A Secret* television show in the 1950s.

North of Riverton via U.S. 69 is the town of **Pittsburg**. Just north of Pittsburg on 69 is the **Mined Land Wildlife Area #1**, formerly a heavily mined area now converted for recreational use, such as fishing. There is also a resident buffalo herd kept there. Just to set your mind at ease, by "mined" they mean that ore excavation took place—as far as we know, there are no undetonated explosive devices in the area.

While in Pittsburg, check out the **Crawford County Historical Museum**, on Highway 69 between 20th and Atkinson, and the **Hotel Stilwell** (7th and Broadway), which was built in 1880 and is listed on the historic register. Pittsburg also hosts the **Oldtime Tractor and Gas Engine Show** in June.

Turn west from U.S. 69 onto State Highway 102 to reach the town of **West Mineral**. Here stands **Big Brutus**, the second-largest power shovel ever built, at 16 stories in height, and with a shovel that with one scoop could fill three railroad cars. One look at Big Brutus will erase any lingering doubts that this part of Kansas owes its livelihood to mining. Each June in West Mineral is the **Big Brutus Miners' Day Reunion**, when veteran miners reconvene here to talk over old times. August gets even livelier, with the **Big Brutus Polka Fest** featuring dueling polka bands. Big Brutus is at 6509 NW 60th St.

Enter Baxter Springs from the north on SE 50th St., then turn left on Third and right onto Military Avenue.

BAXTER SPRINGS

In 1863, at the height of the Civil War, Baxter Springs was the scene of a significant attack on Union forces by Quantrill's Raiders. The Bill Quantrill gang raided a U.S. Cavalry wagon train near here on October 6, killing about 100 men. It became known as the Baxter Springs Massacre. The graves of many of those who died lie in the Baxter Springs National Cemetery on U.S. Highway 166 near Spring Valley Road.

Although some dispute the veracity of the tale, the local restaurant at 1101 Military Ave. (Café on the Route) is housed in a building which was formerly a bank robbed by Jesse James in 1876. In the 1870s, Baxter Springs was widely considered the toughest town in Kansas. Another local restaurant, Murphey's, is located in another former bank, which was also the target of a robbery, though much later (1914).

The **Baxter Springs Heritage Center and Museum** features exhibits on the Buffalo Soldiers, the African-American troops who were heavily involved in the resistance against Quantrill's Raiders. They got their nickname from the local Indians, who likened their coarse hair to that of the American bison. You can also pick up a numbered walking guide to the town, featuring such sites as a log school building dating from 1866; John Baxter's inn and trading post, from which the town eventually sprang; and a replica of Fort Blair, a Civil War-era army post (East Avenue at Eighth). On the grounds of the museum is a small historic marker commemorating the Black Dog Trail.

The **Johnston Public Library** is housed in a building constructed in 1872 and originally intended to be the county courthouse. Though it never served in that capacity, it has seen duty as a city hall, theater, and college (210 W. 10th). On the library's grounds is a monument erected by the Daughters of the American Revolution in 1931.

At Eleventh and Military is **Bilke's Western Museum**. There is a mural on the exterior depicting a longhorn cattle drive, and upstairs is a private collection of old saddles, spurs, and other cowboy-type gear.

At Fourteenth and Grant is the **Little League Baseball Museum**, featuring stars such as regional hero Mickey Mantle, who was from just across the border in Oklahoma. Mantle played a few years with the Baxter Springs Whiz Kids in the late 1940s. It was during that time that he hit a home run into the Spring River and was later approached by a scout for the New York Yankees. The rest, as they say, is history.

One mile west of town on U.S. 166 is a **cemetery** which includes a section designated for Civil War veterans. That plot is bounded by a fence made of cannon barrels protruding from the ground.

FURTHER AFIELD

A few miles outside of town is a small monument at the point where the states of Kansas, Oklahoma, and Missouri all come together. The **Tri-State Marker** was constructed in 1938 by the Youth Work

Administration. Go about six miles east of town on U.S. 166, then turn right just before the state line (SE 118th) and follow it to the dead end.

A little west of Baxter Springs via U.S. 166 is the town of **Chetopa**, proud to call itself both the Catfish Capital and Pecan Capital of Kansas. The town holds an annual pecan festival the third Saturday in November. The **Chetopa Historical Museum** includes a collection of buttons made at a nearby button manufacturing plant as well as information about Osage Chief Che-to-pah, for whom the town was named. The **Bath Funeral Home** at Seventh and Maple occupies a showpiece house built in 1875.

Further west via U.S. 166 is the city of **Coffeyville**. The **Dalton Defenders Museum** is dedicated to the memory of the local citizens who gave their lives in defending the town. On October 5, 1892 in Coffeyville, Kansas, the Dalton Gang tried to do what no one had ever done before: rob two banks simultaneously. The gang of five (some of whom were former residents of the town) split up and entered the Condon and First National Banks that morning. Some of the local citizens recognized them and went to the nearby Isham hardware store for weapons and ammunition. When the robbers emerged, they were met by armed citizens and a shootout ensued. All but one of the gang were killed; also killed were four of the eight town defenders. The museum, at 113 E. Eighth St., also has exhibits pertaining to other local history, as well as mementos of Wendell Wilkie, who lived and taught school in Coffeyville. The **Condon Bank** building still stands and has been nicely restored.

Just a mile south of the site of the shootout, you can visit the Daltons' graves in **Elmwood Cemetery**. Emmett Dalton, the only survivor of the gang, returned to Coffeyville many years after the raid and placed a permanent marker over the graves.

Also in Coffeyville is the **Brown Mansion**. Completed in 1904 and incorporating some Tiffany-designed glasswork, the house is a three-story, 16-room residence built by one of the town's leading citizens, W. P. Brown, who made his money in the lumber and natural gas businesses. The home sits on U.S. 166 at the corner of Eldridge and Walnut. Guided tours are available (admission charged), and reservations can be made for private parties.

Located throughout Coffeyville are **murals** depicting facets of Coffeyville's history, including the Brown Mansion, the Perkins Building, Wholesale Grocery, Walter "Big Train" Johnson, and the Interurban.

At **Pfister Park**, housed in a 1930s-era hangar, is the **Aviation Heritage Museum**. The hangar was constructed in 1933 as a Works Progress Administration project, and was used until 1960 when the Big Hill Airport ceased operation. Vintage airplanes and memorabilia associated with the Coffeyville Air Base are on exhibit.

In Coffeyville each August is the **Coffeyville Inter-State Fair & Rodeo**, with country music concerts, a rodeo, and a demolition derby, in addition to all the traditional carnival-style attractions.

In November, Coffeyville holds an **Intertribal Pow-Wow**, with Native American dancers, exhibits, and other activities.

Somewhere in the vicinity of Coffeyville there's supposed to be a rock formation that resembles a gigantic flushing toilet, known popularly as Toilet Rock. I've been unable to verify this, so if you have any information on this attraction, please drop me a line.

Route 66 travels under the guise of U.S. 69A as it moves south out of Baxter Springs. After sweeping across the Illinois prairie, crossing the mighty Mississippi, meandering through the Ozark region of Missouri, and then sampling the soil of Kansas, Route 66 is finally ready to enter that part of the country with which she is most intimately associated.

Prepare yourself. You are about to enter the Great American West.

OKLAHOMA

The pavement of Route 66 begins in Chicago, but the idea originated here in Oklahoma. When the Joint Board of State and Federal Highway Officials was establishing the system of numbered routes in the 1920s, Cyrus Avery envisioned a major artery passing right through the heart of his own state of Oklahoma. And he worked long and hard to make it a reality.

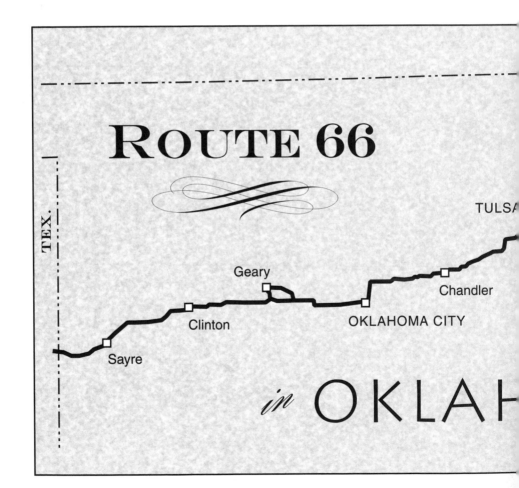

It is no accident that Route 66 cuts such a long, sweeping swath directly through the center of Oklahoma. If you look at a map of the United States and draw a more or less direct line from Chicago to Los Angeles, that path will miss the state of Oklahoma entirely. Even allowing for the curvature of the earth not apparent in a map, the most logical path for such a highway would pass through very little of Missouri, none of Oklahoma, and directly through the heart of Kansas. Indeed, if the highway had been plotted along already-established trails through Middle America, such as the Santa Fe Trail, that path, too, would have made Kansas, not Oklahoma, a prominent part of the route.

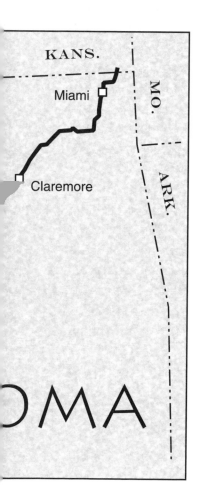

However, U.S. 66 was deliberately calculated to take traveling Americans through Cy Avery's stomping grounds. He reasoned correctly that such a highway would put Oklahoma "on the map" and cause lots of travel-related dollars to be spent all across the state.

This placement of the highway became somewhat fortuitous when the dust bowl years of the 1930s imposed such a hardship on Oklahomans that many of them fled the region for California. Then, all of the surrounding roads became tributaries, adding their flow to the Mother Road, and inspiring the dark *Grapes of Wrath* imagery which the highway still evokes today.

One of the reasons why Oklahoma needed to be put on the map more so than some other states has to do with its unique past. The area had for many years been designated as Indian Territory, and was the home to tribes which had participated in the forced march to the region known as the Trail of Tears. It was only in 1907 that Oklahoma attained statehood; therefore, it had been a state for less than two decades at the time of the establishment of the interstate highway system in the 1920s. By traveling through the state, however, Americans could see for themselves that Oklahoma was no longer a "territory," nor as primitive as that word implied. Route 66, then, would be Oklahoma's ticket to joining the twentieth century as a full partner.

If you've just traveled the old highway's short course through Kansas, you'll enter Oklahoma moving south on U.S. 69. Like the small section of Kansas you've left behind, this district of Oklahoma is mining country, and there's very little to differentiate it at first. The changes, however, will not be long in coming.

Oklahoma, as befits its unofficial status as the birthplace of Route 66, is very 66-friendly. By that I mean that you will have less difficulty in following the old route here than you will elsewhere. Official state maps distributed for free by the Oklahoma Department of Transportation have for years now clearly marked the path of Historic Route 66. Not only that, but one of the later alignments of old 66 as it existed at the time of bypassing by the turnpikes has been designated as Oklahoma 66. That means you can follow the double sixes almost continuously across the state. Keep in mind, of course, that the alignment marked as State Highway 66 is only one of many which the route followed over the years. As always, observation and exploration are your tickets to maximum enjoyment.

Less than five miles past the border, you'll come to the old Route 66 community of Quapaw.

QUAPAW

The village of Quapaw, about four miles from the Kansas state line, is characterized by several buildings with murals painted on the sides. Keep alert for them.

COMMERCE

Commerce is the birthplace of baseball star Mickey Mantle, and the source of his nickname "The Commerce Comet." The main drag (old 66) has been re-named Mickey Mantle Blvd. The house where he grew up is at 319 S. Quincy, and there is a metal-sided barn on the property full of dents where Mickey practiced his hitting. Until a short time ago, there was a plan to build a Mickey Mantle museum here in town, but those plans have been abandoned. Investors decided such a museum will need to be located in a larger community. No decision as to where as yet.

Bonnie and Clyde are said to have had a shootout with police here in Commerce on April 6, 1934.

MIAMI

Named for the Indian tribe, and pronounced *my-AM-uh*, this was formerly known as Jimtown, after four farmers named Jim in the area.

The jewel of Miami is by all accounts the **Coleman Theater** at 103 N. Main. Originally designed in the Italianate style, it was converted to Spanish Mission Revival during construction, resulting in a unique piece of architecture. Opening night was in April of 1929, just six months before the beginning of the Great Depression. The Coleman was on the Orpheum Vaudeville circuit, and saw the likes of Will Rogers, Tom Mix, the Three Stooges, and Sally Rand as performers.

My wife and I were fortunate enough to have been given a private tour of the Coleman in 1994 when it was in the process of restoration. Mr. Jerold Graham was very proud to report that the original "Mighty Wurlitzer" organ, which had been removed many years earlier, had been located in Burleson, Texas (near Fort Worth). Arrangements had been made to have it fully restored and returned to its rightful place here in the Coleman Theater Beautiful (the theater's official name). Since that day several years ago, restoration has continued, and today the Coleman is a truly beautiful must-stop for the Route 66 traveler.

For regional history, visit the **Dobson Museum**, at 110 "A" Street SW, which includes American Indian artifacts, mining items, and other articles relating to the area's early settlement.

The Coleman Theater Beautiful opened in 1929, at the threshold of the Great Depression, Miami, Oklahoma.

On the southern outskirts of Miami, you can still find some portions of old 66 which are even older than the route itself (pre-1926). In this vicinity are some one-lane-wide sections of concrete roadway paved in the early 1920s. It's said that money was tight, and there was only half the amount needed to do the job completely. Rather than cover half the mileage, the decision was made to pave the full distance, but at half the normal width. This meant—and of course it still means today—that driving it requires being very cautious of oncoming vehicles, particularly where visibility is short. Just move your passenger-side wheels off onto the ample shoulder when necessary. To locate this section, just continue straight (on Main St.) at the Steve Owens Blvd. intersection. The more modern alignment bears to the right. You will re-join that alignment at the village of Narcissa. The one-lane section of 66 will demonstrate very clearly to you that early highway alignments were constructed with a considerable number of 90-degree corners. The removal of such harsh turns by re-routing was a major thrust throughout the country during the 1930s.

NARCISSA-AFTON

Between Narcissa and Afton is another of the one-lane 66 sections. To access it, turn right at a street called E. 200 Rd. However, once you've explored this you might want to backtrack a bit on the newer

Afton, Oklahoma.

alignment, which passes the former site of the **Buffalo Ranch**. Buffalo Ranch was a good old-fashioned "tourist trap," featuring trained animals (technically American bison), plus the requisite curio shop, etc. The ranch itself is now gone, replaced by a modern truck stop/convenience store.

One of my favorite Mother Road ruins—the **Rest Haven Motel**—is here in Afton. I hope that great old sign is still there when you read this. If not, you can see a photograph of it on the cover of the National Historic Route 66 Federation *News*, Autumn 1997.

Also in Afton is the restored DX gasoline station and Packard showroom (at First and Locust). The DX station is now an informal visitor center for Mother Roaders. Across the highway from the DX there used to be the World's Largest Matchbook Collection. Unfortunately for all of us, that building burned in the summer of 2003.

FURTHER AFIELD

Not far from Afton is Monkey Island, a peninsula community jutting into the Grand Lake o' the Cherokees, and home to **Darryl Starbird's National Rod & Custom Car Hall of Fame Museum**. The collection features over 40 street rods and other custom-built automobiles, as well as plenty of photographs and other memorabilia. 55251 E. Highway 85A (at Highway 125).

Just east of Afton you can take a side trip south on U.S. 59, across a portion of the Grand Lake o' the Cherokees, to the community of **Grove**. Perhaps the most popular destination in town is **Har-Ber Village**, described as one of the largest antique displays in the country, and which features a reconstructed turn-of-the-century village with over 100 buildings and other exhibits. 4404 W. 20th St.

At 536 W. Third Street (within the Hollywood At Home Video Store) is the **Mickey Mantle Memorial Exhibit and Museum**. Said to be the largest private collection of Mickey Mantle memorabilia, it includes thousands of items of every conceivable variety, and the public is admitted for free.

The town of Grove is also host to the ***Cherokee Queen I & II***, a pair of paddlewheel riverboats which offer tourist excursions on the lake.

In Grove's **Polson Cemetery** is the gravesite of General Stand Watie—the last Civil War Confederate General to surrender, and a full-blooded Native American.

VINITA

One of the oldest settlements in Oklahoma and originally called Downingville, the town was later re-named for Vinnie Ream (1850–1914), the sculptress who fashioned the life-sized image of Abraham Lincoln in the nation's capitol. It is also the birthplace of "Dr. Phil" McGraw of talk show fame.

It was here in 1935 that Will Rogers had planned to attend the town's first-ever annual rodeo. He died, however, in a plane crash at Point Barrow, Alaska, just weeks beforehand. Nowadays, that rodeo is known as the **Will Rogers Memorial Rodeo**, and it is held each August.

Rogers somewhat facetiously called Vinita his "college town," having attended a secondary school here.

Route 66 through Vinita, Oklahoma, still exhibits a lot of charm.

Here in Vinita there is an old cottage-style gasoline station which has been converted to the local Greyhound bus station.

VINITA ATTRACTIONS

The self-guided **Historic Homes Tour** directs you to 35 turn-of-the-century houses built by the area's founding families. Visitor information is available by calling 918-256-7133. Call the same number to get directions to the **Barker Gang Gravesite** and the **Cabin Creek Civil War Battle Site**.

The **Eastern Trails Museum** has a re-created post office, general store, printing office, and doctor's office, as well as items representing Indian history. 215 W. Illinois.

Clanton's is a café (over 70 years old!) with lots of old photos lining the walls. The **World's Largest Calf Fry Festival & Cook-off** is held here in Vinita each September, in which a full ton of the delicacies are annually consumed.

Vinita is also well-known to some as being the location of the largest **McDonald's** restaurant in the United States. It's in an unusual structure that actually spans the turnpike just outside of town.

WHITE OAK-CATALE

In this vicinity is an old tourist court called the Country Court Motel. The first time I passed through, the red-and-white sign was barely visible over the tops of overgrown foliage.

This old motel court is being swallowed up by weeds. Near White Oak, Oklahoma.

CHELSEA

This community dates from 1882. The town includes an example of an underground pedestrian tunnel built to facilitate crossing the then-busy highway. A few miles to the south and west of town is the site of the first oil well in Oklahoma, which was established in 1889. Will Rogers's sister, whom he is said to have visited frequently, lived here in Chelsea.

Signs like this were once commonplace on American roadsides. Chelsea, Oklahoma.

The town also features the site of an original Sears Roebuck pre-cut house purchased in Chicago in 1913 for $1,600 and delivered by railroad car. The **Hogue House** is the only known example west of the Mississippi, and is still owned by descendants of the original purchaser. 1001 S. Olive St., one block west of 66.

BUSHYHEAD

Named for a Cherokee Indian chief, Dennis W. Bushyhead.

FOYIL

Andy Payne, winner of the 1928 Bunion Derby—a cross-country footrace organized as a wildly extreme promotional stunt—was from this vicinity. There is a **bronze statue** of Andy on an old alignment of 66 (Andy Payne Blvd.) at the far edge of town.

Above: Totem Pole Park, in Foyil, Oklahoma, is folk art at its very best. Right: detail at the base of the main totem pole.

Foyil's claim to fame today is that it is the home of Ed Galloway's collection of concrete Native American-inspired structures in what is commonly called **Totem Pole Park**. This is truly a landmark, and a great old-fashioned roadside attraction to boot. Get there by leaving State Highway 66 and turning onto Highway 28A at the Top Hat Dairy Bar. The focal point of this collection is a 90-foot-tall totem pole made of brightly painted concrete. Ed Galloway created this collection of structures in the post-war years (the main totem pole in particular bears a date of 1948) as an expression of his own private passions.

SEQUOYAH

Established in 1871, the name of the settlement was changed to Beulah after the daughter of the postmaster in 1909. The name was changed back in 1913 to honor the famous Cherokee chief, also called George Guess, who developed the Cherokee alphabet. Remarkably, even the most advanced Native American peoples had not developed written forms of their languages until as late as the nineteenth century. Sequoyah, son of a Cherokee mother and a British trader named Nathaniel Gist, became convinced that the white men's superior power and influence derived from their written language. He began developing a system of writing for the Cherokee people in the belief that this would help in maintaining their independence from the whites. About 1820, he developed his syllabary, a system of 86 symbols denoting all of the syllables of the Cherokee language. The system was easy to learn and use, and by 1828 the *Cherokee Advocate* newspaper was being published.

CLAREMORE

This is the county seat of Rogers County, which was named for Will

Rogers's father, Clem Rogers. Claremore was known in years gone by as a place for "taking the waters." There was a well in town that produced a dark, malodorous substance called radium water (even though it contained no radium). This water was touted as being therapeutic for rheumatism and other ailments, and was a big selling point for staying at the **Hotel Will Rogers**, which was known for its baths. The hotel re-opened in 1997 after partial restoration.

As you enter Claremore from the east, there is an older alignment of Route 66 off to your right (J. M. Davis Blvd.) that's pretty easy to recognize. Along that stretch, on the left-hand side, is an old motel court now serving duty as an apartment complex called **Adobe Village**. It appears to be from the 1940s or earlier, and bears a resemblance to the Alamo Courts chain which used to be found scattered about in this part of the country.

CLAREMORE ATTRACTIONS

The most important thing not to miss when in Claremore is of course the **Will Rogers Memorial**, at 1720 W. Will Rogers Blvd. The museum, mausoleum, and grounds are beautifully done, and there's far too much included to even begin to list. Will's body was moved here in 1944, having been interred from 1935 to 1944 at Forest Lawn Cemetery in California. This was property which he had purchased with the intent of finally settling down permanently after the Hollywood career played itself out. Memorial services are held here each November 4th, his birthday.

Will's most famous quote is of course "I never met a man I didn't like," but pithy statements were his stock-in-trade. There are thousands worth repeating, but he seemed particularly to be speaking to people like you and me when he wrote in 1930:

"But if you want to have a good time, I don't care where you live, just load in your kids, and take some congenial friends, and just start out. You would be surprised what there is to see in this

The Round-Up Motel is with us no more. Claremore, Oklahoma.

great country within 200 miles of where any of us live. I don't care what state or what town."

The **J. M. Davis Gun Museum** is also a Claremore mainstay. Included in the thousands of firearms on display are weapons owned by the likes of Pretty Boy Floyd, Cole Younger, Pancho Villa, and others. This is the world's largest privately owned gun collection, with examples spanning six centuries of the gunsmith's art. Besides the guns, there are trophy heads, musical instruments, Indian artifacts, and World War I posters. 333 N. Lynn Riggs Blvd.

The **Lynn Riggs Memorial Museum**, at 121 N. Weenonah, includes the actual "surrey with the fringe on top" made famous in the musical *Oklahoma!*, which was based upon Riggs's novel, *Green Grow the Lilacs*. When the production premiered in the state in 1946, officials declared a state holiday.

On the campus of Rogers State University is Meyer Hall, which houses the **Oklahoma Military Academy Museum**. The academy operated at this location from 1919 to 1971, when its functions were taken over by Claremore Junior College. 1701 W. Will Rogers Blvd.

Several Claremore buildings are listed on the National Register of Historic Places, including the **Will Rogers Hotel**, the **Belvidere Mansion**, and **Meyer Hall** (above). The Belvidere Mansion is a restored pre-statehood Victorian home offering tours by costumed docents at 121 N. Chickasaw. The Belvidere has a ballroom which occupies the entire third floor of the house.

The **Swan Brothers Dairy Farm**, operated by three generations of the Swan family since 1923, has a store and tours at 938 E. Fifth St.

Claremore holds a **Bluegrass & Chili Festival** in September and a Will Rogers birthday celebration each November.

FURTHER AFIELD

Northwest of Claremore via Highway 88 is the town of **Oologah**, Oklahoma. Here, overlooking Oologah Lake, is Will Rogers's boyhood home, known as **Dog Iron Ranch**, with a house, barn, petting zoo, and vintage films and newsreels for your enjoyment. Rogers was born in this log-walled house in 1879. Today, there are 400 acres and a herd of longhorn cattle. The town itself also has a bronze statue—called the *Cherokee Kid*—of its favorite son on horseback, while much of the turn-of-the-century downtown has been restored. The **Bank of Oologah**, built circa 1906, boasts an authentic period interior and furnishings. Today, this bank is touted as having "closed during the Depression." I'm sure that at the time, no one considered it much of a selling point (Maple and Cooweescoowee Sts.). On the same corner is the **Oologah Historical Museum**, with Will Rogers photos and a complete doctor's office on display. Miniatures of the *Cherokee Kid* statue in town are available in the museum's gift shop.

VERDIGRIS-CATOOSA

Just east of Catoosa is the **Nutt House**, a store selling nut candies and such, but which also has an extensive collection of vintage conveyances strewn out front. These include fire engines, a covered wagon, a Clydesdale-style beer wagon, a bus, and a child-sized mock-Roman chariot.

The Port of Catoosa is the nation's largest inland seaport, connecting Tulsa with the Mississippi River and the port of New Orleans. There is a museum, the **Arkansas River Historical Society Museum**, which can educate you on the construction of the project (5350 Cimarron Rd.). You might also want to visit the **Catoosa Historical Society Museum**, at 207 N. Cherokee, for a taste of the city's heritage. Look for the Frisco caboose parked outside.

Near Catoosa is what I refer to as the **Catoosa Whale**, an example of a small-scale mom-and-pop roadside attraction.

Former roadside swimming hole, Catoosa, Oklahoma.

Recently restored, it is a large whale replica, painted blue, which sits in a small pond. In its heyday, visitors could enter the whale's mouth, and then either slide down a chute which exits behind the whale's left ear, or dive off a small platform at the tail and into the surrounding swimming hole. Adjacent is a wooden "ark" that used to house a roadside menagerie. Just across the highway from them both is the former Arrowood Trading Post.

LYNN LANE

This community appears in my 1957 atlas east of Tulsa, a little to the southwest of the current I-44/U.S. 412 junction, just inside Tulsa County. It has been swallowed by the expanding Tulsa city limits, which now run all the way out to the county line. A vestige remains in the Lynn Lane Reservoir nearby.

Enter Tulsa on Eleventh Avenue, an east-west artery that takes you straight into town.

TULSA

A city which owes much to the oil industry, Tulsa was also the home of Cyrus Avery, the man so instrumental not only in the establishment of Route 66, but more particularly in getting it routed through his home state and town. Outlaw Kate "Ma" Barker lived here in 1930 and 1931. That was about the same time that Madison W. "Daddy" Cain bought a former garage at 423 N. Main and called it Cain's Dance Academy, later to become **Cain's Ballroom** and a thriving center for what later came to be called Western Swing.

In 1938, Tulsa gave birth to the **Society for the Preservation and Encouragement of Barber Shop Quartet Singing**. Today, there are chapters from coast to coast.

Hank's is a still-operating burger place on old 66 in Tulsa, Oklahoma.

In honor of Oklahoma's fiftieth anniversary of statehood, a time capsule—which includes a 1957 Plymouth automobile—was buried here under the city's courthouse/city hall lawn in 1957. There is a plaque to mark the location. The car was furnished by a local Chrysler-Plymouth dealership, and will supposedly be awarded to the person coming the closest (in 1957) to guessing the population of Tulsa in 2007. A strange contest, in that most of the contestants probably won't be around for the finish. Experts say that since the car was lowered underground in an air- and water-tight container, it is likely to be in reasonably good condition at the time of its exhumation.

In June of 1921, Tulsa was the scene of a race riot which took the lives of more than 30 people and left the African-American district of town a burning ruin. Today, the **Greenwood Cultural Center** recalls those dark days in the heart of Black Wall Street through photographs and memorabilia. The building, at 322 N.

Greenwood Ave., also houses the **Oklahoma Jazz Hall of Fame**.

Nannie Doss was convicted of murder here in 1954 after having killed 11 people. She said that she was "searching for the perfect mate, the real romance" of her life. Curiously, only four of the 11 victims were husbands. The others included various family members, including her mother, two sisters, and her own infant children. Police got suspicious when her fifth husband died suddenly and his body was found to contain enough arsenic to kill 20 men. She was sentenced to life in prison, and died behind bars in 1964 of leukemia. Her cell was strewn with romance magazines.

For the nostalgia-minded, the **Metro Diner** salutes the Route 66 era through stylish architecture and vintage American road fare. On E. 11th St. (old 66).

The **Crystal City Shopping Center**, at 4233 Southwest Blvd. (west of the river), marks the site of the former Crystal City Amusement Park, a popular entertainment spot during the Route 66 era.

TULSA ATTRACTIONS

The **Philbrook Museum** combines a historical home, extensive art collections, and formal gardens. The Italianate home was built in 1927 by oil man Waite Phillips and has been featured on the program *America's Castles*. Today, the Philbrook is rated in the top 65 art museums in the country, and is surrounded by 23 acres of English gardens. 2727 S. Rockford Rd.

The **Gilcrease Museum** houses one of the world's greatest collections of American Indian and Western art, and rests amid 475 acres of grounds with themed gardens. 1400 Gilcrease Museum Rd.

The **Elsing Museum**, on the campus of Oral Roberts University, features a four-foot jade sculpture among its 60-year-old collection of gems, minerals, crystals, and other stones. Mr. Willard Elsing at one time operated a rock and mineral shop on Route 66 at

Joplin, Missouri. The university is at 7777 S. Lewis Ave. Enter at the giant Praying Hands sculpture, which is about 60 feet tall and weighs 30 tons—a rather arresting sight.

Lovers of Art Deco architecture have plenty to be thankful for here in Tulsa. The most well-known example is the **Boston Avenue Methodist Church**, but there are also a number of deco office buildings in the downtown business district. Church tours are held every Sunday following the 11:00 A.M. service, or by appointment during the week (1301 S. Boston Ave.). You can also take a walking tour of Art Deco by picking up a brochure at the chamber of commerce office at 2 W. Second St.

There is a **Frank Lloyd Wright** creation in a residential

This sign once towered over a corner of 11th Street (U.S. 66) in Tulsa, Oklahoma.

section of Tulsa. It's still a private residence, so no tours are available, but you can view two exterior facades by driving by. On a corner lot at 3700 S. Birmingham Ave.

Mac's Antique Car Museum features dozens of vintage models including LaSalle, Packard, and more. Included is the 1948 Hudson used in the film, *Driving Miss Daisy*. 1319 E. Fourth. Open weekend afternoons only.

The **Sunbelt Railroad Museum** includes restored 1920 passenger cars, memorabilia, videotapes, a reference library, and a working telegraph station. 1323 E. Fifth.

Lovers of miniatures will want to see the **Ida Dennie Willis Museum of Miniatures, Dolls, and Toys** at 628 N. Country Club Drive. The collection includes an ever-changing array of trains, planes, robots, and dolls, all housed in a 1910 Tudor mansion. One of many interesting exhibits is the Gates collection of ethnic and advertising dolls.

The **Tulsa Air and Space Museum** offers the opportunity to take an F-14 Tomcat orientation, hear lectures, watch videos, or experience flight simulator training. You can even sit in the cockpit of an F-14 fighter and have your picture taken. 7130 E. Apache.

The **Tulsa Historical Society Museum** is the official repository of the city's history, including official

Tulsa, Oklahoma.

documents, vintage photographs, and other artifacts. E. Twenty-fifth at Peoria.

If you grew up in mid-twentieth-century America, as I did, then you've heard of **Bama Pies**. Bama is based right here in Tulsa, at 2727 E. Eleventh St. (Route 66).

There's a still-operating drive-in movie theater, the **Admiral Twin**, in the northeastern sector of town, at 7355 E. Easton.

At **Creek Council Oak Park**, a 170-year-old oak tree marks the spot where the Creek Indians arrived in the 1830s after traversing the Trail of Tears, thus establishing the site which would later become Tulsey-town. At 18th Street and Cheyenne Avenue.

There's a 76-foot giant oil worker sculpture, known as the **Golden Driller**, standing outside of the International Petroleum Exhibition (IPE) Building at the Tulsa Fairgrounds. The IPE Building is said to have the world's largest unobstructed interior volume. The roof is suspended by a system of booms and cables, which allows adequate room inside for oversized equipment shows. In fact, the original Golden Driller (he was upgraded in the 1970s) was placed on display inside the IPE Building for a while prior to his outdoor installation in 1966. Twenty-first St. at Pittsburgh.

Also in Tulsa, you'll find the **Center of the Universe**, a sort of acoustical mystery spot downtown. Stand in this spot, recite some words, and you'll hear your voice strongly reverberated back to you. The effect is quite striking. It's a circular feature on the Boston Avenue pedestrian walkway between First and Archer Streets. Just yards away are the Art Deco-inspired **Tulsa Union** railroad depot and a 72-foot sculpture titled *Artificial Cloud*, created in the early 1990s for the city's Mayfest celebration.

At the Tulsa Fairgrounds each March is the **International Auto Show**, featuring new models, prototypes, and aftermarket vendors.

Every August, Tulsa hosts the **Gatesway International**

Balloon Festival, the largest in the state.

Just outside town at **Discoveryland**, the play *Oklahoma!* is performed regularly through the summer months. There is an optional barbeque dinner available, too.

FURTHER AFIELD

About 47 miles north of Tulsa is the city of **Bartlesville**. The city's historic district includes nearly 50 buildings from the oil-boom period of 1900 to 1920.

Bartlesville is also home to the **Inn at Price Towers**, a Frank Lloyd Wright structure from 1956, whose design is said to have been based on the structure of a tree. It's now a hotel and museum with 21 architecturally fascinating guest rooms, some of which are two-story suites. The Inn has its own restaurant and bar. Sixth and Dewey. The **Bartlesville Community Center** was designed by a student of Wright's (W. Peters) and features the world's largest *cloisonne* mural.

On the outskirts of Bartlesville, just west of the airport via U.S. 60, is the home of **Keepsake Candles**. They offer free tours on weekdays, and are located in the old recreation building of what was once a U.S. Air Force radar station. Nearby is the **Red Dirt Soap Company** factory store.

At 1107 SE Cherokee is the **Frank Phillips Home**, a 26-room Neoclassical mansion completed in 1909. Phillips was founder of the Phillips Petroleum Company, the firm which saw fit to brand their gasoline with a highway shield emblazoned with the number 66.

Frank Phillips's country home and guest ranch, named **Woolaroc**, is just outside Bartlesville. The ranch was designed as a sort of Old West preserve, and attracted the likes of presidents, tycoons, and other celebrities of the day as guests. The 3,700-acre compound, established in 1925, features a museum of western art, a collection of Phillips Petroleum memorabilia, a lodge house, picnic areas, nature trails, roaming buffalo, and the Phillips family mausoleum. Southwest of Bartlesville via State Highway 123.

Johnstone Park contains a replica of the first commercial oil well in Oklahoma, named the Nellie Johnstone No. 1. Bartlesville also holds a **Bi-Plane Expo** the first weekend each June.

Not far from Bartlesville is the town of **Dewey**, home to the **Tom Mix Museum**. Prior to his film career, Mix served as marshal in Dewey (1911–12), and the third of his five wives was from here. Mix's film career came to include more than 300 films, some of which are available for viewing in the museum's small auditorium (721 N. Delaware). The **Dewey Hotel**, downtown at 801 N. Delaware, was built in 1900 and serves as a museum. A few miles east of Dewey on Durham Road is **Prairie Song, Indian Territory**, a replica nineteenth-century village of 20 or so hand-hewn log buildings.

As you leave Tulsa, after you cross the river, keep an eye out for the **66 Motel sign** on the western outskirts. The motel itself was razed and replaced with rental storage units, but the owners promised to reinstall the sign for the benefit of roadies like you and me.

Follow Southwest Blvd., which becomes Frankoma Road, en route to Sapulpa via the community of Oakhurst.

SAPULPA

The Liberty Glass Company was established here in the early 1900s by George F. Collins. The idea for the name seems to have come from the fact that 1886, the

Left: On an old alignment of Route 66. Right: OK Motel. Sapulpa, Oklahoma.

year Sapulpa was established, was the same year in which France made the United States a gift of the Statue of Liberty. Jack Rittenhouse makes mention of Liberty Glass at the time of his passing through in 1946.

Sapulpa is fairly well known as the home of **Frankoma Pottery**, on an old alignment of 66 called Frankoma Road. Frankoma has been making earthenware using a local clay source since 1933.

Be sure to explore Sapulpa thoroughly, because an older alignment at the far end of town takes you over a brick-paved iron truss bridge (**Rock Creek Bridge**) and past the **Tepee Drive-In** movie theater. This alignment will take you back in time for a bit and well away from the roar of traffic.

Downtown Sapulpa includes a number of reproductions of antique advertising murals. These appear on the sides of several buildings along old Route 66. There is also a building with the S&H Green Stamp logo painted on the side. This one is not a repro, and it shows the signs of its age.

Housed in a circa-1910 YWCA building, the **Sapulpa Historical Museum** features an 1890s-era kitchen and schoolroom, a telephone exhibit, and items pertaining to the Frisco Railroad. 100 E. Lee St.

KELLYVILLE-BRISTOW

On my earlier trips through here, there was an old store west of Kellyville with a plywood Indian sign out front. The Indian's arm was extended, as if pointing, and lettering on his outstretched arm promised: SOUVENIRS. Long closed, it was a treat for the Route 66 traveler to stumble upon. The sign has since been removed, however, and the remaining structures are nondescript. This is one of many disappearances reminding me to photograph, photograph, photograph.

While passing through Bristow, keep an eye out for a sign pointing to the **Wake Island Memorial**. The town has commemorated those veterans who served in the battle for Wake Island in the Second World War, and there are some nice pedestrian-friendly walking paths in the vicinity.

The **Bristow Historical Museum** is located in the restored 1923 railroad depot and features rotating exhibits pertaining to the area's history, from Indian Territory to the present. 1 Railroad Place.

You can't see it, but along the stretch of road between Bristow and Stroud, there is an enormous underground storage cavity—a depleted gas field—which is used for storage of natural gas during periods of surplus.

What you *can* see is that there are at least three cemeteries along Route 66 between Bristow and Depew, and two more west of Depew, near the junction with the Turner Turnpike (I-44).

DEPEW

The village of Depew seems somewhat isolated. The Mother Road cut off the somewhat circuitous route through Depew early on. Take at least a few extra minutes to drive through town, though. You'll see evidence that this was once a much busier place.

Near Depew there used to be several small vending stands by the side of the road. Not used for that purpose in many years, they were later plastered with the placards of local political campaigns.

West of Depew and east of Stroud, be on the lookout for the **Shoe Tree**—a small tree with shoes tied to the branches.

STROUD

The town was established in 1892. Henry "BearCat" Starr and his gang robbed two banks here in 1915. Starr was the nephew of the famed Belle Starr.

The focal point of Stroud is the **Rock Café**, which is built of stones that were unearthed during the construction of Route 66 in the area, and which features a nice sign that fans of neon will appreciate. A more recent addition to the café is **Mamie's Market**, a gift shop standing just next door.

Also in Stroud is the **Skyliner Motel**, which has a classic neon sign. Look for it near the west end of town. If you keep your eyes open as you pass through town, you might spot the Mother Load Laundromat on one of the side streets.

The town **library** is an example of 1929 Art Deco architecture, and was originally built by Bell Telephone. Seventh St. and Third Ave.

Just a mile or so west of downtown Stroud is **StableRidge Vineyards and Winery**. Their tasting room is in a former Catholic Church built in the years 1898–1902.

Stroud is home to the **International Brick & Rolling**

The Rock Café in Stroud, Oklahoma, is well worth a stop for today's Route 66 adventurer.

Pin Competition and Festival. The competition pits several cities named Stroud against one another in games of skill. The other Strouds are in Canada, Australia, and the U.K.

West of Stroud there is a left turn (at N. 3540 Rd.) you can take which follows the old Ozark Trail highway. This early 66 alignment features an **Ozark Trail Marker** (a tall obelisk, sometimes incorrectly referred to as a pyramid) at one of its intersections. This old path of the highway is more easily spotted when facing east, because the later Route 66 alignment curves to your left, and straight ahead is an obviously older alignment which will take you directly to the marker—that's the way I was first able to find it.

Ozark Trail Markers

The Ozark Trail marker near Stroud is one of several which once stood in the area. There is a similar one—a replica—in the town of Stratford, Oklahoma. That reproduction includes an inscription which is instructive for today's explorer:

Ozark Trail Pyramid

By 1916, plans were underway to promote a network of roads through Oklahoma called the "Ozark Trail." The trails were planned by the Ozark Trail Association. Its mission was to promote a system of better roads connecting the surrounding states. These were the first roads to be classed as public supported highways. Early plans were "grandiose." Originally the Ozark Trail was to be a link from ocean to ocean. The route was to be marked with impressive pyramids and concrete mileage posts. These roads were intended to be "above high water, hardsurfaced, and later oiled." Routes increased rapidly as towns competed to be included on the Trail.

The Ozark Trail Pyramid was one of many marking the trail for travelers in the early 1920s. Oklahoma trails crossed the state, east to west and north to south. They have either become U. S. Highways or follow the same course, such as U.S. 60, U.S. 62, OK 9, the famous "Route 66," and the current Turner Turnpike. This pyramid was one of several placed on the trail from Tulsa to Dallas. Chandler, Meeker, Shawnee, and Sulphur also had identical pyramids marking the trail along this particular route.

Work began on the Stratford Pyramid in December 1921. The buried base was six feet square, the next section was four feet square, the top tapered and stood 22 feet high. The original pyramid stood in the center of Main and Hyden Streets, which is only ½ block to the east. Due to traffic and safety reasons, this replica pyramid could not be in the original location. It was constructed as close to the original site as possible. "Ozark Trail" appeared on all four sides of the upper part of the pyramid and each side listed the mileage for the next towns along the route. In April 1923, the pyramid was wired and lighted. In the early 1940s, it was pushed over and buried where it stood. In the early 1970s, its pieces were exhumed, partially restored, and now stands on a private ranch near Stratford. One other "original" pyramid, which is presumed to be the Chandler pyramid, is located west of Stroud off Highway 66.

This replica was erected in the summer of 1997.

DAVENPORT

Watch for high water in this vicinity. The first time I took Route 66 through Oklahoma, I had to skip Davenport altogether due to the closure of several roads at the time. There is an old Texaco station in town that has an ever-changing array of vintage vehicles parked on the lot.

Be on the lookout for the **Lincoln Motel** as you reach the eastern outskirts of Chandler. Built in 1939 and very much a product of the 66 era, the Lincoln is still in business. Rittenhouse referred to it way back in 1946.

The highway curves to the left near the old WPA-era armory building. The Oklahoma Route 66 Association, whose headquarters are in Chandler, has ambitious plans to convert the armory into an interpretive center.

CHANDLER

Chandler, the seat of Lincoln County, was established with a land run in 1891, and calls itself the Pecan Capital of the World. The town of Cromwell, southeast of here in Seminole County, is reputed to be the site of the last Old West-style gunfight. That was in 1924, and it took the life of Bill Tilghman, former U.S. Marshal at Dodge City and sheriff of Lincoln County, Oklahoma. Poor Bill; he was 70 years old and had been retired quite a few years when he was called upon that one last time. Tilghman is buried in the Oak Park Cemetery on the west side of Chandler.

Close to the center of Chandler is an old cottage-style Phillips 66 station. It is larger than most of its ilk, having been expanded by the addition of garages at some point in its life, probably the 1950s. This station and others like it were the inspiration for the design of Jim Ross's home in Arcadia. Jim is an accomplished

**Work has begun toward restoring this old Phillips 66 station.
Downtown Chandler, Oklahoma.**

author and researcher, and a huge proponent of the Route (but I probably don't need to tell you that). This station here in Chandler has had some restoration work done in recent years.

On the far end of town, just as the road takes a right-hand turn, is a closed restaurant which sports a small Route 66 mural painted on the brickwork.

The **Lincoln County Museum of Pioneer History** showcases Chandler's colorful early history, with an emphasis on their legendary sheriff, Bill Tilghman, as well as hosting **Miss Faye's Touring Historical Marionette Theater** and rare films by cinematographer Benny Kent. During a recent visit, the museum was in the process of creating a meditation garden facing the rear alley, which will result in its having "the best backyard in Chandler." 717-719 Manvel.

The **Oklahoma Route 66 Association** has its offices downtown at 1023 Manvel, Suite A, above the library. They'd love to talk with you about your Route 66 Adventure.

 Between Chandler and Warwick there is a **Meramec Caverns barn**. However, you won't notice it heading west, as the painted side of it faces eastbound travelers in hopes of enticing them to stop at the cave many miles away in Missouri.

Also in this stretch is a sign for the **Read Ranch**, a sort of dude ranch operation offering bunkhouse living, horseback riding, and similar activities.

Phillips 66 station, Chandler, Oklahoma.

WARWICK

Around Warwick, you'll see the **Seaba Station**. The Seaba is an antique shop offering a nice variety of Route 66 gear, and is housed in an old engine-rebuilding shop and former Nev-R-Nox gas station. The current owners of Seaba Station are very supportive of the Mother Road.

WELLSTON-LUTHER

Wellston was cut off from the main route in the 1930s, but there is a loop through town, marked 66B, which follows the older, more circuitous alignment. At the junction of 66B on the east side of town is a café called Pioneer Barbeque. You might want to pull over and take a closer look. The few buildings here constitute the remains of **Pioneer Camp**, which was once a tourist stopover in the early days of Route 66. Most distinctive is the slender totem pole which still stands on the property, the figures of which have glass beads for eyes. Also visible are a pair of stone bases which once supported an archway over the entrance to the camp.

Luther has a small downtown just south of the

Former location of the Pioneer Camp, Wellston, Oklahoma.

highway with vacant storefronts. West of Luther and just east of Arcadia are the remains of a **stone gasoline station** (circa 1920s) reputed to have been the scene of a counterfeit ring. It's small, but it's also one of my favorite ruins on the route, one that I photograph again each and every time I pass through here. Each time I visit, I find that these ruins have deteriorated a bit more.

ARCADIA

There is a historical marker on the eastern outskirts of town designating the eastern boundary of the infamous 1889 land run.

This community is the home of the **Round Barn**, the world-famous Route 66 landmark. Constructed in 1898, the barn was restored several years ago and now houses a small gift shop. The walls are covered with photographs and other memorabilia having to do with unusual barns around the world. These include

Arcadia, Oklahoma.

circular ones, octagonal, and other unconventional configurations. The upper level, above the gift shop, is available for rental for special events.

Also on the National Register is the **Tuton Drug Store** (now Old Country Store).

Keep your sleuth eyes open in Arcadia for a very old alignment of Route 66 which deviates from the main pavement for a short distance and includes the home of Jim Ross. This is the house I alluded to earlier as having been inspired in its design by a vintage Phillips 66 station. You can't help but stare.

Arcadia also has a literary connection. Washington Irving, well-known as the author of the popular tale "Rip Van Winkle," camped here in 1832. He wrote about his travels in this area in *A Tour of the Prairies*, which was published in 1835. Look for the marker east of the Round Barn. Mr. Irving is considered by some to be the United States' earliest professional author, having written *A History of New York* in 1809 under the pseudonym Diedrich Knickerbocker. Like Shakespeare, Irving is credited with putting some phrases of his own invention into the vernacular. He is credited with the expression "almighty dollar," referring to "that great object of universal devotion throughout our land." He also is credited with the expression "happy hunting ground" to refer to the American Indians' life in the hereafter. If that's not enough, then consider that his pen name of Knickerbocker has henceforth been synonymous with New York and New Yorkers since shortly after the publication of his *History* at the age of 26.

Just off the highway in the center of Arcadia is a sort of automotive diorama—a ladybug is about to be devoured by a spider.

FURTHER AFIELD

A real treat awaits you just a short trip north of old 66. A few miles east of downtown Edmond, take either 12th Street or U.S. 77 north

Streetside scene, Arcadia, Oklahoma.

for approximately 20 miles to the very historic town of **Guthrie**, Oklahoma. On the outskirts of the town you'll see a still-working drive-in theater, the Beacon. In business since 1951, the **Beacon Drive-In** had an appearance in the movie *Twister*.

For some 20 years, beginning in 1890, Guthrie was the capital of Oklahoma (or Indian Territory, as it was known at the time). Virtually all of its downtown was constructed during that period, and today Guthrie boasts the largest contiguous urban historical district on the National Register, consisting of 2,169 structures in 400 blocks on 1,400 acres, including 14 city blocks of Victoriana. The territory achieved statehood in 1907, and the capital was moved to Oklahoma City a few years later in 1910. The National Trust for Historic Preservation honored Guthrie as one of its "Dozen Distinctive Destinations" in 2004.

Tom Mix used to bartend at the still-hopping **Blue Bell Saloon**, and just outside the Blue Bell staged gunfights are held in the street for much of the year. Second at Harrison.

Catercorner to the Blue Bell is the **State Capital**

Publishing Museum. This turn-of-the-century publishing house still has lots of the original equipment in place, tons of samples of some of its print jobs from over the years, such as textbooks and legal forms, as well as most of the original furnishings.

The **Scottish Rite Temple** is among the largest of its kind in the world, with an enormous number of stained-glass artworks. Guided tours are available. East of downtown on Oklahoma Ave.

The **Gaffney Building**, near Second and Oklahoma, houses both the Chamber of Commerce and the **Oklahoma Frontier Drug Store Museum**. The folks at the C of C will answer any questions you may have, and the drug store is well worth touring. Not only will you see all the tools of the trade from a circa-1890 pharmacy, but the attendant on duty when we were there was extremely knowledgeable, having been a practicing druggist himself for many years.

Physically connected to one of the 1,946 public libraries endowed by the Carnegie Foundation in this country, the **Oklahoma Territorial Museum** presents a history of Oklahoma during its earliest days, including the Land Run of 1889 and the subsequent influx of settlers. There is even some information about the infamous case of Elmer McCurdy. 406 E. Oklahoma Ave.

Check out **Vic's Place**, at 123 N. Second, for oil and gas collectibles, neon, and other roadabilia.

Also in Guthrie are the **National Four-String Banjo Hall of Fame**, the **Oklahoma Sports Museum**, and numerous bed and breakfasts. In fact, Guthrie is known in the area as the Bed & Breakfast Capital of Oklahoma. Annual events include a **bluegrass festival** in October and a **jazz banjo festival** in May. The old Santa Fe Railroad depot, at 409 W. Oklahoma Ave., houses the **International Model Railroad Museum**.

Don't know how or where to start? Carriage and trolley tours of the city are available.

Elmer McCurdy

For those of you interested in strange stories, this has to be one of the strangest. I have read four or five slightly different accounts of the Elmer McCurdy saga, and each one is as bizarre as the next.

In 1976, a film crew shooting an episode of the *Six Million Dollar Man* was on location at a Los Angeles-area fun house. One of the crew members moved what was thought to be a dummy hanging from the ceiling, but the "dummy's" arm fell off. Inside were what appeared to be the bones and joints of a real human being. That man was soon identified as Elmer McCurdy.

Elmer McCurdy was an outlaw who died in a shootout at the hands of authorities in 1911. His body was taken to a Pawhuska, Oklahoma mortuary where the undertaker, not knowing how long he might need to hang onto the body before it was claimed, added arsenic to the usual embalming fluid and thereby mummified McCurdy's remains. Months passed, and the body still had not been claimed. By this time, McCurdy's corpse had become something of a local attraction, and people came by and paid a nickel apiece to look at it. Many years later, the funeral home had changed hands, the principals in the whole affair were deceased, and no one knew any more that the dried-up dummy in town was a real human body. A carnival passed through and offered to take the "dummy" off the current owner's hands for a small price. A deal was struck, and Elmer McCurdy entered show business posthumously.

No one knows for sure all the places McCurdy's mummified body might have been displayed in the intervening years, until he was discovered that day in the fun house in

1976. Once again, no relatives presented themselves to claim the body. Finally, a historical group arranged for McCurdy's body to be returned to Oklahoma for burial. The Warren Monument company of Guthrie furnished a tombstone bearing the inscription:

ELMER MCCURDY
SHOT BY SHERIFF'S POSSE IN OSAGE HILLS ON OCT 7, 1911
RETURNED TO GUTHRIE, OKLAHOMA
FROM LOS ANGELES COUNTY, CALIFORNIA
FOR BURIAL, APR 22, 1977

Elmer McCurdy was then laid to rest in Summit View Cemetery, Guthrie, Oklahoma. The state medical examiner ordered that two cubic yards of concrete be poured over the coffin before the grave was closed.

Back on Route 66 heading west out of Arcadia, there is little of the Route 66 flavor evident between here and the town of Edmond, although this stretch is relaxing and somewhat rural in character.

EDMOND

Following Route 66 through Edmond means turning left (south) at Broadway. A right at that corner takes you into the smallish business district.

Sanders Camera Shop, at the corner of Second and Boulevard, was at one time the first school in Oklahoma Territory. The building at 1 S. Broadway used to house the city's first movie theater on the ground floor, with the first hospital being directly upstairs.

The **Arcadian Inn**, now a bed and breakfast at 328 E. First St., was originally a one-story private residence built in 1908. Twenty years later, the owner decided to convert it to two stories by lifting the original house and constructing a new first story and basement underneath. How's that for doing things the hard way?

The **Edmond Historical Society Museum**, housed in an armory building constructed by the WPA in 1936, displays photos, documents, and artifacts relating to the town's development. There are also traveling exhibits which change throughout the year. In the 1950s, this building was used for the housing and training of dancing bears for the local circus. 431 S. Boulevard.

Look for the **Blue Hippo** at the AAA Glass Company at 1129 S. Broadway as you head south toward Oklahoma City. Unofficially named Buddy, the fiberglass creature has been known to be temporarily relocated for special occasions, such as weddings and grand openings, or even just relaxing in a local park.

Between Edmond and Oklahoma City is **Memorial Park Cemetery**, just east of U.S. 77 (Kelley) on the south side of Memorial Road (NE 136th). This is the burial place of Wiley Post. Although Post is more widely known these days as the friend of Will Rogers who was piloting the plane in which they both perished in 1935, he was actually very accomplished in his own right. He made the first successful solo flight around the world in 1933 and also designed the first pressurized flight suit. The aviator's likeness and biography are carved in the large stone over the burial plot.

OKLAHOMA CITY

Oklahoma City successfully ousted Guthrie as the state capital in 1910. For many years, the **capitol building** here was unusual for this country, in that it had no dome. A dome was indeed a part of the original design, but it was omitted for reasons of economy. In

Oklahoma City, Oklahoma.

recent years, the citizens of Oklahoma saw fit to finally top their capitol with a dome, so the one you see there today has not been there long. Oil was struck here in 1928, and before the boom was over, there were 24 oil wells pumping on the actual grounds of the Oklahoma state capitol.

Route 66 took many different paths through Oklahoma City

over the years, and so you would do well to explore extensively if you can tolerate the traffic. The best-known route traced present-day Broadway out of Edmond (which becomes Kelley) straight toward the capitol, where it turned west on 23rd, north on May, and west again on NW 39th St. Expressway. Alternatively, a turn from Kelley onto Britton Avenue and then left on Western Avenue takes you through the village of Britton along a rather obscure "beltline" route. Also, be sure not to skip the old 66 alignment which followed Classen Avenue for a time. You'll see a great example of symbolic architecture when you pass the little triangular building with the giant milk bottle on top.

The first automatic parking meter was invented and installed in Oklahoma City by brothers Carlton and Gerald Hale on July 16, 1935. Initially, the meters were placed on only one side of the downtown street. Within three days, the merchants from the other side of the street petitioned to have their side metered also. They liked the constant and rapid turnover that the meters engendered. Two years later, in 1937, Sylman Goldman introduced the shopping cart here on June 4th.

On July 22, 1933, Machine Gun Kelly kidnapped millionaire Charles Urscher from his home here at 327 NW 18th Street. Kelly was the gangster who coined the phrase "G-Man."

You'll leave Oklahoma City via NW 39th. The **66 Bowl** has a sign out front that definitely speaks to us from another era.

OKLAHOMA CITY ATTRACTIONS

Oklahoma City has known tragedy. The worst act of terrorism on American soil—up to that time—occurred here April 19, 1995, at the Alfred P. Murrah Federal Building. You can visit the **Oklahoma City National Memorial** at 620 N. Harvey Ave.

At Reno and Robinson streets in the heart of Oklahoma City

is the **Myriad Botanical Gardens and Crystal Bridge Tropical Conservatory**. Truly an oasis, the gardens cover a 17-acre tract and include rolling hills surrounding a sunken lake. Focal point to the gardens is the seven-story, 224-foot-long Crystal Bridge Tropical Conservatory, a greenhouse providing a habitat for an extensive collection of palms, orchids, cacti, and exotics from around the world.

The **National Cowboy & Western Heritage Museum** (formerly National Cowboy Hall of Fame) is at 1700 NE 63rd Street. This is a large, first-rate complex including major exhibition galleries, a replica turn-of-the-century western town, and several heroic-sized works of sculpture, including a rendering of James Earle Fraser's world-famous *End of the Trail*, which won a gold medal at the 1915 Pan-Pacific International Exposition in San Francisco. Fraser also designed the Indian Head (or Buffalo) nickel, which began production in 1913. Also contained within the museum is the Hall of Fame of Western Film, which includes video clips and other memorabilia associated with the likes of Gene Autry, Gary Cooper, Tom Mix, and Slim Pickens, among many others. There is also a research archive which includes photographs, papers, and personal effects of actor Walter Brennan and several other western notables.

Just down the street from the National Cowboy Museum (above) is the **County Line Barbeque** restaurant. In the 1930s, this place was a speakeasy

Oklahoma City, Oklahoma.

known as the Kentucky Club, and was frequented by Pretty Boy Floyd. The building reportedly has features such as trap doors to facilitate escape in the event of a police raid.

The **Omniplex** is a collection of museums at 2100 NE 52nd. Included are the Hands-On Science Museum, the Kirkpatrick Planetarium, the Red Earth Indian Center, the Air Space Museum, and the International Photography Hall of Fame & Museum. With all of these attractions essentially under one roof, it's a near-overdose for the mind. The photography museum includes the world's largest Grand Canyon photomural, so you can get a preview of the big ditch before you reach Arizona.

The **Paseo Arts District**, centered at NW 30th and Dewey, is a historically rich neighborhood which has been taken over by the city's art community. Several artists have studios and galleries in this area. The district hosts an annual art festival each Memorial Day weekend.

Bricktown is a former warehouse district which has been turned into an entertainment hotspot, with bars, restaurants, and music clubs. Recently added are some canals which are plied by water taxis. The loading area for the narrated taxi rides is across from the Bricktown Ballpark, home of the minor-league Oklahoma RedHawks.

The **Oklahoma Country & Western Music Hall of Fame** at 3925 SE 29th consists of more than 10,000 square feet of items dedicated to Country and Western music performers.

The **45th Infantry Division Museum** is a highly regarded military museum and has something of interest for everyone. Oklahoma's role in the Civil War and Indian wars is represented here, but displays also include items from Hitler's bunker which were captured by the 45th in 1945. There are over 200 original "Willie and Joe" cartoons by artist Bill Mauldin, and outside are dozens of military vehicles, aircraft, and artillery. 2145 NE 36th.

On the grounds of the Will Rogers World Airport is the **Ninety-Nines Museum of Women Pilots**. Amelia Earhart is

prominently repre-sented here—as well as other early female aviators—and there are materials per-taining to women in the space program. 4300 Amelia Earhart Rd.

The **Okla-homa State Fire-fighters Museum**

Vintags police cruiser, Oklahoma City, Oklahoma.

has helmets on display worn by Ben Franklin, John

Hancock, and Paul Revere. Also on display is Oklahoma's first fire sta-tion (1864) as well as 100-year-old fire equipment actually used in Oklahoma communities. 2716 NE 50th St.

The **National Softball Hall of Fame and Museum** at 2801 NE 50th St. covers all aspects of the game, including fast-, slow-, and modified-pitch versions. The museum is housed in the Amateur Softball Association headquarters. The ASA stadium hosts national and world class competition in the sport.

The **Henry Overholser Mansion** was built in 1903 by Henry Overholser at 405 NW 15th St. This Victorian-style home contains 90 percent original family furnishings and is notable for its hand-painted canvas-covered walls.

Built in 1928, the **Governor's Mansion** offers guided tours every Wednesday. The house is said to be haunted by the ghost of Oklahoma's depression-era governor, William H. "Alfalfa Bill" Murray. Outside is a swimming pool shaped like the state's boundaries. 820 NE 23rd St.

The **Harn Homestead and 1889er Museum** is a complex of structures at 313 NE 16th St., in the shadow of the state capitol building. This homestead was claimed in the Land Run of 1889, and includes a stone and cedar barn, three houses, and an 1897 one-room school.

Does pigeon racing tickle your fancy? The **World of Wings Pigeon Center** has dedicated itself to the heritage of the pigeon. A project of the American Homing Pigeon Institute, there is a small museum housed in a 1930s brick house on 10 acres. There are educational exhibits, pigeon lofts, and cultivated gardens. Pigeon races are held in the fall. White pigeons are available here for release at weddings and other special events. 2300 NE 63rd St.

This old bridge is at the edge of Lake Overholser, west of Oklahoma City.

At 2641 NW 10th is the **World Organization of China Painters Museum**. A large collection of hand-painted china accompanies a gift shop, a research library, and classrooms.

The **Classen High School Museum** (1901 N. Ellison) and the **Central High School Museum** (815 N. Robinson) are in competition to see who has the best school spirit. Classen has the country's largest high school alumni organization and boasts of Admiral William Crowe among its constituents. Central High's building (ca. 1910) was designed by the architect of the state capitol and is on the National Register of Historic Places.

Enterprise Square is at 2501 E. Memorial Rd., on the campus of Oklahoma Christian University. Your journey begins with a ride in the Heartbeat Rotunda, a glass elevator that takes you to the fourth floor and a multimedia multi-screen extravaganza extolling the virtues of the capitalist, free-enterprise system. Sales agents include giants, robots, skeletons, and enormous cash registers containing dollar bills with singing presidents' heads on them. Truly a one-of-a-kind attraction. Be sure to spend some of that hard-earned cash in the gift shop by getting an "I Love Capitalism" bumper sticker.

WARR ACRES-BETHANY

The town of Bethany was established in 1906 by members of the Nazarene Church. Today, both Warr Acres and Bethany are embedded in Greater Oklahoma City. The **Bethany Historical Society Museum** is located inside city hall at 6700 NW 36th.

Route 66 is a multi-lane, divided thoroughfare here. Just west of town, it crosses a corner of Lake Overholser. Named for Oklahoma City mayor Ed Overholser, the lake in Rittenhouse's time was a recreational area, which included speedboat rides. Prior to World War II, plans were being made to make Lake Overholser a layover center for seaplane excursions. This, of course, is a mode of travel which never really caught on well. Today, Alaskans use sea-planes very commonly, but they are short on roads up there. Plans are now underway to create a park along part of the lake's shore.

I encourage you to take the old 66 alignment that crosses the vintage Lake Overholser Bridge and then hugs the lake's northern shoreline for a while en route to Yukon.

Yukon, Oklahoma.

YUKON

Singer Garth Brooks and actor Dale Robertson both hail from Yukon, and there is a sign at the edge of town proudly proclaiming Brooks its native son. The Garth Brooks Water Tower is at I-40 and Garth Brooks Blvd.

One of my favorite motel signs on all of Route 66 once stood in front of the Yukon Motel. Unfortunately, a change of ownership at the motel led to the sign's untimely—and baffling— demise.

A major landmark here in Yukon is the **Yukon's Best flour mural**, which is prominently emblazoned on the side of a grain storage facility on the south side of the highway in town, right at the railroad tracks. Also, you are in **Chisholm Trail** country now. Some sources say that Ninth Street through Yukon closely approximates the route of the Chisholm Trail. Other sources say that U.S. 81, which runs through El Reno further west, is more authentic. In truth, being a cattle trail, the Chisholm was of course never paved, and so the precise route varied considerably subject to the vagaries of such things as water availability, prevailing weather, and individual whim. What we can be more certain of is that the trail ran from southern Texas, through central Oklahoma, and on to the cattle markets in Abilene, Kansas. The trail was named for Jesse Chisholm, who was among the first to make regular use of the trail and to advocate its use by others. Yukon holds a Chisholm Trail festival each year, as do many of the towns and cities through which the trail once passed.

There's a park in Yukon (at 2200 S. Holly Ave.) that has a **Chisholm Trail monument** and also contains a "Bank Shot" setup. This is a sort of cross between basketball and miniature golf—it consists of bizarrely shaped backboards on which to test your skill and patience in sinking your "free throws." I've never seen one of them anywhere else.

Yukon's Best Railroad Museum is a static display of a caboose and other rail cars across the boulevard from the Yukon's Best mural. Full tours of the contents of the rail cars are by prior arrangement only.

The **Yukon Historical Society Museum**, at 601 Oak St., is housed in a 1910 school building and includes a doctor's office, Czech history room, and other local history.

North of town is **Express Clydesdales**, at the corner of Wilshire and 11th St. (Garth Brooks Blvd.). Rare black and white Clydesdale horses make their home here in a 1936 barn restored by Amish specialists from Indiana. There is also a gift shop and visitor center.

BANNER

There's little to indicate the community of Banner, but you can go and see what's left of the old town center by taking a right on Banner Rd. and going as far as the railroad track.

EL RENO

El Reno sits at the junction of two famous highways of very different kinds: U.S. 66 and the Chisholm Trail (roughly at U.S. 81), and is the seat of Canadian County. It was reportedly named for a Civil War general, Jesse L. Reno, who was killed in action in 1862.

Look for the **VFW post** as you pass through town; there is a retired airplane out front which saw action in World War II.

Formerly in El Reno was the Big Eight Motel (originally the Beacon Motel), which had a large neon sign. The phrase "Amarillo's Finest" was added to the sign for the filming of the movie *Rain Man* in room 117. The owners left the odd addition there afterward, which caused bewilderment among some travelers. Since then, someone with no sensitivity for the things you and I appreciate took down the vintage sign in favor of one which was duller than words could describe. Renamed the Deluxe Inn, the motel sported a simple plexiglass box on a post, instead of what was once a unique example of the sign maker's art. Go figure. Since that time, the motel closed down altogether and was finally razed.

The **Canadian**

"Amarillo's Finest" was actually many miles away in El Reno, Oklahoma.

County Historical Museum features a jailhouse, depot, one-room school, railroad memorabilia, and other items of historical and cultural interest, including the nation's first Red Cross Canteen. At 300 S. Grand at the old Rock Island depot.

In El Reno is a **BPOE lodge** (Benevolent & Protective Order of Elks), at 415 S. Rock Island, which was part of an exhibit at the 1904 St. Louis World's Fair. The structure was pulled

Old U.S. 66 zig-zagged through downtown El Reno at one time, and today you'll find this mural along the way.

apart and transported here, where it was re-assembled. The 1904 fair was the one in which men were actually held captive in a quasi-anthropological exhibit and which also introduced the hamburger on a bun (see St. Louis, Missouri).

On the first Saturday of each May, the town of El Reno grills a 650-pound **Onion Burger**, and you can get a free bite of the "Big One" as long as it lasts.

There is a visitor center for **Fort Reno**, from which the city of El Reno takes its name, at 7107 W. Cheyenne Street. What remains of the fort itself we'll encounter as we head west along the Mother Road.

About four miles west of El Reno is **Fort Reno**. Although much of it remains, today it looks like many a ghost town. Established in 1875, it was an important post for keeping the Cheyenne and Arapaho tribes at bay during the territorial struggles of the time, and later achieved a reputation for raising a large proportion of the U.S. Army's horses during the pre-mechanized era. It was here that Black Jack, the riderless horse in President Kennedy's funeral procession, was raised. The cemetery contains the grave of one Ben Clark, an accomplished scout and sometime Pony Express rider. During the Second World War, the fort functioned as a prisoner-of-war camp for German and Italian captives, some of whom are also laid to rest in the cemetery.

FURTHER AFIELD

Travel a little to the north of El Reno via U.S. 81, and you'll be approximating the path of the Chisholm Trail. The town of **Kingfisher** is proud of its Chisholm Trail heritage, but a little less proud of its gridiron record. Between 1905 and 1919, Oklahoma U. beat the Kingfisher football team by scores of 55-0, 32-0, 51-0, 46-5, 66-0, 104-0, 40-0, 74-0, 67-0, 67-0, 96-0, 179-0, and 157-0. In 13 games, Kingfisher was outscored by a whopping 1,034 to 5.

Kingfisher was the birthplace of an outlaw named John King Fisher. He was reputed to be a major-league rustler in the 1870s, and is said to have admitted to killing seven men, "not counting Mexicans."

Another outlaw clan, the Daltons, grew up on a farm in the vicinity. Buried in the **Kingfisher Cemetery** are Adeline Lee Younger Dalton, mother of the Dalton boys and cousin of Cole Younger, and her son, Emmett Dalton.

Kingfisher is also where W. C. Coleman, of Coleman Lantern fame, first began selling lamps door to door in the 1890s.

Chisholm Trail museums are to be found both north (Kingfisher) and south (Duncan) of El Reno. There are still visible trail ruts at Monument Hill near Duncan. Information and tours are available at the Chisholm Trail Heritage Center.

Though Route 66 was eventually straightened, for a time it veered north and passed through the town of Calumet. You can take this older course by turning north on U.S. 270.

CALUMET

Prior to the nineteenth century, "calumet" was the name given to what is now commonly called the "peace pipe." It is said to have come from the French *chalumeau*, meaning "reed."

GEARY

The **Canadian River Historical Society Museum**, at Broadway and Main, includes the area's first log jail, a train caboose, and a furnished 1901 home.

North of Geary, on the banks of the Canadian River, at Left Hand Spring Camp, is the grave of **Jesse Chisholm**, the man for whom the trail we crossed a little earlier was named. There is a granite monument marking the site.

Heading south out of Geary, U.S. 281/OK 8 will return you to the "through" alignment of Route 66. If you're feeling adventurous, there is a partially paved road that you can veer onto at the edge of town which parallels the railroad tracks. This was at one time the main highway. After about four miles or so, a right will take you toward Bridgeport and the old river crossing which gave the town its name. You can no longer make the crossing there, however. The other direction takes you back to a rendezvous with the newer 66 alignment, near the convergence of the Canadian, Blaine, and Caddo county lines.

Where U.S. 281 and OK 8 turn south and leave us is what is known as Hinton Junction. There is a ruin of a café there which I'm told was also a bus station at one time. The sign over the door says "EAT."

BRIDGEPORT

Bridgeport was bypassed by Route 66 as the crossing of this branch at the Canadian River was moved further downstream.

FURTHER AFIELD

South of Bridgeport via U.S. 281 is the town of Hinton. The **Hinton Historical Museum** contains one of the state's largest collections of buggies and carriages, as well as nineteenth-century farm machinery.

Just outside Hinton is the **Red Rock Canyon State Park**, reputed to be the haven of horse rustlers and cattle thieves in days gone by. A covered-wagon migratory trail (California Road) once passed through the park, and today one of the many hiking trails will take you to where you can view some of the remaining wagon ruts from those days.

Both before and after Hydro you'll be passing over a stretch of the route which is truly classic. The roadway is segmented concrete, and it rises and falls with the gentle hills in this area. Even though the interstate is only yards away on your left, you get a true taste of what cross-country auto travel was like decades ago. Savor it, and remember it after you've returned home.

To the south of this Bridgeport-Hydro stretch of highway there are some features called **Steen's Buttes** or **Caddo Mounds**. They were reported by army explorers as early as 1840, and were subsequently used as landmarks for '49ers en route to California during the gold rush years. On some maps, one of the mounds is designated "Dead Woman's Mound."

HYDRO

The highway passes just south of the town of Hydro, and at a crossroads called Provine you'll see **Lucille's**, a fixture on Route 66 since 1941. Lucille Hamons and her husband established a gas station and tourist court here. Sadly, Lucille is gone now, and we are all poorer with her passing. She tirelessly took time with each and every traveler who came through here to pass along stories of the road and her many years at its shoulder.

Lucille's, Hydro, Oklahoma.

Johnson's Peanut Company offers seasonal tours, and the gift shop is open all year. Corner of 66 and Arapahoe (Highway 58).

WEATHERFORD

On the outskirts of town is the **66 West Twin Drive-In Theater**.

Being the birthplace of an astronaut has its responsibilities. Weatherford is home to the **General Thomas P. Stafford Airport Museum**, at 3000 Logan Rd., Bldg. 2. It features moon rocks, space suits, rocket boosters, and other memorabilia.

In downtown Weatherford is the **Greek Temple** building, which was known as the German Bank until the first World War came along and made the name an embarrassment. 118 W. Main.

Four generations have plied their trade at the **Cotter**

Blacksmith Shop in the same building since 1910. There is turn-of-the-century equipment here, some of it still in use. 208 W. Rainey.

To the south of Weatherford is **Fort Sill**, where numerous Indian chiefs were imprisoned, and where some of whom, notably Geronimo, are interred.

CLINTON

The town was named for Judge Clinton Irwin. **McLain Rogers Park**, on historic 66 (S. 10th), has a classic enamel and neon sign dating from 1936.

On the east side of town is the **Mohawk Lodge Indian Store & Trading Post**, first established in 1892 and occupying this location since 1940. The original sales counter was brought over and is still in use.

Sadly, Clinton has been losing ground in the struggle against standardization. As of fairly recently, both Pop Hicks' Restaurant, a classic highway eatery, and the Calmez Hotel, an abandoned downtown inn of the old-school tradition, are with us no more.

The **Oklahoma Route 66 Museum** opened here in 1995 (2229 Gary Blvd.) on a later bypass route around town. The building itself is uniquely Route 66-themed, and the exhibits are very professionally done, por-

Clinton, Oklahoma.

The Oklahoma Route 66 Museum in Clinton is a must-stop for every true-blue road warrior.

traying the highway's changing roles in society throughout the various decades of the century. A tiny restored **Valentine diner**, which once served Route 66 travelers in Texas, now sits on the museum grounds. The restoration work on the diner earned Virgil Smith the Cyrus Avery Preservation Award the following year.

Across the highway from the museum and diner is the **Trade Winds Motel**. This was one of Elvis Presley's favorite places to stay, having overnighted in room 215 on many occasions. Elvis was a creature of habit, and Clinton evidently was just about a good day's drive out of Memphis for him. Room 215 is available by reservation.

FOSS

There is a ruin here with red, peeling paint, called **Kobel's Place**. North of town via State Highway 44 is **Foss State Park**.

CANUTE

Canute is notable for its **Catholic cemetery** on the east side of town. The grotto is a Works Progress Administration project from the 1930s.

Also in Canute is the **Cotton Boll Motel**, which is now being used as a private residence. The vintage sign, however, remains.

ELK CITY

Originally called Crowe, the townspeople attempted to persuade Adolphus Busch to put a brewery here by renaming the town Busch. When that plan failed, the name Elk City was adopted, after the nearby Elk Creek. The Dodge City (Kansas) Cattle Trail is said to have passed through here in the nineteenth century (the town was established in 1901). According to Jack Rittenhouse, Elk City was the site of an early experiment in collective health care in the 1940s—perhaps the first HMO. Also in the '40s (August 15, 1946, to be more precise) song composer extraordinaire Jimmy Webb was born right here in Elk City.

In 1998, Elk City introduced the **National Route 66 Museum**, at 2717 W. Hwy 66. This museum covers the route in all eight states through which it passes. Outside is a continually-expanding collection of buildings known as the **Old Town Museum Complex**, which includes both historical and painstakingly reproduced buildings, railroad cars, and other features of interest. The museum is getting more impossible to miss all the time—the exterior now includes perhaps the most enormous Route 66 shield ever conceived. The large kachina figures outside once stood at the Queenan Trading Post, an old-school curio shop on Route 66 that closed long ago.

A brief oil boom period in the area is recalled by a huge oil derrick, **Parker Drilling Rig No. 114**. This stands right next to the old Casa Grande Hotel, which hosted a Route 66 conference way back in 1931. Today, it houses the **Anadarko Basin Natural History Museum** (66/Third St. at Main). A few blocks further down, at the corner of Washington, is an **elk sculpture**.

SAYRE

At Fourth and Elm there are what appear to be storm cellar entrances on either side of the main street (Route 66) as it passes through town. These actually lead to an underground pedestrian walkway which allowed the once-busy thoroughfare to be crossed safely. They are, of course, no longer needed, but there are many other towns along the route whose citizens would have appreciated this same innovation in the days when traffic was incessant.

The **Beckham County Courthouse**, on the town square, made a cameo appearance in the film version of *The Grapes of Wrath*. The post office, at 201 N. Fourth, is decorated with a depression-era mural depicting the Oklahoma land run.

The **Short Grass Country Museum**, at 106 E. Poplar, features changing exhibits pertaining to early life in Beckham County and western Oklahoma's shortgrass country in general.

Sayre, Oklahoma.

Sayre, Oklahoma.

Model railroaders should see the **RS&K Railroad Museum**, featuring hundreds of model trains, including working layouts, as well as railroad memorabilia. 411 N. Sixth.

The **Owl Drug**, at Fourth and Main, has the state's largest antique soda fountain.

South of the city on Fourth St., **Fourteen Flags Park** features a WPA-constructed rock swimming pool.

FURTHER AFIELD

North of Sayre via U.S. 283 is the town of **Cheyenne**. Here are the **Washita Battlefield National Historic Site** and the **Black Kettle Museum**. These sites center around a surprise cavalry attack on a Cheyenne village headed by Black Kettle in 1868. The U.S. troops, the 7th Cavalry, were commanded at that time by Lieutenant Colonel George A. Custer. There is also a sculpture on the grounds of the nearby Roger Mills County Courthouse (in Cheyenne) commemorating the events.

The Sayre-Hext-Erick stretch of old 66 is an open book for you to read. As you drive this corridor you will see that there are two older, disused lanes of highway to your right. They indicate the original alignment of 66 through here, right beside the railroad track. The pair of lanes you are driving on were added later, as eastbound lanes separated from the other lanes by a median, in the days when Route 66 was a major thoroughfare for this area. Later, as I-40 was completed to the south, traffic diminished significantly on 66 and two of its lanes were retired.

What remains of the small community of Hext is between old 66 and I-40 just north of exit number 14.

ERICK

The main street through town has been named Roger Miller Boulevard, in honor of Erick's favorite son, who in turn is most noted for his rendition of the song "King of the Road." The town now has a **Roger Miller Museum** and holds an annual Roger Miller Festival in his honor.

Also hailing from near Erick is performer Sheb Wooley. Sheb was a country music performer in the late 1940s, then went to Los Angeles and took acting lessons to pursue a film career. He got the break he was looking for when he was cast in an Errol Flynn film in 1950. He became better known, though, for his extended role in the television series *Rawhide*.

Stop in at the **Sandhills Curiosity Shop**, located in an old meat market at 201 S. Sheb Wooley. There are tons of memorabilia on display, and you'll experience live entertainment by the Mediocre Music Makers 'til the cows come home.

Open sporadically or by appointment, the **100th Meridian Museum** presents information relating to the oft-disputed boundary line between Oklahoma and the Republic of Texas. At one time, the area you are entering here was claimed by the Lone Star State. Sheb Wooley Ave. and Roger Miller Blvd.

TEXOLA

This town was named for the fact that it rests nearly astride the Oklahoma-Texas border. The more obvious Texoma is already in use elsewhere in the state. Texola can rightly be called a ghost town, having only a tiny fraction of its residences and commercial buildings inhabited. There is a tiny jail (one cell, actually) just a block or so off of Route 66.

 Texola is Oklahoma's quiet farewell to the Mother Road.

Texola, Oklahoma, is best described as a ghost town, and has many buildings in a similar state as this one.

TEXAS

T exas, proud as it is to be the largest state in the contiguous 48, and prouder still of its heritage as a former independent republic, ranks next-to-last in the mileage it can claim along the path of Route 66. That's because the Mother Road crosses the state through what is known as the Texas Panhandle. That panhandle, the northernmost extension of the state, is but an eroded stump

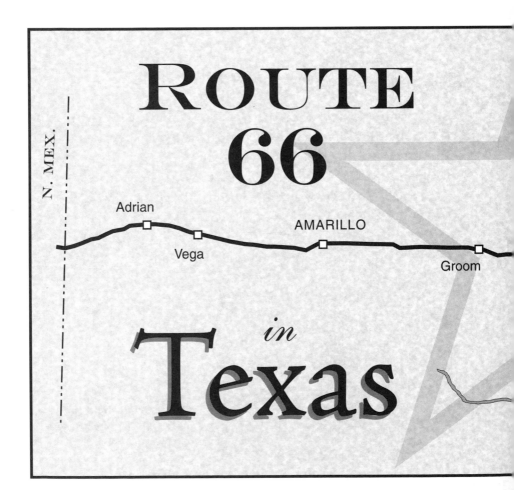

compared to what might have been.

If you took time to stop at the 100th Meridian Museum back in Erick, then you know at least a part of the story. You know that if the Texas-Oklahoma border had been decided differently, the westbound Route 66 traveler of today would have entered the great state of Texas at what is now Erick, Oklahoma. What you might not know is that, if some other political decisions had gone a bit differently, that same traveler would not be leaving Texas until he'd passed through what is now Albuquerque, New Mexico, and crossed over the Rio Grande, some 400 miles to the west.

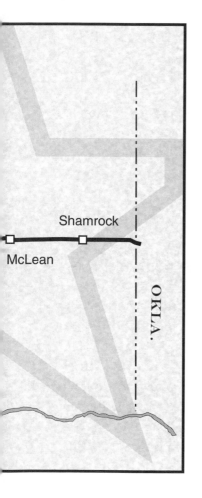

During Texas' early days of statehood (1845–49), it laid claim to territory almost 50 percent larger than its current boundaries, including portions of present-day Oklahoma, New Mexico, Kansas, Colorado, and Wyoming. Since some of this territory was contested by other factions within the U.S., emotions ran high on the subject. At the same time, the former Republic of Texas (1836–45) had incurred significant debts in its struggle for independence. Texas therefore ceded about one-third of its territory in exchange for $10,000,000 in an agreement known as the Compromise of 1850. Much of the territory given up in 1850 makes up the portion of present-day New Mexico east of the Rio Grande.

Texas, as someone once said, is a State of Mind. And fittingly, there's very little to indicate that just moments after leaving Texola, one has entered the Lone Star State. Your first signal, other than the official state line sign erected by the highway department, is the character of the pavement itself. This early stretch of Texas highway is made up of the classic segmented concrete which imparts that rhythmic *thump, ka-thump, ka-thump* to your journey. You'll also note that the road tends to rise and fall with the general lay of the land. If you can succeed in ignoring the raging interstate just a few yards to your right, the rhythm of the road will provide you with that elusive taste of what long-distance highway travel was like decades ago.

Just west of the state line, and right about where old 66 sidles up to the edge of Interstate 40, some maps place the community of Benonine.

BENONINE

My 1957 atlas sees fit to depict Benonine just west of the Oklahoma-Texas state line, but you won't see much from the highway today.

SHAMROCK

Until just a few years ago, as one entered the outskirts of the town of Shamrock from the east, there was a sort of auto graveyard in a field along the north side of the old highway. Those autos have since been removed without a trace. On the left, or southern, side of the road, however, the careful observer may still detect subtle signs that there was once a drive-in movie theater in what is now a pasture filled with livestock, sundry junk, and what looks suspiciously like an old projection booth. There were a great many other ruins along Route 66 in Shamrock not so many years ago. Among them was Lewis Camp, a tourist campground with a general store which has since burned to the ground. A ruin that spoke to me personally was that of an unbranded gasoline station on the east side of town. It had been stripped of virtually all markings, fixtures, and furnishings. However, on the front door three simple words remained: PLEASE COME BACK. That being Day One of my first deliberate excursion on Route 66, I've never been able to get the irony of that sentiment out of my mind. I felt as though ghosts of people long departed were reaching out to me.

But life goes on in Shamrock, albeit at a different pace than in the Mother Road era. As befits a town with such a name, Shamrock puts its all into an annual Saint Patrick's Day celebration. Men grow beards in preparation for the big day—not only is there a prize for the best beard, there is even a price on the head of any adult male failing to sport one.

About midway through town is the junction with U.S. 83, a major north-south highway. Before the interstates came along, the crossing of U.S. Routes 66 and 83 in the center of town was a very happening place, and this intersection was, and still is, dominated by the U Drop Inn.

The **U Drop Inn**, known for a time as Nunn's Café, is an Art Deco masterpiece made all the more impressive by its placement on the Texas plain. The structure, dating from 1936, thrusts two steeple-like projections heavenward. The story goes that, when first constructed, there was a contest to come up with the name for the new enterprise, and that the winner was a youngster who suggested the name U Drop Inn. Fortunately for today's traveler, the U Drop Inn recently underwent a thorough restoration, right down to every last piece of neon tubing. Neon outlines many of the building's design features, which makes it quite an amazing sight at dusk and later into the evening. The local chamber of commerce now has its offices here.

The **Pioneer West Museum** is housed in the former Reynolds Hotel, which dates from the 1920s. The museum has some 20 rooms filled with a variety of exhibits, from Plains Indian culture to NASA moon-mission articles. There are rooms outfitted as doctor

Shamrock, Texas.

and dentist offices, a general store, and a pioneer-era schoolroom. 204 N. Madden St.

There's a fragment of the true **Blarney Stone** on display at Elmore Park, at 400 E. Second Street. The Blarney Stone itself is in County Cork, Ireland, and is reputed to confer eloquence on those who kiss it. Legend has it that the original Lord Blarney was rather accomplished in stretching the truth.

FURTHER AFIELD

North of Shamrock on Highway 83, and just a few miles south of the town of **Canadian**, Texas, is a 50-foot-long **brontosaurus sculpture** crafted by one Gene Cockrell. The brontosaurus overlooks the highway from a small mesa, but the Cockrells' yard is home to many more creations, including a formerly nude (now scantily clad) Dallas Cowboys football team cheerleader. A local story goes that the nearby town of Shamrock once approached Mr. Cockrell about fabricating a 40-foot leprechaun to attach to their water tower, but the Shamrock elders balked at the asking price of several thousand dollars, and the deal was scuttled. No word on whether the leprechaun was to be clothed or not.

Also in Canadian is the **River Valley Pioneer Museum**. Part of the museum's holdings include several hundred glass negatives taken by a local photographer who lived for many years in Canadian starting in 1897. 118 N. 2nd St.

LELA

Lela these days is little more than the crossing of I-40 with Farm Road 1547. You might notice during your time in the Texas Panhandle that people are rather "neighborly" around here. That is, make eye contact with passing drivers and you'll find them giving you "The Wave." The hand that's atop the steering wheel will suddenly have its fingers springing upward into a sort of peacock spread that means "howdy." Please learn to duplicate this maneuver so as not to appear out of place.

Just west of Lela, and on the way to McLean, you can see some trees in the median which are the remnants of the windbreaks referred to by Jack Rittenhouse as he came through here in 1946. It's clear from a look at the shape of these trees that there's a prevailing wind in these parts. It was near here on one of my own Texas 66 forays that I nearly ran over a five-foot snake trying to cross the road.

Before you arrive in McLean, keep an eye out for a pasture where there's an old, old sign full of spaces where the letters have fallen off. Even though it's literally falling apart, there's no doubt about its arresting message: RATTLESNAKES EXIT NOW. The snake I nearly ran over may have been a descendant of one of those captive rattlers from years ago.

McLEAN

Upon entering the town of McLean, Route 66 splits into eastbound and westbound segments, separated by a city block, with two lanes running in each direction. McLean is home to the **Texas Route 66 Museum**, and the town has been quite tenacious in refusing to roll over and die. There are a number of reborn highway businesses, some of which have gone through multiple incarnations attempting to find favor—and a future—with today's motoring public. The Cowboy Café is such a place. McLean even has a couple of small motels, as well as a surprisingly good lunch place in the Red River Café. This is an excellent town in which to get out onto the sidewalk and do some exploring.

The **Texas Route 66 Museum** and the **Devil's Rope Museum** share an address on Kingsley Street, in the block between east- and westbound lanes of Route 66, and the place is well worth a stop. You certainly can't help but be impressed with the enormous

Long-abandoned gift shop in the town of McLean, Texas.

balls of barbed wire on display out front. This building formerly housed a brassiere factory, which was known as Marie Foundations. The Route 66 Museum exhibits include a mock 1950s-era diner and a large snake sculpture which once graced the property of the Regal Reptile Ranch in Alanreed, just several miles west of here. Although I'm not knowledgeable at all on the subject of barbed wire (devil's rope, that is), I have it on good authority that this museum houses one of the finest collections in the world, and believe me, there are people who take this stuff very seriously indeed—almost as seriously as you and I take old Route 66, for example.

The restored **Phillips 66 Station** is right on the highway (westbound) and is an irresistible photo opportunity. It's the classic, tiny, cottage-style variety of Phillips station, a larger example (with attached garages) of which we saw in Chandler, Oklahoma earlier.

RATTLESNAKES EXIT NOW: The snake pit is gone, but the sign remains for today's Route 66 adventurer. East of McLean, Texas.

This one was restored by the Texas Route 66 Association, circa 1991.

The **McLean-Alanreed Area Museum**, at 117 N. Main, houses panhandle history exhibits as well as artifacts relating to the prisoner-of-war camp located near here during the war years.

McLean, Texas.

ALANREED

Alanreed has been known by several names over the years, including Prairie Dog Town and Spring Tank. But Gouge Eye is by far the most colorful, and was obtained in connection with a barroom brawl. At one time there was a community to the north of Alanreed called Eldridge (or Elderidge). That town was established prior to Alanreed, and even had an established post office. However, when the railroad came through a few miles to the south, the lure of those steel rails and the promise of commerce made the citizens of Eldridge pack up their belongings (and their post office) and relocate to the Alanreed townsite.

You can still see a remnant of the community of Eldridge by going north on Highway 291. About five miles north of I-40, turn west on a dead end called County Road X. A short distance brings you to a small cemetery that once served the town. There are few marked graves there, and fewer still with actual names. One of the markers states that it is thought to be the grave of a 12-year-old girl who died from a rattlesnake bite.

While in Alanreed, be sure to travel along the older highway alignment that takes you right through the heart of the village of

Alanreed. There are some very old café ruins here, as well as a restored gas station, the **66 Super Service Station**. The station bears a plaque: "Built by Bradley Kiser 1930—then in downtown Alanreed." When one peers around Alanreed today, it's a little difficult to think of it as ever having a "downtown" district, but if you're at Mr. Kiser's old station, you're standing in the middle of it, what with the ruined Magnolia Café only a few yards away.

North of the "old" alignment, and right alongside the interstate, there is a newer bypass-style Route 66 alignment which now acts as a sort of frontage road. It was there that the Regal Reptile

Depression-era Texaco station, downtown Alanreed.

Ranch once lured families out of their iron chariots with the promise of a close-up look at rattlesnakes, Mexican beaded lizards, and other natural curiosities of the American Southwest. The Regal is now gone, a victim of time and the bulldozer. Only a few years ago, there were still a few ruined buildings and quite a bit of fencing with some of the original lettering visible.

On the west side of Alanreed there used to be some ruins of motel courts which have since been completely removed, leaving only an empty lot. I bring this up as a reminder to you that what you see today may be gone tomorrow, so keep your camera handy and use it—not only for the enrichment of your own experience, but perhaps for the sake of posterity as well.

"Colorful Raccoons." Alanreed, Texas.

FURTHER AFIELD

West of Alanreed, the Highway 2477 North exit will take you on a side trip to Lake McClellan, an old stopover with WPA-era structures, now designated the Lake McClellan National Grassland Park.

You'll notice that once you've left Alanreed heading west, the Texas landscape begins to change as the lower plains of the eastern panhandle give way to the Caprock. The so-called Caprock is an elevated plateau from which the rest of Texas slopes noticeably downward toward the southeast and the Gulf of Mexico. As you climb, the landscape seems to open up to ever more impressive views of the surrounding country.

Also in this vicinity, you might initially be confused by some signs along the roadside first announcing Donley County, then Gray County, and then Donley again. It's not that the shape of those counties is so irregular; rather, the highway wanders back and forth across a political boundary which was designed by a man with a ruler in his hand. The highway's path, on the other hand, makes some allowances for the lay of the land.

Once atop the Caprock, you are on the *Llano Estacado*, or Staked Plain. There are multiple theories on how the area got its name, but the one given the most credence comes from the days of Coronado. When his entourage began crossing the region, they drove stakes into the ground as a substitute for natural features (trees, boulders) which in this area are rare-to-nonexistent. This was done to prevent needlessly retracing their steps. The staked plain begins roughly at the Caprock escarpment and continues to just east of the Pecos River Valley in New Mexico.

JERICHO

At Texas Hwy 70 South, the only remaining thing to be seen is a ruined motel court and a nearby cemetery. The cemetery has some unique features and is worth a look. The area around Jericho, however, earned an ugly reputation during the days of Route 66 travel

These structures are nearly all that remain of the community of Jericho, Texas.

as being something of a quagmire. There was an unpaved section, or muck in the pavement, which could be difficult to navigate under wet conditions. Travelers were advised to take extra care in the vicinity of Jericho Gap, lest they become another ledger entry for the folks making a living towing stranded vehicles out of the gap.

BOYDSTON

Little is left of this community—located about two miles west of the Highway 70 North junction—other than an interstate exit for Boydston Road. However, my 1957 road atlas portrays it on a par in size with other neighboring communities, such as Alanreed or Groom. There is still a tiny cemetery in this vicinity, about two miles south of I-40.

GROOM

Exit Interstate 40 at the first Groom exit, the one with the leaning water tower. I wish I had a nickel for every time I've heard someone describe this water tower as having "one leg shorter than the others." To the keen-eyed observer, this is pure hokum. Look carefully and you'll note that there are five appendages—four legs and one central water conduit. The end of that water pipe was intended to be beneath the surface of the ground, so it is in fact longer than the four true legs, which is why the tower sits at such an angle. The legs are actually all the same length, just as they should be. The owners of the Britten Truck Stop that once operated here thought that the spectacle of the leaning tower made for a good gimmick; and besides, it would've been unnecessarily expensive to install the thing properly.

Make a left turn under the interstate here to enter the town of Groom. The road will soon bear to the right, and you'll be surrounded by the spirit of old Route 66. Groom has that lonely and delicious air of a town that was robbed of its life by the bypassing of the old highway. The road is extremely wide through town, and the traffic very light, so take your time. There are a pair of more-or-less identical motels in town that were called Golden Spread, but their signs have long since been removed and the premises converted to other uses. One of them has been transformed into a mini-warehouse rental facility. Golden Spread is an old term referring to the relatively rich resources to be found here in the high plains region of the country, including rich soil, mineral

The 66 Courts have since been demolished. Groom, Texas.

deposits, and plentiful subterranean water for irrigation.

My favorite Groom landmark—now demolished—was the remains of the 66 Courts, just across the road from the grain elevators. It was at one time a combination motel court and Magnolia gasoline station. For years, there was an Edsel parked beneath the 66 Courts sign that made for a great photo opportunity, as did several other retired road warriors scattered on the property. It was the 66 Courts which provided the inspiration

Streetside scene in Groom, Texas.

for the vaguely Art Deco-flavored design of one of the new I-40 rest areas near Alanreed.

A modern addition to the community of Groom is the **giant cross**, which can be seen from quite a distance. It's said to be the largest in the Western Hemisphere, at 190 feet tall. The complex includes sculptures depicting the various Stations of the Cross, and the whole affair is lit at night.

Groom is home to the **Blessed Mary Restaurant**, a non-profit entity where you pay what you want for your meal, with the proceeds going to charity.

CONWAY

If you're on I-40 as you approach Conway, make sure to exit at Highway 207. As you enter Conway, there is a complex surrounded by chain link fencing on your right. Standing amid the rusting automobiles is a small neon sign—CABINS—just in front of what

Old tourist court complex at Conway, Texas.

is left of the main office. Nearby, and pressed up close to the side of the highway, is a separate building which acted as a sort of general store and café. There is lettering on the side that can only be faintly read, part of which says "Eat." The opposite (west) side clearly says "Buddy's Café."

A little further on you come to a crossroads and what was at one time a mom-and-pop-style gas station or convenience store. A right turn here quickly returns you to the interstate. Continue straight ahead (Hwy 2161) so as not to join the mad rush any sooner than necessary.

Also in Conway is a more recent addition to Mother Road lore: **Bug Ranch**. This is a spoof of the famous Cadillac Ranch art installation several miles ahead in Amarillo. It consists of a set of Volkswagen Beetles buried nose-first in the earth.

AMARILLO

As is the case with most cities of significant size, the path of Route 66 through Amarillo varied over the years. The easiest alignment to follow is one of the later incarnations, which more or less bypassed the core of the city via what is now Amarillo Boulevard. This version of the route takes a northerly detour around the city, and this alignment still retains plenty of evidence of its having been a major thoroughfare in the pre-interstate era. Most of this part of Amarillo has been neither maintained nor restored over the intervening years, and gives the traveler a genuine taste of the seedier side of the highway life cycle. The majority of the motels which remain now accommodate a longer-term clientele, and most of the other buildings have been recycled many times over and enlisted in lines of work their original owners and designers neither envisioned nor intended.

An earlier alignment of the highway went directly through the heart of the city, during the years when that was common practice. A section of Sixth Street, roughly between Georgia and Western Streets, has recently seen some revitalization work in order to make the most of its Mother Road heritage. This has resulted in some modest gentrification of the neighborhood, with a collection of antique shops, cafés, and boutiques now lining this stretch of the route.

Amarillo was first settled as a buffalo-hide tent camp in the 1880s, and named for the nearby Amarillo Creek, which was in turn named for the yellowish soil and wildflowers that were prevalent in the area. Curiously, Amarillo is closer to four other state capitals (Santa Fe, Denver, Topeka, Oklahoma City) than it is to its own (Austin). This undoubtedly contributes to the region's independent-mindedness. The city is considered the Helium Capital of the World, producing about 90 percent of the world's supply of the unique element. There is a six-story structure at 1200 Streit—just off Amarillo Blvd. in the western part of town—which commemorates the centennial of the discovery of helium in the area. When it was first erected in 1968, articles were collected to create four time capsules, the last of which is not slated to be opened until A.D. 2968, 1,000 years (!) after its interment. Included in the capsule is a $10 passbook savings account at a local bank which will then be worth at least one quadrillion dollars, assuming the bank—and money, for that matter—are still in existence.

Amarillo is one of the quirkiest towns on Route 66, if not the entire country. A disproportionate amount of that quirkiness seems to be attributable to one man, Stanley Marsh 3 (starting with that Arabic numeral in his name). He's the man behind something collectively referred to as the Dynamite Museum, a series of mock road signs scattered throughout the city and proclaiming odd bits of philosophy, poetry, or just plain nonsense. Conceived by Mr. Marsh and erected by his merry band of part-time collegiate aspiring artists, they appear in front of small businesses, in residential neighborhoods, and in places that might aptly be described as no place in particular.

Stanley Marsh 3 is even better known for having commissioned *Cadillac Ranch* in 1974, which has since become a sort of
Mecca for Route 66 pilgrims. Ironically, the construct, which was
assembled by an art co-op calling themselves the Ant Farm, came
along too late to be contemporary with Route 66 in the region.
Instead, it was placed in a field beside I-40, the highway which had
supplanted U.S. 66. That said, no trip through the Texas Panhandle

Public art in Amarillo, Texas.

is complete without taking a walk out into that field to absorb some of the energy contained in those upended Cadillacs, which are said to be positioned at the same angle as the sides of the Great Pyramids of Egypt.

Another Marsh commission is *Floating Mesa*, a sort of topographic illusion about 11 miles out of town on Ranch Road 1061.

In terms of its significance in Route 66 lore, the only thing in Amarillo that's in the same league with *Cadillac Ranch* would be the Big Texan. After serving steaks to Mother Road travelers for many years, the **Big Texan Steak Ranch** responded to the shift in American travel habits by relocating to the shoulder of Interstate 40 in 1968. There, they continue their long-standing tradition of serving a 72-ounce steak at no charge, provided the person ordering it can consume it (and all of its accoutrements) in less than 60 minutes. There is a sort of Hall of Fame on the premises where you can read the names of those patrons who have been successful in meeting that challenge over the years. As the sign outside says, "The

Roadside stand, Amarillo, Texas.

Public Is Invited Come One Come All."

Included in the Big Texan restaurant and motel complex is a gift shop which has a display case featuring live rattlesnakes, a latter-day nod to the reptile ranch traditions of the glory days of 66. And just to make sure you notice the place, there is usually an enormous model of a beef steer on a small trailer parked out front. The steer features a painted-on saddle blanket emblazoned with "Big Texan Steak Ranch Motel."

AMARILLO ATTRACTIONS

Encroaching suburbia led to the relocation of **Cadillac Ranch** a short distance to the west in 1997. It now sits in a field between I-40 exits 60 and 62 on the west side of town. For those of you who never visited it at its original location, it must seem improbable that such an installation would be literally picked up and moved after 20-odd years, but that's exactly what happened.

The **American Quarter Horse Association (AQHA) Heritage Center and Museum** is a world-class facility dedicated to the history and the continued appreciation of the American Quarter Horse. The AQHA is the world's largest horse breed registry, and has had its headquarters (right next door to the museum) in the panhandle town of Amarillo since the 1940s. There is even a research library and archive for the serious enthusiast. 2601 I-40 East (exit 72A).

The **gallery** of artist Lightnin' McDuff is at 508 S. Bowie St. There is a veritable menagerie of creatures made from scrap iron, old farm implements, and so forth. He is also the creator of the *Ozymandias* sculpture outside of town (see Further Afield).

If burgers are your thing, you'll want to pay a visit to the **Arnold Burger**. This is the place to come when you need something special, such as a 10-pound, 18-incher that'll feed 15 people. Or perhaps a largish burger that's shaped like the outline of the state

Amarillo, Texas.

of Texas is more your style. Either way, it's at 1611 S. Washington St.

Railroad buffs might want to check out **Santa Fe Park**, at the Tri-State Fairgrounds (Third St. at Grand). On display is one of only five "Texas Type" Baldwin locomotives, and this one is the original prototype of the 2-10-4 configuration dating from 1930. This locomotive was nicknamed the "Madam Queen," after a fictional character from the *Amos 'n' Andy* radio series.

FURTHER AFIELD

Northwest of town via Ranch Road 1061, about 10 miles past Amarillo Blvd., is *Floating Mesa*. It's an art installation which creates an illusion of a natural feature, a mesa, which has been sliced horizontally so that its top hovers above the base with no visible means of support. For the best effect, start looking for it at around seven miles from the Amarillo Blvd. junction. As you get closer, you'll see it more clearly and the illusion is less effective.

Just south of Amarillo, near the town of **Canyon**, is the

Amarillo, Texas.

Palo Duro Canyon. The first time you lay eyes on it, you're guaranteed to be surprised and impressed. The bright red cliffs are stunning. Cut by the Prairie Dog Town Fork of the Red River, the Palo Duro Canyon runs for many miles and is hundreds of feet deep. The drive through it is around 16 miles, but also available are horseback excursions, hiking trails of varying levels of strenuousness, and even a scenic railroad. Visitor center at 806-488-2227. The city of Canyon is home to the **Panhandle-Plains Historical Museum**, housed in a WPA-era building and the largest history museum in Texas. It's truly first-rate, with sections dedicated to art, western heritage, petroleum, transportation, and paleontology. Included are several dinosaur fossils, a wood-bodied Model A Ford (serial no. 28), and a replica Pioneer Town. Canyon also was once the stomping grounds of artist Georgia O'Keeffe, who was a member of the Art Department at the local college for a time.

West of Canyon, Texas on U.S. 60 is a **giant cowboy** statue at the Cowboy Café. "Tex" is said to measure 47 feet in height and seven tons in weight.

Commissioned by Stanley Marsh 3 and inspired by the

timeless Shelley poem, the ***Ozymandias*** sculpture, a piece by Lightnin' McDuff, is several miles south of Amarillo on I-27 at Sundown Lane. True to its poetic inspiration, it's a pair of torso-less legs recalling the temporary nature of man's works. There's even a tongue-in-cheek (but very official-looking) historical marker at the site advising that this was the actual ruin which inspired Shelley's poem, and that the face of the statue was removed and placed in the Amarillo Natural History Museum—which is of course nonexistent.

If you're willing to drive a little further, the town of **Hereford** is about 45 miles southwest of Amarillo via U.S. 60. Hereford is home to the **National Cowgirl Hall of Fame**, which of course includes exhibits pertaining to female rodeo stars. The town still holds an annual women's rodeo. 515 Avenue B.

North-northeast of Amarillo, near the shore of Lake Meredith, is **Alibates Flint Quarries National Monument**. Here, thousands of years before the Egyptians constructed the Great Pyramids, ancient Americans were quarrying a distinctive type of flint from which they made tools and weapons which were subsequently used in trade with their neighbors throughout much of North America. These quarries were utilized continuously from about 10,000 B.C. to A.D. 1800. Contained on the grounds are pueblo ruins and petroglyphs (rock art). Free guided walking tours (about 1.5 miles) are available.

BUSHLAND-WILDORADO

There is little to note in the neighboring communities of Bushland and Wildorado. Bushland took its name from one W. H. Bush, who owned the land on which the town site was founded. Wildorado is marked by some cattle feed lots. There is also a vintage example of roadside signage from the Route 66 era: a neon creation for Jesse's Café still adorns the north side of the highway.

VEGA

Opinions differ as to the midpoint of Route 66—for every person who claims it's in Vega, there's another who says it's actually in Adrian, a few miles further west. What seems certain is that the halfway point of Route 66, as it wends its way from Lake Michigan to the Pacific Ocean, lies somewhere here in the Texas Panhandle.

East of Vega, Texas.

Unraveling this disagreement is not as simple as it may appear. While you will see some rather exacting figures published for the total mileage of Route 66—2,448 being one of the most popular—that "precision" is more smoke than substance. The route itself, and the total mileage that comprised it, was always in a state of change and flux. While in one town the road might add some miles in order to bypass the downtown area, at the same time hundreds of miles away in another state the highway department would be rounding off some corners, replacing them with curves, and thereby shortening the overall length. Such changes occurred again and again, all along the route, and continued over the course of decades. In fact, even though U.S. 66 officially no longer exists, the roadway you drive today continues to undergo some of those same processes in its current role as a collection of secondary roads.

The town of Vega was established in 1900 by the Chicago, Rock Island & Gulf Railroad, and is the Oldham County seat, a post it took over from the nearby town of Tascosa in 1915. South of the courthouse is a 1920s-era Magnolia gasoline station which has recently been restored, partly through funding from the Route 66 Corridor Preservation Program.

Stretch your legs awhile in Vega by popping into **Dot's Mini Museum** at 105 N. Twelfth St., near a dead-end segment of the route in the heart of town. Dot has an extensive collection of artifacts accumulated over a lifetime on Route 66. The **Vega Motel** is an original Mother Road tourist court which is still in operation.

FURTHER AFIELD

About 40 miles north of Vega on U.S. 385 is **Old Tascosa**, a Western-style ghost town. In the 1870s, Tascosa was a lively place, and functioned as a supply depot for some large area ranches, such as the XIT and the LIT. It was the seat of Oldham County, was heralded as the Cowboy Capital of the Plains, and boasted its own newspaper, the Tascosa *Pioneer*. Such famous characters as Kit Carson and Billy the Kid were known to walk its streets. Billy the Kid was eventually killed by Pat Garrett, sometime sheriff of Oldham County (you can see Billy's grave later on, at Ft. Sumner, New Mexico). Tascosa's decline came with the advent of fenced property and its being bypassed by the railroad in 1887. The county seat was moved south to Vega in 1915, it being said at the time of the balloting that there were only 15 residents of Tascosa left. The last of those residents, Mrs. Mickey McCormick and her dog, finally departed around 1940.

It was about then that Cal Farley, champion wrestler and successful Amarillo businessman, entered the picture. He founded the Boys Ranch in 1939, with its center at the old Oldham County Courthouse (now Julian L. Bivins Museum); the old townsite is now on the grounds of **Cal Farley's Boys Ranch**. Mr. Bivins donated the first acreage around the old town, which resulted in the establishment of this home for wayward and homeless boys. The compound has since expanded to include some 10,000 acres and cares for about 300 boys and girls annually. Visitors to the ranch are welcome daily. In September, the youngsters (4-18 years of age) participate in an annual Labor Day rodeo.

Before leaving Tascosa/Boys Ranch, be sure to visit the classic Old West cemetery, aptly named **Boot Hill**.

About seven miles or so west of Vega is the exit for Landergin. It was never really a town, but rather a railroad siding, a location given a name by railroaders for their own convenience.

Landergin was the site of the "Run to the Heartland" celebration in 1996, the first of many national Route 66 celebrations to come. What with both Vega and Adrian laying claim to the Midpoint of the Route, Landergin made an ideal compromise, situated as it is between the two rivals for the title. George and Melba Rook, true Route 66 celebrities, used to run the store here

Memorial to *The Grapes of Wrath,* Landergin, Texas.

and had a great Okie-style truck parked outside the premises. That celebration was the scene of the first presentation of the John Steinbeck Award, Michael Wallis being the first such honoree. Not much happening at this place the last few years, however.

ADRIAN

Again we are—or still continue to be—at the midpoint of Route 66. In the battle of one-upsmanship, the former Zella's Café in Adrian (circa 1928) is now known as the **Midpoint Café**, and has a slogan to match: "When You're Here, You're Halfway There." There is a small monument to that effect across the street from the café, and many travelers find it an irresistible photo-op. The city of Adrian has even painted their new water tower to proclaim it the midpoint of Route 66.

The Midpoint Café is a terrific place to stop in and sample some local hospitality. The staff will make you feel welcome, the food is great, and there is a gift shop where you can spend your money on terrific Route 66 stuff. If you like dessert, you'll love the "ugly crust" pies for which the Midpoint is justifiably known.

While in Adrian, keep on the lookout for the **Bent Door**. Years ago, someone used parts from an airport control tower in the construction of this roadside business. As in so many other cases, there has been talk for some years of returning the place to its former glory. I have seen a postcard of this place from the 1960s, at which time it was operating as Tommy's Café, with a yellow-and-red sign similar to the one in front of the Midpoint today.

In Adrian recently there has been an outbreak of the same fever so prevalent in Amarillo—various installations of the **Dynamite Museum** now abound here. Among them is my personal favorite: "Art is what you can get away with."

GLENRIO

Glenrio can rightly be called a ghost town. Each time I have ventured here it has been deathly quiet, except for the barking of the junkyard dogs that commences a few moments after my arrival. Barking dogs, with no human owners in evidence, do not make for pleasant exploring. Glenrio today consists of a few ruinous buildings of unknown identity, and the equally ruinous Last Motel in Texas. If you pass by it and then look back from the west, you'll see that the sign read First Motel in Texas for the eastbound travelers arriving from New Mexico.

All in all, Glenrio is a somewhat spooky locale, which makes it all the more startling to learn that in the 1940s this was a thriving, bustling place. A current resident of Fort Worth tells me that he worked for the Texas Highway Department here at Glenrio at an offi-

This lonely stretch of highway is at Glenrio, which straddles the Texas–New Mexico border.

cial welcome station in 1941–42. He witnessed firsthand the so-called "Okies" traveling westward with all of their earthly possessions tied to the roofs of their automobiles. At that time, they were headed for work at the shipyards and defense plants of California.

Glenrio was founded in 1903, shortly after a railroad line was established in the vicinity. Many have observed that the name is formed from the English glen (for "valley") and the Spanish rio (for "river"), while the actual town site is located neither in a valley nor along a river.

According to a former resident of Glenrio, a film crew spent about three weeks in the town filming portions of *The Grapes of Wrath* in 1938. At that time, full-time residents of the town numbered about 30.

Somewhere in the middle of Glenrio is the New Mexico border, but the *Llano Estacado* continues as far as the eye can see, having no respect for political boundaries.

NEW MEXICO

New Mexico—Land of Enchantment. The name is fitting, in that the place, its people, and its traditions have a way of winning the hearts of all those who visit. Those of us fortunate enough to spend time in New Mexico invariably speak again and again of our experiences here, and perhaps even talk of making it our permanent home.

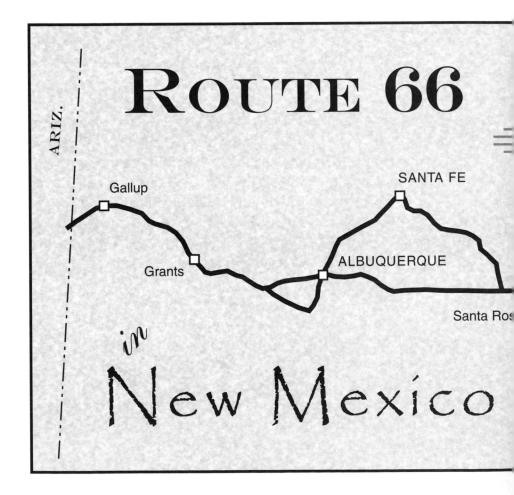

The land itself is beautiful, with its spreading plains, purple mountains, and colorful, overarching, cloud-filled skies. These in themselves are alluring, but beyond that there is the profound sense of respect one feels for the centuries of history and tradition that permeate the land. Perhaps nowhere is there a more successful commingling of disparate cultures to form a unique whole than there is here in New Mexico. Tread softly, for you are on hallowed ground.

The *Llano Estacado* continues to the Pecos River Valley. This land was formerly a part of Texas, but was ceded to appease jealous rivals who worried over the enormous influence a vast Texas might wield as a state. The land has seen and been inhabited by every walk of mankind: farmer, rancher, miner; Indian, Spaniard, Anglo; the base, the virtuous, and the merely foolish. All have left their marks, and those marks are here for you to see.

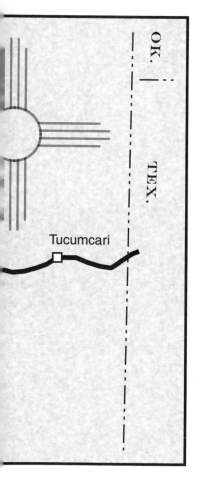

Here in the West, scars on the earth are slow to heal. New Mexico is a treasure chest of archaeological discoveries, some uncovered long ago, others waiting to be revealed. Here in New Mexico are the stone ruins of centuries-old civilizations and the still-visible wagon ruts of trade routes rendered obsolete by the iron horse. Also to be seen are the scars left by abandoned stretches of Route 66.

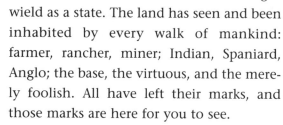 Unless you have a four-wheel-drive vehicle, or you are absolutely certain there has not been recent rain to make the dirt road hazardous, you should not attempt your entry into New Mexico by way of the spur of 66 that passes through

Glenrio. You are safer to return to I-40 and cross the border that way. You'll see a sign advising you that you are entering Mountain Time, a very real-world indication that you are now starting a new chapter in your Route 66 Adventure.

Part of that new chapter involves cuisine. In this part of the country, virtually every restaurant has a "Mexican" or "New Mexican" section of the menu. This can make for some strange bedfellows, such as the Chinese buffet that offers tacos, or the sandwich shop that has refried beans as a side order. And be prepared for the first time you are asked the Official State Question: "Red or Green?" The choice of either red or green chili sauce with your southwestern meal is such a profound—and yet ordinary—question in these parts that the state of New Mexico passed a bill in 1999 adding the question to the list of other officially recognized items such as the state flower, state bird, and so forth. (Incidentally, if you have difficulty choosing, you may want to answer "Christmas," ensuring that you get some of each.)

ENDEE

The name of this community was most likely adopted from the name of the N D Ranch, which was established in the area in the 1880s. If you took the unpaved road out of Glenrio, you'll come upon Endee about five miles west. If you had to use the interstate, you can exit at NM 93 and turn south to visit Endee.

The old route from Endee to San Jon is also unpaved. Depending on conditions, you may need to go north and pick up I-40 for the ride into San Jon. If so, don't feel bad; my 1957 atlas shows Endee as having already been bypassed at that time in favor of a newer alignment to the north, where today's I-40 roadbed is located.

BARD

Although Bard usually shows up on older (1930s–'40s) maps of the area, there is not much for today's traveler to see. I've been unable to find out much of anything about it in my own research. Try some exploring south of I-40 at exit 361, which is about four or five miles east of San Jon.

SAN JON

There are still several abandoned motels on the old route through town, among them the Western Motel. On a recent trip through here, there was an early '60s Plymouth sedan rusting in the parking lot of the Western.

You can eschew the interstate and take old 66 all the way into Tucumcari from San Jon.

San Jon, New Mexico.

TUCUMCARI

This is the town that changed my life by starting me on a quest to see all of Route 66—more on that in a moment.

Formerly called Six-Shooter Siding, there are at least two stories circulating as to how Tucumcari (two-come-carry) got its modern name—one romantic and one less so. Legend states that an Indian maiden named Kari was so grieved over the death of her lover, Tocom, at the hand of a rival, that she took her own life. Her father, upon discovering the tragedy, exclaims "Tocom! Kari!" A wonderful fable, with shades of Romeo and Juliet, but sober heads inform us that the name comes from a Commanche word, *tuka-mukaru*, meaning "to lie in wait," as in an ambush.

Speaking of sober heads, I lost mine permanently in 1992 on a trip through here on my way to Fort Worth, Texas, from Greeley, Colorado. My wife and I were on the stretch of I-40 west of Tucumcari, heading east, when we started seeing billboards shouting *TUCUMCARI TONITE!* and *ON HISTORIC ROUTE 66!* Since it was around nightfall, we decided on the spur of the moment to stay the night in Tucumcari, a long-standing tradition for Route 66-ers that we were unaware of at the time. Pulling off the interstate and prowling through Tucumcari absolutely floored me. We saw a souvenir stand in the shape of an Indian teepee, and then we came across a restaurant shaped like a Mexican sombrero. I thought: "I can't believe there are still places like this! This is amazing!" I've been coming back to Route 66 year after year ever since. And it *still* amazes me.

Tucumcari has lots of Route 66 spots that folks around the globe recognize. There's **Teepee Curios**, of course, which in the

1940s was actually a gasoline station. The Mexican restaurant we ate at that night was La Cita, and it has since been painted to make it even more dazzling to the eye. The real cornerstone of Tucumcari highway businesses, though, has got to be the **Blue Swallow Motel**. Built in the 1940s from surplus WWII cabins, the motel was later presented as an engagement present to Lillian Redman, the proprietess for many years, by her husband-to-be, Floyd. That was in 1958. Lillian kept things going for many a year and

Quite possibly the most spectacular sign on all of Route 66 is in Tucumcari, New Mexico.

only recently (in Mother Road terms) has it fallen into other capable hands.

The **Redwood Motel**, dating from around 1954, was recently placed on the state register of historic properties—it has authentic redwood used in its construction. Another landmark is the **Trails West Lodge & Package Store,** whose distinctive sign

Signage in Tucumcari, New Mexico.

appears in the Route 66 upholstering fabric that's been so ubiquitous the last few years, making the Trails West familiar even to those who haven't yet made it to Tucumcari.

Tucumcari truly has a wealth of vintage roadside businesses that reach far beyond the scope of this book. You should plan to spend hours just exploring, not only along the old route with its dozens of classic neon signs, but also downtown, where there is a still-running depression-era theater and a large railroad depot. As if Tucumcari didn't have enough going for it already, in recent years they've added several **murals** scattered throughout downtown, including a Mother Road-themed one on the side of Lowe's grocery.

South of town you'll see Tucumcari Mountain, tattooed with a big letter "T." The **Tucumcari Mountain Cheese Factory** is a few blocks north of 66, on Main Street. It is housed in an old Coca-Cola Bottling Plant building which dates from 1951. Also in town is the **Mesalands Dinosaur Museum**, run by the Mesa Technical College. Notable is the fact that the dinosaur models on display are cast in bronze (rather than more fragile plaster or resin as is more common), and visitors are invited to touch. These bronze castings are made right here at the college by students and volun-

Tucumcari, New Mexico.

teers. The dinosaur museum is at 222 E. Laughlin. At 414 S. Adams is the **Tucumcari Historical Museum**, which, of course, includes an exhibit on Route 66 through the area.

On the west end of town, as you're passing the convention center, pause to admire the **Route 66 monument** by artist Thomas Coffin. The piece was installed in 1997, and incorporates a 1950s-style automotive tail fin, a mock-adobe base, and the double sixes.

You'll have to enter I-40 at the west end of Tucumcari, but be sure to leave it at exit 321 for the run into Montoya.

MONTOYA-NEWKIRK

Route 66 crosses a fair number of other routes of significance over its course; for example, we crossed the Chisholm Trail back in Oklahoma, which was used primarily for the transport of cattle. Another cattle trail is at hand now. The **Goodnight-Loving Trail** crosses our path somewhere between the communities of Montoya and Newkirk. One of the best maps I've seen places it very close to Newkirk, and so the highway that stretches northward out of Newkirk, numbered 129, must be the closest thing we have to an actual road that follows that course. The Goodnight-Loving Trail passed through Fort Sumner to the south of us before going on to the markets in Denver and Cheyenne to the north.

CUERVO

Cuervo has been what can only be called a ghost town for many years. Although there are still some inhabitants, large tracts of the town are now deserted, with broken windows and gaping doors.

SANTA ROSA

While New Mexico is generally an arid place, Santa Rosa is the exception. Thanks to a collection of artesian springs in the area, it's a veritable garden spot, and nicknamed the City of Natural Lakes. The most famous of the springs here is the **Blue Hole**, which attracts scuba divers from far and wide to indulge their hobby. The Blue Hole is more than 80 feet deep and 60 feet wide, with water temperatures hovering around 64 degrees F. It's about a half-mile south of 66 on Blue Hole Road.

The **Club Café**, long a fixture at Santa Rosa, has been closed for years now. There were a great number of billboards along 66 (and I-40) in New Mexico with the Smiling Fat Man logo. Speaking of billboards, there may yet be some weathered concrete billboards visible on the eastern side of town just west of the airport on an old 66 alignment. I don't know what they once might have advertised.

If you're into classic cars and related stuff, check out the **Route 66 Auto Museum**, at 2866 Will Rogers Drive, in the east part of town. Look for the yellow car atop a pole.

The Pecos, a river prominent in the lore of the American West, is crossed here at Santa Rosa. This reportedly is also the place where Coronado made the crossing in 1541 (Route 66 through town is named Coronado Avenue in recognition). From the Pecos River crossing, the highway begins climbing toward the continental divide, more than 200 miles to the west.

FURTHER AFIELD

About 10 miles south of Santa Rosa via State Route 91 is **Puerto de Luna**, an abandoned Spanish settlement. Along the way the road follows the Pecos River Valley, and there is some very attractive canyon country.

About 45 miles southeast of Santa Rosa via U.S. 84 is **Fort**

Sumner, both the military post and the town. It was here in 1881 that Billy the Kid was shot and killed by Pat Garrett, and his gravesite is here at Fort Sumner—or at least we think that it is (more on that in a moment). Billy the Kid (or William Bonney) was a hired gun in the Lincoln County (New Mexico) range wars, and in that capacity killed a man for every year of his life "not counting Indians and Mexicans" by his own account.

Fort Sumner was constructed in 1862, and was a major stop on the Goodnight-Loving Cattle Trail, which ran from Texas to Wyoming. In 1869, the land the fort stood on was sold to Lucien B. Maxwell, who converted the officers' quarters to a private residence. That was where Billy was killed by Garrett years later. Judging from conditions in Fort Sumner today, if anyone could get their hands on Billy's corpse now, it would be torn into at least two pieces. An explanation is in order.

In downtown Fort Sumner is the **Billy the Kid Museum**, at 1601 E. Sumner Drive. This museum originated in the 1950s, and really shows its age. There are disintegrating mannequins of Billy the Kid and Pat Garrett, a stuffed two-headed calf, old farm implements, and antique typewriters—the flotsam and jetsam that a down-to-earth museum curator accumulates over the decades. Outside is a graveyard with markers for Billy and two of his cohorts, surrounded by a chainlink fence. Fastened to the fence, however, and located so that it appears in virtually every snapshot taken of the gravesite, is a small sign that states: REPLICA. What's going on? The lady at the museum states that the replica had to be created because the real grave is in such a poor state. But where is the real grave—and Billy—if this gravesite is a replica?

Drive about seven miles southeast of the town of Fort Sumner (U.S. 84 East to NM 212 South) to the **Old Fort Sumner Museum**, established in 1932. This museum also has Billy the Kid artifacts, such as Billy's letters to the governor asking for amnesty. Outside is what is billed as "The Real Grave of Billy the Kid." As at the replica in town, there is also a pair of companions. This grave is completely covered in a metal cage to prevent vandalism. It seems that the original headstone was stolen in 1950 (remember the lady at the replica grave saying the real one was in bad shape?) and not recovered until 26 years later. Then it was stolen again in 1981 and again recovered. Now they take no chances. The ground over the grave has even been encased in concrete, just to make sure there's no funny business.

Adjacent to The Real Grave of Billy the Kid and the Old Fort Sumner Museum is the **Fort Sumner State Monument**. This is the site of Navajo and Apache confinement at the hands of the U.S. military in the 1860s.

Leaving Santa Rosa, the old highway we love so much has pretty much been buried by the interstate. Several miles west of Santa Rosa, you'll come to a crossroads. Not so much in the physical sense, as in the spiritual sense. What you do encounter physically is the junction where U.S. 84 splits off and goes to the north. That northerly route more or less follows the older Route 66 alignment, which for several years wandered up through Santa Fe. Straight ahead is the alignment born in the 1930s, when a straighter course was carved through the countryside, shaving significant miles and time from the passage through New Mexico. The two alternate paths will meet again in Albuquerque.

The narrative immediately following takes you along the older route through Santa Fe. If you choose to take the later route straight to Albuquerque, you can pick up the account for that segment below at the Flying C Ranch.

ROMEROVILLE

The town of Romeroville was named for Don Trinidad Romero, who entertained President Rutherford B. Hayes at his home, and whose father founded the Romero Mercantile Company, a firm which became one of the leading wholesalers of the region.

From Romeroville onward, Route 66 closely approximates the track of the **Santa Fe Trail**. The trail originated in central Missouri (at Old Franklin) and took a northerly tack through Kansas and Colorado. It was a very significant trade route for several decades of the nineteenth century, connecting the ancient city in newly independent Mexico with the western United States.

FURTHER AFIELD

Las Vegas, New Mexico, founded in 1835, is a very special place indeed. Over the past four centuries, the area has been inhabited by Native Americans, Spanish conquerors, Anglo settlers, desperadoes, robber barons, and dance-hall girls, all of whom have wielded their respective influence. Doc Holliday and his girlfriend, Kate Elder, moved here in 1879 and opened a saloon; they were followed a few months later by their friend, Wyatt Earp. Butch Cassidy once worked in town as a bartender. Bob Ford, a Las Vegas saloon-keeper, was the man who later became known for killing Jesse James. In 1915, Tom Mix made several of his westerns here. And filmmaking in the town didn't stop there. The town fire station appears in a scene from *Easy Rider*, where Jack Nicholson's character makes the decision to hit the road with Peter Fonda and Dennis Hopper. Scenes from *Charlie Siringo* and *Red Dawn* were also made here.

Las Vegas boasts more than 900 (!) buildings on the National Register of Historic Places. Two of the most notable are **La Castaneda Hotel**, an example of the Harvey House collection of fine railroad-era hotels, and **El Fidel Hotel**. Walking tour information is available at the local chamber office (727 Grand Ave.).

The **City of Las Vegas Museum and Rough Rider Memorial Collection** commemorates Teddy Roosevelt's famous Rough Riders, who distinguished themselves in the Spanish-

American War in Cuba, as well as exhibiting Indian artifacts and items pertaining to the local history of Las Vegas. The museum is housed in a WPA-era structure which was originally intended to serve as the city hall. When the Roughriders were originally formed, the largest contingent from any one state or territory came from New Mexico; later, in 1899, Las Vegas hosted the group's first reunion. Over the years, many attendees of those reunions donated various mementos of the campaign, and so established the collection now held at the museum. Also housed here is the Las Vegas/San Miguel Chamber of Commerce, at 727 Grand.

The **Bridge Street Historic District** offers an impressive array of architectural styles, including Victorian, Italianate, and nineteenth-century commercial.

A series of several *acequías*, or early irrigation channels, are preserved here in Las Vegas.

Five miles northwest of Las Vegas (via NM 65) stands **Montezuma Castle**, an opulent resort hotel from the 1880s on the grounds of the Armand Hammer United World College of the American West.

About 28 miles or so to the northeast of Las Vegas is **Fort Union National Monument**, a significant stop on the old Santa Fe Trail. Fort Union was the chief quartermaster depot for nearly 50 other western forts during the late 1800s, and its troops stood guard here as protection for the settlers in the region and for travelers on the Santa Fe Trail, the two major branches of which—the Mountain Branch and the Cimarron Cutoff—converged in this vicinity. Just outside the fort is the largest network of visible Santa Fe Trail **wagon ruts** still remaining. Fort Union was also the intended objective of Confederate forces in the Battle of Glorieta Pass, which occurred west of here and which is sometimes called the "Gettysburg of the West." There is a 1.25-mile tour trail which explores not only ruins of the fort, but also adobe villages nearby. There is also a visitor center with a museum.

Back on Route 66, go southwest out of Romeroville. The modern highway (I-25/U.S. 84) closely adheres to the path of the old Santa Fe Trail. Near a community called Rowe, you can exit the main highway and use State Highway 63 to enter the town of Pecos.

PECOS

This is a very old pueblo which once held over 2,000 residents. It was abandoned circa 1838, at which time the remaining inhabitants reportedly went to Jemez.

Kozlowski's Ranch was a stage station on the Santa Fe Trail, and was located in this vicinity.

Just outside Pecos Pueblo is the **Pecos National Historic Park**, which includes the ruins of two Spanish Colonial missions, as well as ancient pueblo features. Unlike most pueblo ruins, the kivas here are accessible to the public. The ruins are also very scenic, and there is an easy self-guided trail sprinkled with interpretive plaques to explain all of the features.

There is a Benedictine Monastery located on the northern edge of Pecos pueblo. Continue out of Pecos westward on NM 50 toward Glorieta.

GLORIETA

Just after passing through the town of Glorieta, you will come to Glorieta Pass, the passage through the mountains which made this circuitous route to Santa Fe a necessity in the days of the old trail. It was here, at a Santa Fe Trail stopover called Pigeon's Ranch, that the Battle of Glorieta Pass occurred in March of 1862 during the American Civil War. There is still one adobe structure remaining from the 18-room stage station complex. The **battlefield** is a National Historic Landmark.

SANTA FE

Santa Fe is the oldest capital city in the U.S., having been designated as such in 1610, when the plaza was laid out and the Palace of the Governors was established. It is also the focal point of the famous Santa Fe Trail, a primarily trade-oriented route which was at its most important from about 1821 until 1880, when railroad transport effectively supplanted it.

Your entry into town is along the same path as the old trail, and the modern-day street is so named: Old Santa Fe Trail. A monument to mark the end of that trail was placed at the southeast corner of the central plaza by the Daughters of the American Revolution in 1911. It was not until a year later, in 1912, that New Mexico attained statehood. Today, the **La Fonda Hotel** (circa 1920) occupies the site of the old inn which marked the end of the trail and which served as a mass meeting place for those who'd made the arduous journey. It is said that Billy the Kid washed dishes in that inn for a time.

Oddly, the Sangre de Christo Mountains near Santa Fe were the set for the filming of the "Oh What A Beautiful Morning" scene from the movie *Oklahoma!*.

At Cerrillos Road and St. Francis Drive is an establishment that actually refers to itself as a "tourist trap": the **Tin Nee Ann Trading Company**. You'll find Southwest arts and crafts, jewelry, wooden Indians, t-shirts, moccasins, geegaws, and just plain junk for the kids. Stock up here on "stuff" before continuing your odyssey.

SANTA FE ATTRACTIONS

The **Museum of New Mexico** is actually a set of four museums: the Museum of Fine Arts, the Palace of the Governors, the Museum of International Folk Art, and the Museum of American Indian Arts and Culture. Also part of the family are five historical monuments across the state. The Palace of the Governors, at 105 W. Palace Ave. on the plaza, has seen five governments in its 400-year history, and is the oldest continuously occupied public building in the United States.

Georgia O'Keeffe, whose nearby museum is housed in a renovated adobe mission church, is one of only a very few widely disparate American artists with memorial museums: Norman Rockwell, Frederic Remington, and Andy Warhol among them. 217 Johnson St.

Canyon Road is Santa Fe's gallery district, lined on both sides with upper-echelon art galleries, coffee houses, and so forth.

An interesting tale awaits you at the **Santa Fe National Cemetery**. Among the rows upon rows of simple, identical head-stones on these hallowed grounds stands the lifelike statue of Private Dennis O'Leary. The statue depicts the young O'Leary lean-ing against a tree while wearing his army uniform. Legend states that he was a lonely and unhappy soldier stationed at Fort Wingate, and that he carved the likeness himself in his free time. According to the story, he wrote a suicide note describing the location of the statue and asking that it be placed over his grave. He then shot him-self with his own pistol. Army records, however, list his death as having been a result of tuberculosis. When Fort Wingate was decommissioned in 1911, Private O'Leary and several others were re-interred here.

You can take the **Santa Fe Southern Railway** on a day trip. The 36-mile, four-hour round trip runs from the historic depot (410 S. Guadalupe St) to the nearby town of Lamy. The old Santa Fe Depot, established in 1880, has been an inspiration to artists and photographers for generations.

The **Miraculous Staircase** is located in the Loretto Chapel, at 207 Old Santa Fe Trail. There is a very interesting story involving a "mysterious carpenter" who constructed the unusual staircase in the latter part of the 1870s. He appeared with a donkey and a toolbox, constructed the staircase over the course of several months, then abruptly vanished without pay or thanks. The staircase was innovative for its time, incorporating two full turns (720 degrees) and showing no obvious means of support. The Miraculous Staircase has been the subject of numerous articles over the years, as well as an episode of *Unsolved Mysteries*.

Also on Old Santa Fe Trail is the **Chapel of San Miguel por Barrio de Analco**, referred to as the oldest continuously occupied church. The chapel was constructed in 1626–28. Nearby, on DeVargas Street, is the **Oldest House**, which dates from approximately A.D. 1200.

The **Mission of San Miguel of Santa Fe** was constructed in 1610, and has on display a bell which was cast in Spain in 1356 and then brought here by oxcart in the early 1800s.

The **Awakening Museum** is something a little different. Artist Jean-Claude Gaugy created a monumental work of inspirational art on some 400 wooden panels over the course of 13 years. The artwork covers 11,000 square feet of walls and ceilings. What's extra-amazing about it is that the whole collection was relocated from the artist's home in West Virginia to Santa Fe in 2000. 125 N. Guadalupe St.

FURTHER AFIELD

Fans of Georgia O'Keeffe may want to be aware that about 45 miles or so north of Santa Fe, at **Abiquiu**, is the **Georgia O'Keeffe National Historic Site**. The 5,000-square-foot adobe structure here at Ghost Ranch was the artist's home and studio for more than 40 years.

Further north of Santa Fe, and certainly more than just a side trip, is the very historic and distinctly artsy district of **Taos**, Taos Pueblo, and Ranchos de Taos. The Church of San Francisco de Asis is one of the most painted and photographed buildings in the United States. Note that the Taos Pueblo charges a fee for admission, for parking, and for photography, and that the pueblo has no modern conveniences, such as electricity and plumbing.

Nearby is the **Kit Carson Home and Historical Museum**, where the famous frontiersman kept his residence from 1843–68. Kit Carson and his wife are both buried nearby. Or visit the home of Ernest L. Blumenschein, artist and co-founder of the original Taos Society of Artists.

Narrated trolley tours of Taos are available, as are walking tours of Taos Pueblo. The Taos area is also a hub for skiing in winter and river rafting in summer.

To the north of Taos, at **Arroyo Hondo**, is the **D. H. Lawrence Ranch and Memorial**. The Lawrences spent about two years here in the 1920s, and the surroundings are said to have had significant influences on a number of his books. When Mr. Lawrence died in 1930, his wife scattered his ashes here at the ranch. The ranch is nestled in the Sangre de Christo Mountains on 160 acres.

West of Santa Fe, Route 66 encounters yet another very old highway: the famous **El Camino Real**. This old road (circa 1581–1800) connected Mexico City with Santa Fe and continued to San Juan Pueblo to the north. The old trail is thought to have crossed today's I-25/old 66 near the La Cienega interchange. There is a monument near the community of Los Lunas (a little further in our journey).

DOMINGO

Here, the Santo Domingo Indian Trading Post was featured in *Life* magazine and visited by President John F. Kennedy in 1962. Unfortunately, the trading post burned to the ground a number of years ago.

ALGODONES

Leave the superslab at the exit for NM 313, which takes you through the communities of Algodones, Angostura, the Pueblo de Santa Ana, and El Llanito. Just south of El Llanito is the town of Bernalillo.

BERNALILLO

Behind the Sandoval County Courthouse sits a 19th-century **stone jail** which once served the area. Also in town is **Silva's Saloon** (in the 900 block of S. Camino Del Pueblo), which opened the day after prohibition ended in 1933, and has been run by the same family ever since. There is plenty of memorabilia displayed on the walls— over 70 years' worth—including a hat collection.

Just a mile or so northwest of Bernalillo by way of NM 44 (co-numbered U.S. 550) is the **Coronado State Monument**. The famous Spanish explorer is said to have stayed here during his expedition of 1541–42. Today, there is a park overlooking the Rio Grande, as well as a river walk and museum gallery. Parts of the village of Kuaua were excavated here as part of a WPA project in 1936, and there is a self-guided trail taking you through the ruins, which include a kiva and a pre-Columbian mural. To get there, cross to the west side of the Rio Grande via 550/44, and then turn right (north) on Monument Road.

FURTHER AFIELD

Bernalillo is also your launch pad for a terrific detour: the **Jemez Mountain Trail National Historic and Scenic Byway**. Take NM 44 northwest from Bernalillo to San Ysidro. From here, NM 4 is the Jemez Mountain Trail. The Scenic Byway designation means that the trail has scenic, historical, and cultural importance, and is one of only a handful in the state. It winds through 5,000 years of human history, millions of years of geologic time, and four climatic zones. The trail takes you to Jemez Pueblo, Jemez Springs, Jemez State Monument, Soda Dam, Battleship Rock, and Bandelier National Monument.

Jemez Pueblo features a visitors' center, which is a destination in and of itself. **Jemez Springs** is known for its mineral waters and bath houses (some of which are clothing-optional), and features a number of galleries for you to stop and enjoy. **Jemez State Monument** is the prehistoric site of the Pueblo of Giusewa ("boiling waters"), which includes the ruins of the 17th-century Church of San Jose de Los Jemez. Marvel at the walls of these ruins, some of which are eight feet thick. **Soda Dam** is a natural dam formed on the Jemez River from mineral deposits built up over thousands of years. The river emerges through a hole in the dam, forming a waterfall.

Further north is **Battleship Rock**, which towers over you as you wend your way through rugged terrain formed by volcanic activity ages ago. **Bandelier National Monument** is one of the most-visited collections of Indian ruins in the nation. Miles of trails leave the visitor center and radiate outward to dozens of cliff dwellings. Nearby is **Los Alamos**, America's "Secret City" and birthplace of the nuclear age. It was here that the Manhattan Project was undertaken during World War II in order to develop the atomic bomb. You can learn more about it at the **Bradbury Science Museum**, located in downtown Los Alamos at 15th and Central.

South of Bernalillo, and just east of the old highway, is the Sandia Pueblo.

About halfway between Bernalillo and Alameda, but on the opposite side of the Rio Grande from you, is the community of Corrales. This community was named Sandoval (the same name as the county you are now in) at the time my 1957 atlas was printed.

There is an old church there, the **Old San Ysidro Church**, which is a favorite subject for painters and photographers. Built in 1868, it now serves as a community center. Nearby is **Casa San Ysidro**, a restored Spanish Colonial ranch house now operated by the Albuquerque Museum.

As you continue to head toward Albuquerque, keep an eye out for some **impressive gates** just off the roadway. These mark the entry to El Pinto, a restaurant touting its cuisine as "New Mexican."

ALAMEDA

As you approach the northern outskirts of Albuquerque, you will pass through a community called Alameda. For a nice side trip, a right at the State Road 528 junction will take you across the river to the town of **Rio Rancho**. In Rio Rancho is the **J&R Vintage Auto Museum** (at the Stagecoach Stop RV Park) and the **Intel Museum** on Rio Rancho Drive (Hwy 528). Also here are the grounds where each year the **Friends and Lovers Balloon Rally** is held. Note that this is a separate event from the Kodak-sponsored balloon event held in Albuquerque. This is the one famous for the hot-air balloons that dramatically fire up periodically against the night sky.

The loop of old Route 66 which passed through Santa Fe was a rather circuitous route necessitated by the challenging terrain and limited road-building budgets and equipment of the time. However, it was recognized very early on that a straighter, more direct route from Santa Rosa to Albuquerque should someday be completed. In 1934, then-New Mexico Governor Clyde Tingley, a personal friend of President Roosevelt, secured a number of New Deal projects for the state. Among those projects was the straightening of Route 66. That new alignment opened in 1937, running into

Albuquerque along Central Avenue, and leaving the state capital high and dry. A further tale relates that preliminary steps in the bypassing of Santa Fe were taken by a spiteful outgoing governor, A. T. Hannett, who lost re-election in 1926 just as the federal highway system was coming into being.

In taking the newer alignment, you proceed due west out of Santa Rosa, and continue straight ahead (on I-40) past the U.S. 84 split.

FLYING C RANCH

"The Flying C" is of course not a town in the traditional sense, but it certainly is pure Route 66. At exit 234 you'll find what's left of a once-proud roadside complex that offered pre-interstate motorists food, fuel, lodging, and entertainment. In later years, they called themselves Bowlin's Running Indian, a name for which they invented a distinctive sign.

CLINES CORNERS

Clines Corners is just that: an intersection. Today there is an enormous gift shop that purveys such classics as rubber tomahawks, beaded belts, and cedar geegaws of every description.

The I-40 exit 203 is the **Longhorn Ranch** interchange. The Longhorn Ranch is often regarded as having been the ritziest, glitziest tourist trap on the route. It was a full-blown tourist compound including motel, gas station, museum, curio shop, restaurant, and bar. The whole operation was packaged in the guise of a Wild West movie set. Most of the structures are gone, save for the Longhorn Bank building.

BUFORD-MORIARTY

NM 333 takes you on the old route through this community. Buford shows up on some early maps of the area, but it has been taken over or absorbed by modern-day Moriarty. Look for the Buford Courts as evidence of the former community of that name.

The sign at **El Comedor** in Moriarty was fortunate to be the target of neon restoration work recently. Described as a rotosphere, it consists of two halves of a ball rotating in different directions, with numerous Sputnik-style spikes protruding all around. The whole affair revolves, too.

The **Love House** is an old home in Moriarty constructed of discarded oil cans bonded together with mortar. It's on Main St. near the eastern end of town, and is no longer occupied at last report.

The **Moriarty Historical Society Museum** is located at 777 Old U.S. Route 66 SW, in the town's first fire station.

Moriarty Airport is home base for the **Albuquerque Soaring Club**. The group chose this area for its unbeatable thermal conditions that result in many flights in excess of 250 miles each year. The airport is also home to the **U.S. Southwest Soaring Museum**.

Moriarty calls itself the Pinto Bean Capital—there's a pinto bean festival held here in the fall. In November, the town plays host to an annual meeting of the Sherlock Holmes Society even though there is no known connection between the town's name and that of Holmes's notorious rival.

Stay on NM 333 as you leave Moriarty and head toward Edgewood.

EDGEWOOD

At Edgewood is **Wild West Nature Park**, a 122-acre facility harboring non-releasable wildlife, including deer, coyotes, and mountain lions. The park is a project of the New Mexico Wildlife Association, and is staffed by members and volunteers of the state's Youth Conservation Corps.

TIJERAS

Balanced Rock, an unusual rock formation destroyed by the highway department in 1951, used to reside somewhere in the Tijeras Canyon area. The reasoning behind its destruction was that the vibrations brought about by passing traffic posed the danger of toppling the formation; however, it's been widely reported that the job took considerably more explosives than anyone predicted, and so it may have endured for quite some time if it had been left alone. At one time there was a painted sign on the rock directing the passing motorist to **Queens Rest Camp**, 6200 Central Avenue, six miles ahead in Albuquerque.

FURTHER AFIELD

A great side trip from Tijeras is the **Turquoise Trail** (NM 14), a beautiful scenic byway which runs northward towards Santa Fe, and takes the traveler through turquoise mining country, complete with three revived ghost towns: Golden, Madrid, and Cerrillos. Madrid, established in 1914, was a ghost town for many years until, in the 1970s, it began to be resettled by artists. A few miles further north is Cerillos, which fits the bill as the stereotypical Old West town—it had over 20 saloons at one time. These days, that western atmosphere is being exploited by the film industry, with *Shoot Out* (1972) and *Outrageous Fortune* (1987) being filmed in the area. Cerrillos is also home to the Casa Grande Trading Post and the Cerrillos Turquoise Mining Museum.

Just off the Turquoise Trail via NM 536 is **Sandia Crest**, with an elevation of over 10,000 feet. The view is spectacular, and you can hike the numerous trails in the Sandia Mountain Wilderness which treat you to one gorgeous view after another. You can either drive to the top of Sandia Peak, or take the 30-minute trip by chair lift from the Sandia Peak ski area. The adventurous can take along (or rent) mountain bikes, then ride down from the observation area on a 15-mile trail. Alternatively, there is a popular tram ride (the longest of its kind at 2.7 miles) that departs from Albuquerque, with spectacular views of the Land of Enchantment.

From NM 536 in the Sandia Crest area, you can follow Highway 165 north toward **Placitas**. About halfway to Placitas is the site of an archaeological dig where evidence of very early man has been discovered. The **Sandia Man Cave**, a self-guided hiking tour, is the earliest known archaeological site in the Southwest (20,000 B.C.).

Also on NM 536 is the town of **Sandia Park**. This is the home of **Tinkertown**, the creation of a man named Ross Ward. Tinkertown consists of worlds in miniature, such as an animated miniature western town, a tiny three-ring circus, and other dioramas, all surrounded by a collection of over 40,000 bottles. The motto at Tinkertown: "We did all this while you were watching TV."

ALBUQUERQUE

There is a huge array of **vintage motels** on Central Avenue along the eastern approach to the city. The city must have appeared almost oasis-like to the traveler decades ago who'd just come the 100-plus miles from Santa Rosa, the last stopover of any size. Central Avenue is the nation's longest main street, at 18 miles east to west. In the 3200 block of Central, keep your eyes peeled for **Kelly's Brewery**, a modern-day brewpub housed in a restored Streamline Moderne-style auto dealership dating from 1939.

Albuquerque is the hometown of the fictional Ethel Mertz (indeed, Vivian Vance actually lived here for a time herself). It is also home to the **New Mexico Route 66 Association**, which is headquartered at the **66 Diner**, a 1940s-era streamline-style structure at 1405 Central. The 66 Diner burned in 1995, but fortunately for all of

The 66 Diner in Albuquerque also serves as headquarters for the New Mexico Route 66 Association.

us it has been lovingly restored to its former glory.

Architecturally, the city is marked by fine examples of the Pueblo Revival style, including several buildings at the **University of New Mexico campus** (even the UNM campus is on Central). The city also boasts the **KiMo Theater**, at 423 Central Ave. NW. The KiMo was built circa 1927 and designed by the same team of architects that conceived the one-of-a-kind Coleman Theater in Miami, Oklahoma: Carl and Robert Boller. Its design, sometimes referred to as Pueblo Deco, was intended to reflect the three major cultural influences in the area: Indian, Hispanic, and Anglo. Details include painted murals and terra-cotta buffalo skull wall sconces. Some say that the KiMo is haunted by the ghost of a small boy who died there in 1951, when a hot water heater exploded.

The old (circa 1936) **Monte Vista Fire Station**, at 3201 Central Ave. NE, has been converted to a restaurant. **La Posada Hotel** (1939) was formerly a Hilton and one of Albuquerque's most prestigious hostelries. It was here that Conrad Hilton married Zsa Zsa Gabor on April 10, 1942. La Posada is one block north of Central on 2nd St. and includes a 1930s-era coffee shop.

You can take a **self-guided walking tour** of Pueblo Deco architecture beginning at the KiMo Theater, and also taking in the Maisel Building, Wright's Trading Post, the J. A. Skinner Building, and several others.

Check out Albuquerque's **Old Town**, where the city was first settled around 1705. The area is actually believed to have been inhabited prehistorically. The 300-year-old San Felipe de Neri Church stands on the corner of the plaza, and nearby is the 1912 Bottger Mansion, now a bed and breakfast, which once played host to Machine Gun Kelly and his gang. Free maps are available in Old Town for self-guided walking tours. You can also see one of the **Madonna of the Trail** monuments, at Fourth and Marble NW.

Part of the ambience at the Aztec Motel in Albuquerque, New Mexico.

Madonna of the Trail

In the 1920s, the National Society of the Daughters of the American Revolution (DAR) commissioned the design, casting, and placement of 12 monuments commemorating the spirit of the pioneer woman. All 12 monuments were located alongside the National Old Trails Highway between Washington, D.C., and Los Angeles, California. Originally, the ambitious plan called for more than 3,000 individual mile markers approximating the route of the National Road, the Santa Fe Trail, the National Old Trail, and others. Working with the National Old Trails Road Association, which at the time was headed by Judge Harry S. Truman of Independence, Missouri, the groups finally settled on the idea of one marker to be placed in each of the 12 states through which the route passed.

The monuments were dedicated at (from east to west): Bethesda, MD; Beallsville, PA; Wheeling, WV; Springfield, OH; Richmond, IN; Vandalia, IL; Lexington, MO; Council Grove, KS; Lamar, CO; Albuquerque, NM; Springerville, AZ; and Upland, CA.

ALBUQUERQUE ATTRACTIONS

Petroglyph National Monument, with thousands of ancient examples of rock art on thousands of acres, is near the western edge of town, on Unser Blvd. north of I-40. Visitors can hike several trails of varying levels of difficulty to view the rock art, which is strung out along some 17 miles of volcanic escarpment.

The **National Atomic Museum** is located just north of Old Town, and has replicas of Fat Man and Little Boy on display, as

As of this writing, the El Vado Motel is in danger of meeting the wrecking ball. Albuquerque, New Mexico.

well as a film on the Manhattan Project. The museum has ambitious plans to expand, relocate, and rename itself in 2009. 1905 Mountain Rd. NW.

The **Unser Racing Museum** celebrates four generations of a family that has become a household name in auto racing. 1776 Montaño NW.

Pimentel & Sons have been crafting handmade custom guitars for more than 50 years. Each is made by one craftsman, and typically includes inlay made especially for the individual customer. The Pimentels say that the New Mexico air is like a kiln, and perfectly seasons the wood in 10 to 15 years. The shop and showroom are at 3316 Lafayette Dr. NE.

The **American International Rattlesnake Museum**, at 202 San Felipe NW, has the largest collection of captive-born rattlesnakes. The museum is the largest of its kind ever developed, and its specimens include the rare albino rattlesnake.

The **Albuquerque Skateboard Museum** is housed in Skate City Supply, at 1311 Eubank NE. Lots of models are on display, including the Skee Skate of the 1950s.

The **Telephone Pioneer Museum** of New Mexico contains three floors of telephone history, including photographs, literature, and physical exhibits dating back to 1876 and covering more than a century of telephone development. See the actual switchboard that was used to warn of Pancho Villa's attack in 1916! Place a call to the Elvis novelty phone to hear how it rings. 110 Fourth St. NW.

Exhibits at the **New Mexico Museum of Natural History and Science** include full-scale dinosaur models, an ice age cave, a walk-through volcano, and a saltwater aquarium. 1801 Mountain Rd. NW.

The **Institute of Meteorites**, in Northrop Hall on the University of New Mexico campus, was established more than 30 years ago as an educational resource for the state. In its permanent collection is one of the largest stone specimens on record. Also on display is a spectacular 1,600-pound iron meteorite, which is on long-term loan from the Field Museum in Chicago.

Ernie Pyle, the famous World War II correspondent, once lived in Albuquerque at 900 Girard Ave. SE. His former residence has been converted to the **Ernie Pyle Memorial Branch Library**, which houses a small museum dedicated to the Pulitzer Prize winner who was killed in action in Okinawa.

The **Kodak Albuquerque International Balloon Fiesta** is held the first two weekends in October, and is considered one of the world's most-photographed events. Balloon entries have mimicked boats, bottles, houses, animals, ad infinitum.

Since 1988, Albuquerque has been home to the **National Fiery Foods & Barbeque Show** every March. This show is for both the professional trade and the public, and participants include retailers, wholesalers, growers, and just plain aficionados. There are product and cooking demonstrations; anything goes if it's even remotely chili-related.

On the western edge of Albuquerque is the Rio Grande (Spanish for Large River). It was here, on the east bank of the river and on the south side of old 66 that there used to be a sort of neighborhood bathing pool called Tingley Beach. There is an echo of that era in the name of The Beach Apartments just west of the **El Vado Motel** (at this writing, there are plans to demolish El Vado). As you cross the Rio Grande, you are finally leaving the old territory of the Republic of Texas that you entered in western Oklahoma all those miles ago.

West of Albuquerque, the highway begins its climb up out of the Rio Grande valley and onto the Colorado Plateau. The plateau continues until about halfway across Arizona.

The hill on the horizon is **Nine Mile Hill**, so named because its summit is located that many miles from the town center of Albuquerque.

It should be noted here that the early alignment of the route, which entered Albuquerque from the north via Santa Fe, continued southward out of Duke City and passed through Isleta Pueblo, Los Lunas, Rio Puerco, and Correo. The later alignment heads due west. To drive the *older* alignment, leave Central Avenue at Fourth Street and turn left (south). Then turn right (west) onto Bridge Boulevard, cross the Rio Grande, and follow the signs for NM 314 to Los Lunas. There, turn west on NM 6, which is Los Lunas' Main Street. The two alignments will come together again near the village of Mesita.

ISLETA PUEBLO

The **mission church** at Isleta Pueblo is a heavily buttressed structure built in approximately 1613, making it one of the oldest in New Mexico. It was partially destroyed during the Pueblo Rebellion, and then restored after the 1692 re-conquest. Since that time it has been in constant use. Isleta is where Thomas Edison made the very first motion picture, a short piece called *Indian Day School*, using his newly invented Kinetoscope around 1898. These days, the pueblo engages in several commercial enterprises, including a casino and golf course.

LOS LUNAS

The **Luna Mansion** is an elegant structure on the National Register that is now a restaurant and bar. There is also a **Saint Patrick's Day Balloon Rally** held in Los Lunas each year.

Just south of Los Lunas is the town of **Belen**. In Belen is a **Harvey House** which has been turned into a museum operated by the Valencia County Historical Society (VCHS). A walking/driving tour of the city sponsored by the VCHS includes such features as the **Central Hotel**, which figured prominently in the 1970 film, *Bunny O'Hare*, and **Gabino Gilbert**'s home, which was constructed with two-foot-thick adobe walls. Between Los Lunas and Belen is Tomé Hill, at the foot of which is a **steel structure** commemorating El Camino Real.

RIO PUERCO

It was here that a stuffed polar bear was displayed for some years. One day it was stolen and found several miles away torn to pieces. Some believe that local Indians performed the deed in a gesture designed to free the poor animal's spirit.

CORREO

Correo is a Spanish word meaning "mail." The community was earlier known as Suwanee.

MESITA

At Mesita, use NM 124 to follow old Route 66. Keep your eyes peeled for **Owl Rock**, an outcropping very close to the side of the road which has been pictured in many a postcard over the years.

LAGUNA

Laguna is the site of a very photogenic church up on a hill—the **Saint Joseph of the Lake Mission Church**. This is where Kirk Douglas's character hurriedly picked up a priest in the movie *Ace in the Hole/Big Carnival*.

Old Paraje trading post, Paraje, New Mexico.

PARAJE

Route 66 passes the old, long-abandoned Paraje Trading Post here.

FURTHER AFIELD

West of Paraje is a community named Casa Blanca. From here, a side trip to **Acoma Pueblo** is possible, about 13 miles or so to the south. Acoma Pueblo, or "Sky City," has been called the oldest continually inhabited pueblo in America. These days, only about 50 individuals live here full time, but many more gather on traditional feast and festival days. Guided tours are available, which take visitors to the pueblo atop Enchanted Mesa (about 350 feet up). There is a mission church there, the Mission de San Esteban Rey, which is the setting for Willa Cather's book, *Death Comes to the Archbishop*. The church was constructed in 1629, and all of the materials had to be carried to the mesa top by the builders. This includes the roof beams, which have been traced to Mount Taylor, some 30 miles away.

BUDVILLE

The **Budville Trading Company**—a former gas station, garage, and general store—still stands today, 70 years after its construction in 1935. The tiny community was named for H. N. "Bud" Rice, who started an automotive service business hereabouts in 1928.

CUBERO

Cubero proper was an early victim of bypassing sometime in the 1930s. Afterward, the **Villa de Cubero** appeared—a cluster of enterprises at the new highway junction, including tourist court, café, etc. The Villa de Cubero Tourist Courts found itself host to a number of notable events: the filming of *Desert Song* took place here; Lucy came and stayed here after leaving Desi; and, Papa Hemingway came to stay awhile and wrote *The Old Man and the Sea* while a guest here.

SAN FIDEL-MCCARTY'S

At McCarty's is the site of a 1933 **Spanish Colonial Church**, a half-sized replica of the church at Acoma.

About five miles west of McCarty's is the exit for NM 117. South of here is the eastern access to **El Malpais National**

Monument. El Malpais, or badland, is the largest contiguous lava flow in the U.S., at about 400,000 acres. Features include Sandstone Bluffs Overlook, Big Tubes, and Chain of Craters. Also here is La Ventana, one of the Southwest's largest freestanding natural arches. El Malpais can also be accessed via NM 53, south of Grants. The city of Grants has an El Malpais information center at 620 E. Santa Fe Avenue. Wear rugged footgear if you go, as the lava is very hard and sharp.

GRANTS

First settled in 1872, the local Indians refer to Grants as "Place of Friendly Smoke" as a result of a peace pact reached here between

The Grants Motel and its excellent sign have been demolished since this photograph was taken. Grants, New Mexico.

Kit Carson and Chief Manuelito. In 1887, Indians robbed a Santa Fe train of about $100,000 which was never recovered. Some think it may be buried in the area. In modern times (1950), uranium was discovered nearby at a place called Haystack Mountain.

It was outside Grants in 1958 that Liz Taylor's then-husband, Michael Todd, met his death in a plane crash.

The main drag through Grants is called **Santa Fe Avenue**, and it is lined with a number of vintage motels and other structures. However, one of my personal favorites, the Grants Motel, was demolished several years ago.

On Iron Street at the

Grants, New Mexico.

corner of Santa Fe Ave. is the **New Mexico Museum of Mining**. Said to be the only uranium mining museum in the country, it includes a simulated underground mine allowing visitors to explore tunnels and get more of a taste of the mining experience.

FURTHER AFIELD

Some 40-odd miles southwest of Grants, via NM 53, is **El Morro National Monument**. Also known as Inscription Rock, the main feature is a 200-foot sandstone cliff rising from the valley floor and bearing inscriptions

dating back centuries. The rock sits along an ancient east-west trail which has been frequented by travelers since prehistory. The earliest "European" inscription belongs to Juan Oñate, the first colonial governor of New Mexico, who made his mark in 1605. But there are petroglyphs which are of course a great deal older. A half-mile trail takes the visitor

This well-weathered mural adorns the side of an old trading post near Prewitt, New Mexico.

on a tour of the inscriptions, and a longer trail takes one to the top of the mesa, where there is a pueblo ruin. Interesting, isn't it, that once graffiti gets old enough, it's considered a cultural treasure?

Also on NM 53, and on the way to El Morro, is the **Bandera Volcano and Perpetual Ice Caves**. It's said that Zuni guides brought Coronado here, and that the place has been a destination ever since. A study in contrast, this privately held attraction includes the 500-foot extinct volcano with a hiking trail, as well as nearby caves which glisten with ice all year round. Trails begin at the historic **Ice Cave Trading Post**.

MILAN-ANACONDA-BLUEWATER-PREWITT

Heading west out of Grants, you pass through country which, in the time of Rittenhouse, was a major carrot-producing area covering thousands of acres between here and Bluewater. Route 66 (or the modern-day NM 122) passes between the towns of Anaconda and Bluewater, which are on opposite sides of both 66 and I-40.

Between Bluewater and Prewitt is the **Route 66 Swap Meet**. There is a wall covered with license plates facing the interstate.

As for Prewitt, I once saw a matchbook cover for sale on e-Bay which advertised Justin's Western Shop & Fountain "On Highway 66" in Prewitt. It looked as though it was printed in the 1940s. The telephone number, believe it or not, said "phone Prewitt No. 2."

THOREAU

This town was originally named Mitchell, but later renamed for the author, Henry David Thoreau. Thoreau is home to the Zuni

Mountain Kachina Company as well as the Frontier Trophy Buckle Company, manufacturer of oversized belt buckles for rodeo champions.

FURTHER AFIELD

North of Thoreau is the town of **Crownpoint**, which is famous for its monthly Navajo rug auctions, held at the local elementary school. Crownpoint is also a potential launching pad for an excursion to **Chaco Culture National Historic Park**, although this is not the preferred approach (it is more advisable to access Chaco from the north). Chaco Canyon is one of the key attractions in the Four Corners region exemplifying prehistoric culture in America. There are dozens of impressive sites here, two of the major ones being Pueblo Bonito and Chetro Ketl; the area was settled as early as the ninth century, and the culture reached its apex around A.D.

Prewitt, New Mexico.

1150. Archaeologists have determined that these people established a network of roads connecting them not only with the other villages in this canyon, but with a broader community extending for many miles. The complexity of architecture, community, and social organization is astonishing. Chaco Canyon is quite isolated—plan on bringing plenty of food and drink if you go.

CONTINENTAL DIVIDE

Around five miles west of Thoreau is a community named after the backbone of the North American continent. There is a sign here explaining that rainwater which falls west of this dividing line flows westward to the Pacific, while that which falls to the east flows toward the Atlantic via the Gulf of Mexico.

This was also formerly home to Top O' the World, a dance hall, bar, tourist court and boarding house.

The **Continental Divide National Scenic Trail** crosses Route 66 here as it wends its way along the divide from the Mexican border in the south all the way to the Canadian border north of Glacier National Park, a distance of more than 3,000 miles.

About 15 miles or so west of Continental Divide is the turnoff for **Fort Wingate** to the south (State Highway 400). Fort Wingate was established in 1862 at a site near San Rafael (south of Grants) as a base for Colonel Kit Carson's campaigns against the Navajo, when he rounded up thousands and marched them 300 miles to Fort Sumner in what has become known as the "Long Walk." The fort was moved to its present site in 1868, the same year Carson died. He is buried near Taos.

About four miles west of the Fort Wingate turnoff is the turnoff for **Kit Carson Cave**, which is a few miles north of old 66 via NM 566.

GALLUP

Old Route 66 through Gallup is unmistakable, paralleling as it does the railroad tracks, which are only yards away.

The jewel of Gallup is the **El Rancho Hotel & Motel**. Boasting the "Charm of Yesterday and the Convenience of Tomorrow," the El Rancho is truly one of a kind. The lobby decor is extraordinary, and the guest rooms are all named after Hollywood personalities who used to stay here in the glory days of filmmaking, when Gallup was a sort of Hollywood South-

Gallup, New Mexico.

west: Clark Gable, John Wayne, Claudette Colbert, and dozens of others are enshrined here. Photographs of stars line the walls. There is also a restaurant, lounge, and gift shop on premises.

Downtown Gallup invites pedestrian exploration in an area of several blocks including old Route 66 and Coal Street (formerly part of 66), which is one block to the south. Check out the former Rex Hotel, the McKinley County Court House, and the El Morro Theater.

Downtown Gallup, New Mexico.

GALLUP ATTRACTIONS

The **Gallup Cultural Center** is located in the restored Santa Fe Railroad depot at 201 E. Highway 66. A project of the Southwest Indian Foundation, the center hosts a variety of events, and includes a gallery, cinema, museum, bookstore, gift shop, and café.

The **Navajo Code Talkers' Room** is housed in the chamber of commerce building at 103 W. Highway 66. Here you can learn the fascinating story of how American strategists during World War II were stumped at finding a way to beat the Japanese code-breakers. Since the Navajo language is so different from other known languages—it's of such complexity that it cannot be learned without extensive training—and because in the 1940s virtually all Navajo speakers were living in remote areas of the American Southwest, it was determined that this might be a way to develop an unbreakable code for transferring military secrets

without fear of enemy interception. When put to the test, the Navajo Code Talkers convinced the U.S. military of their effectiveness and confounded the enemy, thus helping to win the war in the Pacific.

Red Rock State Park, just east of town, is home to the Intertribal Indian Ceremonial gathering in August and the Red Rock Balloon Rally in December. More than 30 tribes from throughout North America participate in the Intertribal gathering, which has been held since 1922 and is the largest gathering of its kind, attracting some 50,000 visitors. Near the entrance to the park is **Mr. Wilson's Red Rock Trading Post**, a National Historical Landmark. The park's red cliffs have been the setting for many movie productions over the years, including *Sea of Grass*, starring Spencer Tracy and Katherine Hepburn in 1946.

The Gallup Historical Society operates the **Rex Museum**, which specializes in railroad and mining history in the area. 300 W. Highway 66.

Code Talkers

The Navajo language proved an important strategic advantage to the American forces in the Pacific during World War II. The U.S. Marine Corps employed some 400 Navajo speakers to transmit messages that would be undecipherable to the Japanese. This was possible largely due to the fact that the Navajo language is one of extreme complexity; it has no alphabet and is unwritten; it is spoken only in the American Southwest; and at the outbreak of World War II was understood by no more than 30 or so non-Navajos—none of them Japanese. For decades following the war, the U.S. military kept this part of history largely under wraps in case they might have need of this capability again. Finally, in 1992 the information was made public and the hundreds of code talkers so vital to the war effort were recognized and honored for their unique contributions. In 2002, MGM Studios released a feature film on the subject, *Windtalkers*.

FURTHER AFIELD

Gallup sits at the junction of U.S. Routes 66 and the former 666. The highway which carried the apocalyptic designation (now known as 491) heads north out of Gallup toward the **Four Corners** region of the country. About 80 miles or so north of Gallup lies the town of **Shiprock**. It was named for the very distinctive remains of an

This sign at the Lexington Hotel has since been fully restored. Gallup, New Mexico.

extinct volcano situated a few miles outside of town and resembling a many-masted sailing ship. From Shiprock, access to a huge wealth of ancient ruins throughout the Four Corners region is possible. These spectacular Anasazi sites include Salmon Ruins, Aztec National Monument, Chaco Canyon, Mesa Verde National Park, Hovenweep National Monument, Canyon de Chelly, and many lesser-known archaeological treasures. There is also the Four Corners Monument itself, right at the juncture of New Mexico, Arizona, Utah, and Colorado, where one can actually stand in four states at once. And, straddling the Arizona-Utah border is Monument Valley, with an array of interesting geological features many of us recognize immediately from their appearances in John Ford's Westerns.

The route (NM 118) dead-ends here at Defiance. You'll need to cross to the south side of I-40 for a few miles.

West of **Manuelito,** and just before the Arizona state line, the old highway passes the site of the filming of *The Big Carnival* (a.k.a. *Ace in the Hole*) in 1950. The caves are in the cliffs on the north side of the highway. Many years ago, there was a sign near the border as one headed east advertising "Cliff Dwellings" one-half mile east of the Arizona border.

ARIZONA

Quietly, New Mexico gives way to Arizona as you continue to motor west. The character of the land here is harsher than any you've seen earlier in your journey. There certainly are green and inviting places in Arizona, but at this moment you could be forgiven for not believing it.

And yet, there are many who are profoundly drawn to this

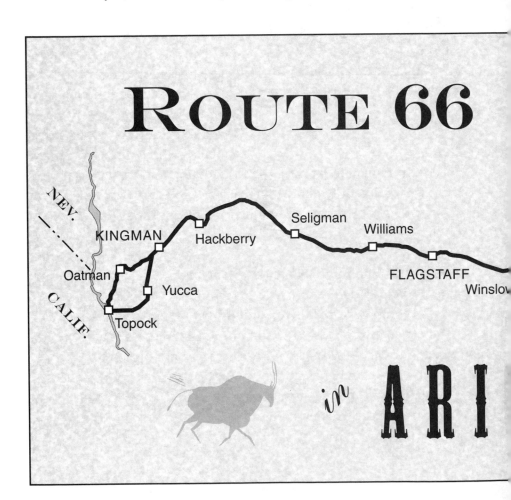

place. I first glimpsed it myself many years ago in what is called the Arizona Strip, that northwestern portion of the state which is cut off from the rest by the Grand Canyon. There, far from the bright lights of any metropolis, I lay on the ground one evening and saw more stars in the sky than I had ever thought possible—I could swear they overlapped.

Water, that most precious of commodities, is in short supply. You could say that water in this area is an acute condition, rather than a chronic one—you will see a great many dry streambeds which gush to life on only a few occasions during the

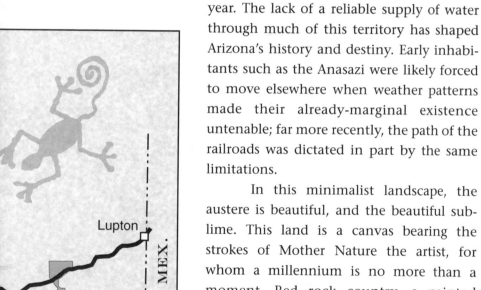

year. The lack of a reliable supply of water through much of this territory has shaped Arizona's history and destiny. Early inhabitants such as the Anasazi were likely forced to move elsewhere when weather patterns made their already-marginal existence untenable; far more recently, the path of the railroads was dictated in part by the same limitations.

In this minimalist landscape, the austere is beautiful, and the beautiful sublime. This land is a canvas bearing the strokes of Mother Nature the artist, for whom a millennium is no more than a moment. Red rock country, a painted desert, and the scar from a meteoric collision all await you in a place where trees turn to stone and volcanic eruptions shape the countryside.

Just across the New Mexico-Arizona border you'll encounter the community of Lupton.

LUPTON

From Route 66, Lupton looks to be mostly a sort of "strip" comprised of trading posts offering tourist-oriented souvenirs. The most notable thing about them is their garish appearance, including bright primary colors and replicas of teepees. At least one of them features a wooden Indian chief standing outside. The Yellowhorse Trading Post even has animal figures arrayed on the cliffs above. This area is an excellent place to pick up that bullwhip or rubber tomahawk you've been wanting.

About 25 miles or so to the north of here via Highway 12 is **Window Rock**, a natural feature consisting of an aperture carved in a large sandstone formation by the forces of wind, dust, and water. There is a viewing area at the Window Rock Tribal Park on Highway 12. The nearby community of Window Rock has been the official capital of the Navajo nation since 1938. There is a museum nearby on Highway 264.

Traveling Route 66 in Lupton, you quickly cross to the south side of I-40 for the run toward Sanders. Here you'll see **Ortega's Indian Galeria**, which is housed in a geodesic-domed building. There's a similar structure, also a trading post, which you'll see later at Meteor City.

HOUCK-SANDERS

Around Houck is something called Fort Courage, built as a replica of the fort used in the television series *F Troop*. If you're driving on I-40 when you reach exit 346, leave the interstate here and follow the north frontage road. You'll run out of pavement, but not to worry. This old alignment takes you past the Querino Trading Post, as well as the ruins of the **Old Querino Trading Post**. These ruins have been rapidly deteriorating, so by the time you read this there may be very little left, but this slow-moving branch road is good for the soul anyway.

In Sanders, check out the **66 Diner**, which is housed in a building manufactured by the renowned Valentine.

CHAMBERS-NAVAJO

Rejoin the interstate here, and continue west.

FURTHER AFIELD

About 37 miles north of Chambers via U.S. 191 is the village of Ganado and the **Hubbell Trading Post National Historic Site**. Established in the 1870s, this is the oldest continuously operating Navajo trading post, and is now run by the National Park Service. John Hubbell's grave overlooks the site from nearby Hubbell Hill.

Thirty-six miles further north from Hubbell's Trading Post is **Canyon de Chelly National Monument**, which contains probably the most-photographed ruin in the United States—the

White House Ruin. The ancient cliff dwelling ruin is reached by an arduous trail, about 2.5 miles round trip, which may leave you breathless on the ascent but which is well worth the effort. The trail goes past an active farmstead and across a small stream before reaching the bottom of the canyon, where the ruin is built into the canyon wall. This is the only ruin in the park which is accessible without a guide.

Back on Route 66, you'll want to make a point of leaving the superslab at exit 320 for a trip into the past. There is a much older alignment of 66 which will take you to the ruins of the old **Painted Desert Trading Post**. After exiting the interstate, go north a short distance to a crossroads. Turn left, and you are on an early stretch of the Route. Go slowly, as the road is quite rough. Your patience will be rewarded as you approach the white walls of the old trading post on a graceful curve in the road. Just beyond the ruin is a mostly dry river bed (the Dead Wash) which contains the wrecks of several old cars pressed up against the sandy bank in an elbow in the river. You'll need to turn around and return to the main road the same way you came in, and continue on I-40 westbound.

No longer accessible from what remains of old 66, the **Painted Desert** and the **Petrified Forest**, a pair of natural attractions straddling the highway, must be accessed from I-40. However, in this vicinity you can use the I-40 overpasses to look at the adjoining terrain and pick out where the Highway 66 pavement used to run. The paving was removed in this area, but out here, scars are slow to heal, and you can often spot differences in the color and character of the vegetation which signals where the old roadbed was. Keep alert and you'll see what I mean.

The **Petrified Forest National Park** is about 26 miles east of Holbrook. It was established in 1906 during the Teddy Roosevelt administration and designated a national park in 1962. This area was once a dense and humid forest eons ago, and conditions were such that fallen trees became transformed into mineralized versions of themselves. The agate and quartz which comprise these fossils still exhibit the visible characteristics of wood, such as grain and growth rings. The park includes natural formations, such as undisturbed fallen trees, as well as some man-made structures, such as Agate House, a pueblo which was fashioned from the rare material. Other features include the Puerco Indian Ruin, a 100-room pueblo dating from about A.D. 1300, and Newspaper Rock, which is covered in petroglyphs.

The **Painted Desert** is just north of the highway and connects with the Petrified Forest to the south. Plenty of photo opportunities are provided by the colorful mineral deposits which give the area its name. These are particularly impressive in the early-morning or pre-dusk light. The **Painted Desert Inn**, at Kachina Point, was built in the 1920s and then restored in the '30s by the Civilian Conservation Corps. Later, it became a part of the Harvey House chain.

Both the Petrified Forest and the Painted Desert are bona fide Route 66-era attractions, so be sure to take advantage of the opportunity to experience them.

HOLBROOK

Holbrook is well known to 66 travelers as the home of the **Wigwam Village Motel**. There were at one time seven such villages, all built between 1933 and 1950, with the original one being in Horse Cave, Kentucky. The sister set of units near San Bernardino was the last to be built. Each village consists of several individual room units designed to resemble Indian teepees. Furthermore, all units of each village originally had pay-per-listen radios, the receipts of which were forwarded to the originator of the concept, Frank Bedford, as a sort of royalty fee.

The **Rainbow Rock Shop** has a collection of dinosaur

sculptures outside to catch your attention; however, there's a penalty—signs are posted insisting that you pay the owners a fee for any photographs you take of their enterprise. Also in town is the **Holbrook Wild West Museum**.

If you haven't had enough petrified wood yet—or if you skipped the Petrified Forest completely—you might want to exit at Geronimo's (exit 280) where they have what they boast is the **World's Largest Petrified Log** on display.

JOSEPH CITY

This community was originally established by Mormons circa 1876—America's centennial year, and exactly 50 years before the

Here It Is: the most famous billboard on all of Route 66, Joseph City, Arizona.

establishment of U.S. 66 and the rest of the federal highway system.

Nearby is the famous **Jackrabbit Trading Post**. The billboard proclaiming *HERE IT IS* has to be one of the best-known sights along the route. I, for one, find myself transported backward in time whenever I see it. Aside from the billboard, the Jackrabbit is also justly famous for its cherry cider, and for its slogan: "If you haven't been to the Jackrabbit, you haven't been in the Southwest." Lots of travelers over the years have had their photographs taken sitting astride the giant jackrabbit figure on the premises.

MANILA-HIBBARD-HOBSON

Manila shows up plainly as a town directly on Route 66 in my 1957 road atlas, as does Hibbard. Hobson by that time had already been bypassed, and appeared just south of the route. Hobson is still down there, though, right on the railroad tracks, as befits a very old alignment. The memory of Hibbard persists thanks to the I-40 exit sign—exit 264 is called Hibbard Road. Today, the community at this exit is called Havre.

If you have a rugged vehicle and are feeling adventurous, take the Hibbard Road exit, go to the north side of the interstate, and follow the road west. You will lose the pavement for most of the way, but you will be passing through what was once a well-traveled piece of backcountry. At the Highway 87 junction, cross to the south side of I-40 for the run into Winslow.

WINSLOW

As you enter Winslow, the highway splits into east- and westbound portions at a rest stop/picnic area. As always, when the highway splits like this through any town, I recommend you double back after you've passed through town in order to see what's on the other side.

Winslow received mention in the Eagles' song "Take It Easy" many years ago, and the town has latched onto this bit of trivia for all it's worth. Go check out the "corner in Winslow, Arizona" yourself, where you'll see a sign quoting the famous line as well as a piece of modern sculpture standing nearby.

The **Old Trails Museum**, at 212 Kinsley, houses a collection of Winslow historical artifacts and Route 66 memorabilia.

La Posada, a former Harvey House property, is at 303 E. Second St. This masterpiece was created in 1928 by top-drawer architect Mary Colter, widely regarded today as having been far ahead of her time. Offering a modest number of guest rooms in a space larger than Hearst Castle, this Spanish hacienda-style jewel was restored in the late 1990s and features a museum, gardens, and meeting spaces.

As you leave Winslow heading west, keep an eye out for the ruins of the Tonto Drive-In movie theater. The screen, projection booth, ticket booth, and marquee sign are all still standing.

Winslow, Arizona.

FURTHER AFIELD

Just outside Winslow on AZ 87 is **Homolovi Ruins State Park**. This is a 4,000-acre preserve with more than 300 archaeological sites and numerous petroglyphs. Homolovi is a Hopi word meaning "place of the little hills." The four major pueblo sites here are thought to have been occupied from A.D. 1200 to 1425. The park is an active archaeological site, with archaeologists working here Monday through Friday in June and July revealing agricultural features and pit houses.

LEUPP CORNERS-DENNISON

According to my trusty 1957 atlas, Leupp Corners was a small community at the Route 66 junction with a gravel road going north to the town of Leupp. That road (or the closest thing to it) is what is today marked State Highway 99.

METEOR CITY

At exit 239 is Meteor City, a geodesic dome-style trading post by

Outisde the Meteor City Trading Post, Meteor City, Arizona.

the side of the highway. There is actually a partially paved road which heads south and eventually wanders over toward the crater to the southwest, but this is not the official approach and is not recommended.

RIMMY JIMS

Rimmy Jim was the moniker of the man who originally ran the Meteor Crater concession. The crater itself is about six miles south of I-44 here at this exit (233). Statistics for the crater include: 570 feet deep, one mile across, three miles in circumference. The crater was created from an object that was traveling 45,000 mph at impact. There is a gift shop, snack bar, interpretive exhibits, and observation platforms. You can hike around the crater via a guided tour, but you

Ruins of the former observation tower near Meteor Crater.

cannot enter it. Since the object causing the crater originated in outer space, there is also a sort of Astronaut Hall of Fame on the premises. A segment of 1984's *Starman* was filmed at the crater.

Nearby, on a disused stretch of old road, is the Meteor Crater Observatory, a stone ruin of the primitive observation tower used in the old days.

TWO GUNS

Today, access to Two Guns is often impossible, due to the fact that it rests on private property that the owners seem to prefer to keep gated and locked. Two Guns was a town only in the loosest sense; it was actually a made-to-order tourist trap, with several cages of captive animals, such as coyotes and mountain lions, to lure the motorist off the highway. This is the stuff of which lasting memories are made for young boys traveling with mom and dad.

FURTHER AFIELD

Go south from exit 225, between Two Guns and Twin Arrows, and you can find the **Raymond Buffalo Ranch**, which supports a herd of bison maintained by the Arizona Game & Fish Department.

TWIN ARROWS

Twin Arrows is an abandoned tourist complex featuring a café, trading post, and fuel station, distinguished by a pair of enormous arrows sticking out of the ground. I've been hoping for years that someone will make a go of it here, but so far those hopes have not been answered. I just love those larger-than-life arrows embedded in the earth. This is the type of feature which so distinguishes the old highway's attractions from today's cookie-cutter copies.

WINONA

This is the place made somewhat famous for its reference in Bobby Troup's classic song, wherein he exhorts: "Don't forget Winona." There's not a great deal to see in Winona, other than the big, gleaming, vintage trestle bridge here which used to carry the highway. From Winona, you can take an early alignment to Flagstaff by using Townsend-Winona Rd., then turning south at Highway 89. To use the later alignment, return to the interstate and exit at Walnut Canyon Rd.

COSNINO

Once the Townsend-Winona Road loop mentioned above was bypassed, Route 66 took a slightly more direct path toward Flagstaff, which passed through the village of Cosnino.

FLAGSTAFF

Nestled at the feet of the San Francisco Peaks, Flagstaff enjoys nearly the same elevation as Denver, and so has a considerable skiing season in the winter months. The same slopes in summer make for excellent hiking, affording views which sometimes extend into neighboring Utah to the north. There is a Flagstaff anecdote which says that Cecil B. DeMille almost made Flagstaff the center of filmdom instead of Hollywood. However, the day he arrived from the east there was snow falling, and so he decided to stay on the train and continue to California and sunnier climes. The rest, as they say, is history.

Entering Flagstaff from the east, prior to arriving downtown you'll see a vintage roadhouse known as the **Museum Club**. Built in 1931 to house a taxidermy collection and other artifacts, it was

The Monte Vista Hotel in Flagstaff, Arizona, opened in the 1920s.

originally called the Dean Eldridge Museum. Later it evolved into a honky-tonk nicknamed The Zoo because of all the animal trophies on display, and has seen the likes of some top-tier performers over the years. There are a few stories of ghost hauntings here, with one of the former owners having committed suicide in front of the fireplace. Look for the guitar-shaped neon sign out front.

In downtown Flagstaff, you'll find a lot of vibrancy, mixed together with plenty of vintage architecture and neon. The **Hotel Monte Vista** first opened its doors on January 1, 1927, and has played host to the likes of Jane Russell, Spencer Tracy, Humphrey Bogart, Teddy Roosevelt, and many, many others of similar celebrity stature. It's said that Zane Grey did some of his writing here at the hotel. The adjoining bar has a terrific neon marquee which says simply: *COCKTAILS*.

Route 66 runs right alongside the railroad tracks through

Flagstaff, and so you'll see the old Santa Fe depot as well. There is a colorful **commercial strip** along here which includes the Grand Canyon Café, Joe's, and Wigwam Curios (now closed).

FLAGSTAFF ATTRACTIONS

Walnut Canyon National Monument, established in 1915, is home to the ruins of a small Sinagua community. The 13th-century community is comprised of some 300 rooms. There is a steep, self-guided walking trail which meanders through the canyon past numerous cliff dwellings. I-40 exit 204, east side of town.

The world-famous **Lowell Observatory**, established in 1894, is at 1400 W. Mars Hill Road. It was here that astronomers in 1930 discovered the planet Pluto, and the telescope used at that time is still on display. Also here is the original 24-inch refractor used in the 1890s. Guided tours and lectures are available.

Riordan Mansion State Historic Park features the 40-room Riordan Mansion, built in 1904 in the Arts and Crafts style. The architect, Charles Whittlesey, also designed the Grand Canyon's El Tovar Lodge. This house was built for two close-knit families—the Riordan brothers married two sisters from another prominent family and both couples lived and raised their own families here. The house features log-slab siding, volcanic stone archways, and hand-split wood shingles. Interior appointments include handmade furniture and stained-glass windows. A truly unique feature of the house is the set of photographic windows in the Rendezvous Room. A prominent photographer, John K. Hillers was commissioned by the owners, and his photographic transparencies were fused to panes of translucent glass, so that the photos are illuminated by the incoming sunlight. These windows were painstakingly restored in the 1990s using Hillers's original glass negatives found at the Smithsonian Institution. 409 W. Riordan Rd.

The Arizona Historical Society's **Pioneer Museum** is located north of downtown at 2340 N. Fort Valley Road in what was formerly a hospital for the indigent from 1908 until 1938. Also on the grounds are a barn and root cellar that were utilized by the hospital, and a cabin which was moved to the site in 1967 from elsewhere in Flagstaff. From November to February each year, the museum presents **Playthings of the Past**, an exhibit of toys from the 1880s through the 1960s. Each June, there is a **Wool Festival** featuring sheep, goat, and llama shearings, as well as wool spinning, dyeing, and weaving demonstrations.

Annual **Winterfest** in February includes dogsled races, llama games, ice skating, and snowmobiling.

FURTHER AFIELD

About 15 miles north of Flagstaff (take U.S. 89) is **Sunset Crater Volcano National Monument**. This cinder cone was formed around A.D. 1064, and was active intermittently for the next 200 years or so. The Lava Flow Nature Trail begins at the visitor center and offers a 45-minute walk which traverses some of the lava flows and affords some nice views. For the stout of heart, the Lenox Crater Cinder Cone Trail is steep and strenuous.

From Sunset Crater, a paved road crosses the lava flow and connects with **Wupatki National Monument**. Established in 1924 by Calvin Coolidge, a president known for working four hours per day at most, Wupatki is composed of several ruins on 35,000 acres thought to have been inhabited by ancestors of the Hopi. Most impressive is the Tall House, a 100-room complex with a nearby amphitheater and ball court. Self-guided walking trails take the visitor through each of the ruins.

To the south of Flagstaff (30 miles) is **Sedona**. A sort of New Age sanctuary, Sedona is famous for its red rock scenery, which changes in appearance throughout the course of each day. The nearby **Red Rock-Secret Mountain Wilderness** is a red-hued, canyon- and pinnacle-filled landscape with cliffs, ruins, and rock art. Sedona also hosts an **International Film Festival** each March.

Beyond Sedona, but still on ALT 89, is the old mining community of **Jerome**. This mining town, perched on the side of Cleopatra Hill, was just about gone until being resurrected as a sort of art colony. Today, the town bustles with guests browsing the assortment of galleries, shops, and historic buildings. While in Jerome, check out the old **Douglas Mansion** at Jerome State Historic Park. The museum traces the history of Jerome, and the Douglas family in particular, through photos, minerals, and artifacts. Just walking the streets of Jerome is an enjoyable experience.

Very close to Jerome is **Tuzigoot National Monument**. Here you can tour a pueblo once inhabited by the Sinagua people that rests on the summit of a ridge some 120 feet above the surrounding valley.

Southeast of Jerome and Sedona near I-17 are **Montezuma Castle National Monument** and **Montezuma Well**. Named by early explorers who assumed it was Aztecan in origin, the castle structure is about ninety percent intact, and is at the end of a paved trail which makes an easy stroll. The well is about 11 miles away, and consists of a spring at the bottom of a canyon-like depression. The sides of the canyon are filled with small pueblo ruins.

Farther south on ALT 89 from Jerome is the city of **Prescott** (pronounced "press kit"). Prescott is worthy as a destination in itself. There is a beautiful historic downtown district ideal for walking around. Prescott has more Victorian-era buildings than any other community in Arizona. The **Sharlot Hall Museum** alone has twelve buildings on three acres evoking the flavor of territorial Arizona. Included are the old Territorial Governor's Mansion, Fort Misery Cabin, and the Bashford House, considered a premier example of western high Victorian style. Prescott also is home to the country's oldest rodeo each July, which has been held consistently since 1888. And, if you appreciate western art, don't miss the

Phippen Museum of Western Art, named for the founder of the Cowboy Artists of America.

 Back on Route 66 heading west out of Flagstaff, the road will eventually force you onto the interstate. Leave the interstate again at exit number 185.

BELLEMONT

The name Bellemont means literally "pretty mountain."

PARKS

This tiny town (formerly called Maine) was cut in pieces and left to die by the interstate. It includes the **Parks in the Pines General Store**, established in 1921, years before the highway was designated Route 66.

WILLIAMS

Williams was the last town to be bypassed by the construction of the interstate in 1984. It therefore had the last active stretch of Route 66 and the last stoplight on I-40.

This vintage motel is still serving guests in Williams, Arizona.

The town is named for Bill Williams, a well-known fur trapper widely regarded as the first white man in the area. There is a mountain south of

Signage, Williams, Arizona.

town also bearing his name, as well as the Bill Williams Trail, also to the south of town.

Williams has a very nice stretch of vintage 66 running through town, lined with small motels and other tourist-related businesses. Williams, though small, was very well-developed for the motoring public, due in large part to its proximity to the Grand Canyon. Williams is the traditional launching pad for **Grand Canyon National Park**, which lies about 60 miles or so to the north.

The renovated **Frey Marcos Hotel** was formerly a Harvey House and doubles as the depot for the **Grand Canyon Railway**, perhaps the most tradition-rich way of going to the canyon. The railway was established in 1901. From then until 1927, more than half of all canyon visitors came by train. Today, you can get a taste of the Old West by taking the train from Williams. The Grand Canyon Depot, at the end of the run at the canyon's south rim, is one of only three remaining log-constructed depots in the U.S., and is on the National Register. It was built in 1909 of rustic logs in order to complement the adjoining Ponderosa pine forest. At the Grand

Canyon, facilities are plentiful, including a laundromat, post office, general store, and bank. The 1905 **El Tovar Hotel** is nearby. Activities include hiking, camping, mule rides to the bottom of the canyon, helicopter tours, and white-water rafting.

Someone's got the Route 66 spirit in Williams, Arizona.

Highway 66 through Williams is divided into east- and westbound portions, so don't forget to turn around when you reach the end of town and drive it in the other direction. Notable businesses include the **Turquoise Teepee** and **Rod's Steak House**, a fixture on the route since 1945.

ASH FORK

This is the self-proclaimed Flagstone Capital of the World. Again, Route 66 splits itself into eastbound and westbound segments, separated by a city block. Make sure to turn around and check out the eastbound portion before you move on.

 Important: Between Ash Fork and Seligman is the Crookton Road exit. This is the one to take in order to cruise the longest unbroken portion of old 66 remaining—Seligman to Topock. From now on, and all the way to the California border, you will remain on old Route 66 and not have to use any interstate highway at all.

SELIGMAN

Now you are on the section of 66 of which the Route 66 Association of Arizona is so justifiably proud. Here begins the stretch that was so completely bypassed by I-40 that it is today as unspoiled as any section of the road anywhere, all the way to Topock at the Colorado River.

Seligman is home to the Delgadillo brothers, Angel and Juan. Angel used to run the barber shop in Seligman, and Juan (now deceased) operated the **Snow Cap Drive-In**. Juan's son now continues the tradition. Open or closed, be sure to get out of your car and do some exploring on the grounds of the Snow Cap. It is chock-full of interesting artifacts, humorous signs, and other surprising touches. A little ways past the Snow Cap is Angel's **Route 66 Visitor Center**. The **Copper Cart** is also a great vintage restaurant, and has a big, one-of-a-kind sign out front.

Seligman, Arizona.

AUDLEY-PICA-YAMPAI

This is a series of small communities strung out along Route 66 when the predecessor to the alignment you are now driving was still current. They are all just to the south of the modern-day road.

GRAND CANYON CAVERNS

Here's a good old-fashioned roadside attraction. Called Coconino Caverns on some old maps—and later, Dinosaur Caverns—the cav-

Outside the Grand Canyon Caverns—formerly known as Dinosaur Caverns. West of Seligman, Arizona.

erns themselves are accessed by an elevator which takes you 21 stories underground. Aside from the normal cave formations, attractions below include a mummified bobcat. Outside, you'll see dinosaur replicas lining the walkway to the front door. There is a restaurant and gift shop, as well as an airstrip.

As you approach Peach Springs from the east, keep your eye out on the north horizon. There is a point at which you can see all the way to the south rim of the Grand Canyon, which makes its closest approach to the highway along here.

It is possible to take Highway 18 from this vicinity (just east of Peach Springs) to a relatively untrammeled part of the Grand Canyon, and stay at the **Havasupai Lodge** on the Havasupai Reservation.

PEACH SPRINGS

The Hualapai tribal headquarters are located here in Peach Springs.

TRUXTON

The old **Frontier Restaurant** still operates here. Out front is a pair of street signs. One says Will Rogers Hwy; the other says Historic Route 66. Also be on the lookout for a wrecked car serving as a milepost marker for various Route 66 destinations (see photo on page 296).

CROZIER

Although the town of Crozier appears plainly on the path of Highway 66 in my 1957 atlas, Rittenhouse already reports it as "bypassed" in 1946.

VALENTINE

A scene from the movie *Easy Rider* was filmed here, on the south side of the highway, just west of the Indian Agency. Peter Fonda fixes a flat in the background, while a cowboy shoes a horse in the foreground to demonstrate that some things don't really change.

Valentine, Arizona.

HACKBERRY

The **Hackberry General Store** is a must-stop. The current operators, John and Kerry Pritchard, are attempting to return the place to something close to its original state. For years, this location was Bob Waldmire's International BioRegional Old Route 66 Visitor Center.

Hackberry, Arizona.

Shortly after the Hackberry Store, you begin what is reputed to be the longest continuous curve on all of Route 66 (several miles).

LOGASVILLE

According to local residents, there once was a town called Logasville located at what is now the eastern part of

Kingman back in the 1950s. It is said to have been bordered by Bank Street, Shangri-La, and Route 66. This community does not appear on my 1957 atlas, however, and it was at some point annexed by the city of Kingman.

KINGMAN

This settlement was named for Lewis Kingman, a civil engineer with the Santa Fe railroad, in 1880. Today there's no mistaking Kingman thanks to the huge beige-colored tower that's been painted with these words: "Welcome to Kingman, the Heart of Historic Route 66."

Kingman is the hometown of well-known character actor Andy Devine, who grew up at the Beale Hotel, which his parents used

to run. Each September, the city holds Andy Devine Days in his honor. Clark Gable and Carole Lombard got married at the local Methodist Church here in Kingman, and then raced down Route 66 to honeymoon in nearby Oatman. In the downtown area, one block

Classic car show, Kingman, Arizona.

from the route, there is a nice neon sign at the Kingman Club.

The **Quality Inn** here in Kingman (over at the interstate) has a couple of its rooms named in honor of George Maharis and

Martin Milner, stars of the early 1960s television series *Route 66*. There is even a memorabilia display in the lobby area. Although very little of the television series was actually filmed on Highway 66, it is in retrospect a very interesting series nonetheless, with early guest appearances by such later notables as Alan Alda, Robert Duvall, Joey Heatherton, and Burt Reynolds.

The **Power House Visitors' Center** is headquarters for Arizona's Route 66 Association, and has an extensive gift shop on premises. 120 W. Andy Devine.

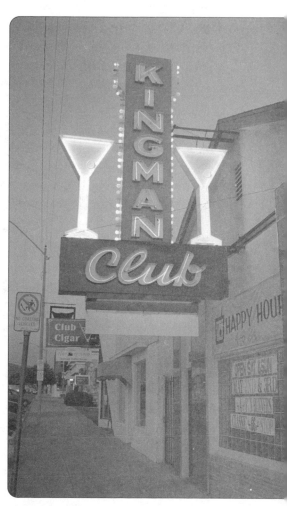

The **Bonelli House** is a two-story mansion built in 1915. It was built on the site of an earlier dwelling which had burned down. Therefore, this structure was built of locally quarried tufa stone, a material valued for its fire resistance and its insulative, cool-in-the-summer characteristics. At 430 E. Spring Street. The home is maintained by the **Mojave Museum of History and Arts**, located at 400 W. Beale St., which also includes items relating to favorite son Andy Devine.

Downtown Kingman, Arizona, has some great-looking neon.

Route 66 TV Series

In the fall of 1960, the CBS television network launched a weekly series called *Route 66*. In it, two young men (portrayed by Martin Milner and George Maharis) traveled around the country in a Chevrolet Corvette and became involved in the lives of the people they met each episode.

Although only a small number of the more than 100 episodes were actually filmed on U.S. 66, the series is notable for a number of reasons. The early 1960s were a transitional period in America, and the series took on themes which were unconventional—even daring—for the time. The two protagonists came into contact with a runaway heiress, a dying blues singer, and a heroin addict, to name just a few. They tackled issues such as gang violence, racism, labor unions, and mental illness at a time when most television stayed on safer ground.

Also notable about the show were the logistical challenges involved. The series was shot on location throughout the country (even in Canada), and required a crew of 50 to 60 people, along with two tractor-trailers full of equipment. It was probably the largest mobile filming operation in television history up to that time.

Guest stars on the show included some fading film stars such as Joan Crawford, but more interesting today is the roster of up-and-coming talent that was featured, including such now-familiar names as Rod Steiger, Suzanne Pleshette, and Robert Redford.

FURTHER AFIELD

South of Kingman is **Hualapai Mountain Park**. Established in the 1930s, the park has several cabins constructed by the Civilian Conservation Corps. The scenery is beautiful, and there are several trails for hiking, as well as a campground.

North of Kingman is the near-ghost town of **Chloride**, Arizona, founded in 1862. To reach Chloride, take U.S. 93 North. A sign will direct you to turn right on a county road to the small, now-quiet town of Chloride.

Also north of Kingman via U.S. 93 are **Lake Mead**, the **Boulder Dam**, and **Las Vegas**. Opinions on Las Vegas, Nevada, are generally of two kinds: "Love it" or "Hate it." I count myself among the very few who don't feel strongly one way or the other. I don't care for the casino scene, but what I do like about Las Vegas is its location. My wife and I have used Las Vegas as a convenient launching pad for a number of other destinations. Easy day trips out of Las Vegas include Death Valley, Lake Mead/Boulder Dam, Zion National Park, the ghost town of Rhyolite, and—of course—Route 66.

The other redeeming feature to Route 66 fans, at least as I see it, is that if you think the Mother Road has some wild and kitschy signs and architecture, then Las Vegas has to be the record-holder. In Las Vegas there are casinos and other businesses which mimic Hawaiian islands, pirate ships, castles, pyramids, miniature cities of the world, and much, much more, most of it open 24 hours a day and brightly lit all through the night. If Las Vegas should fall into disuse over the next generation or two as Route 66 has, then it will make for some fine exploration one day for the ruin-hunters among us.

For those of you who want to taste a little of Las Vegas, here are a few suggestions, including a few attractions you may not have heard of:

The older part of Las Vegas—the downtown district known as **Glitter Gulch**—was semi-enclosed a few years ago and has received other infusions of cash to improve its image and desirability. This is where you'll find such venerable fixtures as the Golden Nugget and the Four Queens.

The Strip, where the majority of Las Vegas development takes place these days, dates from much later, when Bugsy Siegel built his Flamingo Hotel out there in the 1950s and began promoting the **Vegas Strip** heavily.

There is a **Liberace Museum** at 1775 E. Tropicana. Not only that, but there is a Liberace Play-Alike Competition held at Carlucci's Piano Bar each year on Liberace's birthday, May 16th. Judging of the contest is based on technique, material selection, performance style, and (of course!) costume.

The **Gun Store** is at 2900 E. Tropicana. For 10 bucks plus ammo, you can shoot an impressive array of handguns, and for $30 you can shoot a real tommy gun.

The **National Canvention & Breweriana Show** [sic] is held each March and includes an exhibition and the sale of beer-related memorabilia.

The **Vegas Ventriloquist Festival** in June includes workshops on improving technique, building your own dummy, developing your own brand of comedy routine, and more.

There's a park near the western edge of town which includes a retired steam locomotive from the Santa Fe line. It's here where you'll need to bear left in order to take the old Route 66 alignment into the hills toward Oatman via McConnico and Goldroad. Soon after leaving Kingman on old 66 near the chamber of commerce, the scenery and terrain begin changing. Be mindful of the conditions out here; there are lots of dusty, gravelly switchbacks and plenty of low places in the road where flash flooding can occur.

McCONNICO

According to my 1957 atlas, roughly around the town McConnico, there was a fork in the road. The older stretch of road went on to Oatman from here, but that alignment had already been bypassed. By 1957, official Route 66 went southward through Griffin and on to Yucca, Haviland, Powell, and Topock. That, of course, is the same alignment which was later upgraded to become Interstate 40.

Not long ago it was just a ruin, but **Cool Springs Camp** has recently made a comeback, thanks to caring owners. Look for it about 15 miles past the McConnico/I-40 junction. About a mile past Cool Springs is what remains of Ed's Camp.

GOLDROAD

Sitgreaves Pass, just east of Goldroad, was a very hard climb for vehicles in days gone by. Some cars and drivers had a very difficult time of it, and so there were wreckers in the area solely to haul hapless motorists over these crests. Some vehicles could make it in reverse, if not forward. The reason for this was two-fold: one, reverse is a substantially lower gear than first; and two, moving in reverse could overcome the shortcomings of early gravity-fed fuel delivery systems.

There was gold mining taking place here at Goldroad for decades before the fluctuations in the price of gold made mining here impractical. There's said to be considerably more ore here, if only the economic conditions change sufficiently. Meanwhile, the **Goldroad Mine** now offers one-hour walking tours of an actual gold mine.

OATMAN

Mining was big business here through the 1930s and right up until the onset of World War II.

You can't get lost in Oatman, as there's really just one road through it: old Route 66. This is a true Old West mining town which went through a ghost town phase and is now clinging to life as a tourist town. There are wooden plank sidewalks in Oatman, and the town's most celebrated inhabitants are the burros, descendants of forebears that were brought here in gold-mining days as beasts of burden. There are feed dispensers scattered around town so that you can indulge them. Get out of your car and do some walking here.

The old **Oatman Hotel** is where Clark Gable and Carole Lombard came for their honeymoon in 1939. You can view their suite (Room 15) and lots more of the place just by wandering upstairs.

In the early 1960s, portions of *How the West Was Won* were filmed in Oatman and environs. Each July, Oatman holds an annual **Egg-Frying Contest**. Entrants use every solar-based gizmo imaginable trying to fry an egg in 15 minutes or less. I've been told

Oatman, Arizona.

that the town's population sometimes increases tenfold for this event.

GOLDEN SHORES-TOPOCK

Neither of these communities qualifies as much of a town. Golden Shores is really no more than a housing subdivision. Topock comes from the

Unofficial street sign, Oatman, Arizona.

Mojave word meaning "water crossing," so is certainly appropriate.

There is an arching bridge (ca. 1916) which crosses the Colorado River, but today it carries no vehicle traffic, only a pipeline. Today's Route 66 adventurer is forced to make the crossing on the I-40 bridge.

FURTHER AFIELD

Consider a side trip down Highway 95 to **Lake Havasu City**. It was there in 1971 that the London Bridge was re-assembled piece by piece and turned into a tourist attraction. This, after having been painstakingly dismantled and all of the parts carefully labeled. The man who masterminded the plan originally thought that he was buying London's Tower Bridge, which is much more picturesque, but after learning of his mistake, he decided to go through with the deal anyway.

Route 66 has now passed through seven states on its journey west, and is poised at the crossing of the Colorado River. The promised land of California awaits on the opposite shore.

CALIFORNIA

fter traversing the Illinois prairie, the Missouri Ozark country, the Indian Territory of Oklahoma, the Panhandle of Texas, the old Spanish colony of New Mexico, and then the harsh landscape of Arizona, Route 66 finally arrives at the doorstep of California.

California, the land of milk and honey; the land where

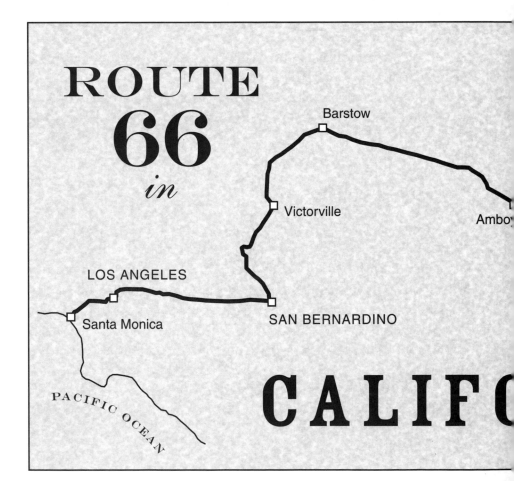

dreams live, where fortunes are built, and where the soul longs to be. Surely this is where the end of the rainbow must lie. But Nature can be a cruel provider. The Colorado River, threshold to the Golden State, is a welcome sight to the traveler who has arrived after crossing the desert of western Arizona, but the fabled land on the other side looks no more inviting than that which has tested him for more than 100 miles already.

How cruel must it have seemed to the fleeing Okies of the depression that even in California the land appeared barren and forsaken. Greeting them here at the border was no Xanadu, but rather the needles for which the nearby town is named, and many more miles of Mojave Desert yet to be crossed. The river is not an end to the desert, only a reference point.

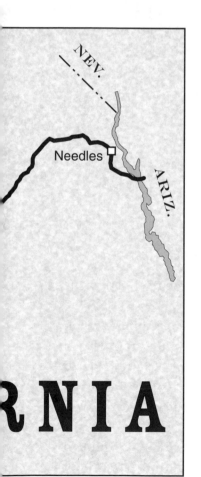

The actual location where Route 66 crosses over the Colorado River changed over the years. Unfortunately for Mother Road devotees such as you and me, the older bridges which used to carry the highway are either gone or inaccessible to traffic. You will be forced to use the I-40 bridge to make the crossing into California.

NEEDLES

Established in 1883 as a stop on the railroad, Needles is known for being one of the hottest places in the United States. Temperatures frequently exceed 100 degrees Fahrenheit. Named for the rocky outcroppings across the river in Arizona, Needles was once the home of *Peanuts* cartoonist Charles Schulz, who often used Needles and the surrounding

Needles, California.

desert as the setting for Snoopy's cousin, Spike. The river bath scene in *The Grapes of Wrath* was filmed here back in the 1930s.

As you enter the town from the east, there is an old wagon in the median which is said to be the same 20-mule team wagon used in the *Death Valley Days* television show, which starred Ronald Reagan. On the right-hand side of the highway is the **Old Trails Inn**, which in the Route 66 era was known for many years as the Palms Motel.

On Front Street, an older alignment of Route 66 through Needles, sits **El Garces**. This Santa Fe depot and hotel was built shortly after an earlier structure was destroyed by fire in 1906, and was designed with distinctive columns and balconies, which are unusual for this part of the country. Across the street from El Garces is the **Needles Regional Museum**, which includes exhibits pertaining to Route 66.

Keep an eye out for the 66 Motel, which has a neon sign in fine condition. As you pass through the town of Needles, there are still a number of buildings to see which are from the Route 66 era.

HOMER-GOFFS-FENNER

The loop which includes Homer, Goffs, and Fenner was cut off from Route 66 at an early date. The later alignment took a more direct path from Needles to Essex. Take this older loop (now U.S. 95) in order to avoid the interstate. When you reach the railroad crossing, turn left to follow the track of old Route 66.

At Goffs is a **schoolhouse** dating from 1914 which was meticulously restored in 1998–99 by the Mojave Desert Heritage & Cultural Association. The association maintains what may be the largest collection of Mojave Desert historical materials anywhere. Aside from the materials and exhibits displayed inside the schoolhouse, there are dozens of artifacts, including vehicles and mining equipment, on display outside in a self-guided tour format.

ESSEX

It was here in the Mojave Desert near Essex that U.S. troops under General Patton trained for desert conditions in preparation for the anticipated confrontation with (the Desert Fox) General Erwin Rommel's troops in North Africa. There is a public well (now dry) which offered free drinks of water to Route 66 travelers generations ago.

FURTHER AFIELD

Northwest of Essex is **Mitchell Caverns**, in Providence Mountains State Park, offering 1.5-hour guided tours. Caving is a refreshing activity here in the desert, with underground temperatures remaining in the 60s throughout the year. This state park sits in the midst of Mojave National Preserve, an area twice the size of Yosemite and which is at the confluence of three desert regions: the Mojave, Sonoran, and Great Basin Deserts. Features include rock art, abandoned mines and ranches, and over 300 known species of wildlife.

CADIZ SUMMIT

The remains of a small tourist complex rest here, with the ruined buildings now festooned with graffiti.

CHAMBLESS

In the vicinity of Chambless you'll see the rusting metal framework of what appears to have been a roadside billboard. Also, the remains of a huge restaurant sign with a roadrunner logo are baking in the desert nearby.

West of Chambless there is a berm, or small bank, along the north edge of the highway, which for several miles is covered with graffiti. Individuals have placed small stones and other detritus in such ways as to spell out words, make outlines, or otherwise communicate with future passers-by. Among the symbols are peace signs, various initials, a Route 66 shield, and many more which are difficult to either describe or to comprehend. You can easily become entranced by looking at this artwork for mile after mile through your side window.

AMBOY

For many years, the property owners here tried to capitalize on Amboy's isolated highway-side atmosphere. I saw some magazine ads extolling the virtues of the place for location filming, commercials, and so forth. I agree; in fact, I think this would make an excellent setting for an episode of *The Twilight Zone*. The **Roy's Motel & Café** complex definitely has that certain something.

In 2005, however, the whole town was bought by a new owner—lock, stock, and barrel—and I've yet to pay another visit. According to the most recent reports on the Route 66 e-group, little to nothing has changed thus far with the new ownership. It's rumored that the new owner wants to restore some features, add public restroom facilities, perhaps even re-open the cafe. We're waiting with bated breath, and only time will tell what sort of changes will unfold.

Roy's Motel & Café,
Amboy, California.

FURTHER AFIELD

Amboy Crater is just a mile or two south of the highway. There is a turnoff to the dormant volcano just west of Amboy proper.

For the truly adventurous, south of Amboy near Twenty-Nine Palms is **Joshua Tree National Monument**. Featured are a number of hiking trails, including one about four miles in length leading to the largest group of palms. A shorter trail (less than two miles) takes you to an oasis at Forty-Nine Palms Canyon. There is also a restored ranch within the confines of Joshua Tree, through which park rangers offer guided tours.

North of Amboy, at the town of **Baker** (near Death Valley), is a **135-foot-tall thermometer**. Around here, having respect for the temperature can mean the difference between survival and the alternative.

BAGDAD

Here's the inspiration for the name of the film *Bagdad Café*, which was actually shot a little further down the highway at Newberry Springs. Once upon a time, there actually was a Bagdad Café here, with a changing cast of road-weary travelers making up the clientele. Nowadays, you'll be hard-pressed to find much of anything.

SIBERIA

It seems an odd name for a community in the Mojave Desert, but it's somewhat in keeping with the community of Klondike nearby (and a short distance off of 66). I suppose one name inspired the other. Today, only a few foundations remain in Siberia.

LUDLOW

Established circa 1882 by the Ludlow Mining Company. Most of the
Mother Road-era part of town is now privately owned by the rail-
road and is slowly wasting away. Be sure to take a look at the classic
Ludlow Mercantile Company building, which was constructed in
1908. Also nearby are a number of other ruins, including the old
Ludlow Café.

Ludlow, California.

At Ludlow,
you can cross to the
north side of the inter-
state to avoid superslab
driving. Just north of
here are the remains of
World War II-era camps
used for training
American soldiers
(Crucero Rd.).

Cross the inter-
state again (to the south
side) at Lavic Road. My
1957 map of the region shows no community by that name, only
the Lavic Dry Lake to the south.

NEWBERRY SPRINGS

At Newberry Springs, pull over for awhile at an old Whiting Brothers
station now named Dry Creek Station. There are some wonderful old
pumps standing in front, and the desert setting is perfect.

The Bagdad Café is here also (formerly the Sidewinder). As
mentioned earlier, this is where the movie of the same name was
filmed.

On the road just east of Daggett, to the north of the highway, is what is called a Solar Concentrator. This is one of the latest high-tech methods for converting solar heat into useful energy.

Old Whiting Bros. Station, Newberry Springs, California.

DAGGETT

In Daggett stands the **Stone Hotel**, frequented in its day by the likes of Tom Mix, Death Valley Scotty, and John Muir. The hotel has walls which are some two feet thick. Also in town is the **Desert Market**, which in its day was the place local miners came to exchange their findings for legal tender.

There is a building at the corner of Route 66 and Daggett-Yermo Rd. with an unusual shape to its roof. This is locally known as the "Ski Lodge Roof House," and was originally opened as a visitor information center in 1926, the same year our beloved highway

was designated num-
ber 66.

The **Daggett Museum** is at 33703 Second St., and includes a collection of railroad china and Navajo Code Talkers' memorabilia.

Daggett, California.

FURTHER AFIELD

North of Daggett (use Daggett-Yermo Rd.), near the small town of **Yermo**, is the **Ghost Town of Calico**. Calico was a silver-mining town and also a source of borax, a mineral which has been known since ancient times and which has many applications, including pottery glazing, fertilizers, and detergents.

Calico, California.

A true Old West mining town dating from 1881, one-third of Calico's buildings are original, with the rest being carefully re-created to evoke the late nineteenth century. The town site covers about 60 acres, and includes a downtown business district, miners' quarters, tours of an actual mine, and an operating narrow-gauge railroad.

Calico has been the location for numerous television and film crews over the years, thanks to its authentic look and feel. The town hosts a number of festivals, including the Calico Spring Festival in May, which features a chili cookoff, music festival, and the World Tobacco Spitting Championship. Calico Days occurs every October, and counts a parade, burro races, and the National Gunfight Championship among its highlights.

A little to the east of Yermo and the ghost town is the **Calico Early Man Archaeological Site**. This archaeological dig, begun in 1964 by Dr. Louis Leakey, has pushed back the date for the presence of man on this continent thousands of years. Stone tools as much as 200,000 years old have been found here, making it one of the oldest tool-bearing sites in the Western Hemisphere. Public tours of the facility are available year-round.

BARSTOW

Named in 1886 for William Barstow Strong, who owned the Santa Fe Railroad, Barstow has a number of vintage Route 66-era signs and buildings to make you slow down and explore. Not the least of these is the **El Rancho Barstow Motel**, with its 100-

Barstow, California.

foot-tall neon sign supported by twin towers. Much of the motel was constructed using discarded railroad ties from the defunct Tidewater & Tonopah Railroad.

Be sure to see the Village Hotel & Café, the Katz, and the sign for the Palm Café.

Barstow is also home to another fine example of the Harvey House hotels from the glory days of rail travel: the **Casa del Desierto**. Located inside are the **Barstow Route 66 Mother Road Museum** and the **Western America Railroad Museum**. 685 N. First Street.

LENWOOD

Lenwood is just west of Barstow, and has largely been erased. There is still a Lenwood Drive, however, and a few businesses which continue to use the name Lenwood as part of their own.

HELENDALE

Most of Helendale is off the highway, but you will see the landmark **Helendale Market** alongside 66. Next door is a mostly empty lot selling firewood that has an antique sign for the Polly brand of gasoline as part of the décor. It occupies the site of a former fuel station.

Just outside Helendale on a former goat ranch is the **Exotic World Burlesque Museum & Hall of Fame**, truly something special. Here in the desert between Barstow and Victorville is one woman's tribute to strippers and exotic dancers. There are thousands of pieces of memorabilia from the glory days of burlesque, including photographs, costumes, and even the ashes of Miss Sheri Champagne, one of burlesque's all-time greats. Other well-known performers represented include Lily St. Cyr, Tempest Storm, the Eyeful Tower, and Chesty Morgan. Admission is free, but donations and

Barstow, California.

West of Helendale, California.

gift shop purchases are of course sincerely appreciated. Exotic World is at 29053 Wild Road.

Just past Helendale is a veritable **forest of bottle trees**, the creation of Elmer Long, who lives on the property and has been fashioning his brand of folk art since about the year 2000. Some of the bottles are old and dusty, while others are quite new and shiny, revealing the fact that this is indeed a work in progress.

You'll see a sign marking the turnoff for the **Roy Rogers Double R Bar Ranch**, formerly a private retreat owned by the King of the Cowboys, and now offering a variety of services and events through the year.

ORO GRANDE

Oro Grande has a very small former business district right on the highway. The most notable structures in Oro Grande are an enormous cement plant and a small building with a curved front currently doing business as Club 66.

Oro Grande, California.

VICTORVILLE

You need to stop and spend a little time in Victorville. Here's where you'll find the **California Route 66 Museum**. The folks here are friendly and knowledgeable, so you can get whatever materials and tips you'll need for the remainder of your journey. D Street, between Fifth and Sixth.

Part of the display at the California Route 66 Museum in Victorville.

Formerly here in Victorville was the Roy Rogers Museum, which moved to Branson, Missouri in mid-2003. You can still see a hint of the museum's influence, though, in the sign at the nearby New Corral Motel. The rearing stallion in the motel sign is a distinct echo of the figure of Trigger which used to stand in front of the museum.

Victorville, California.

Leaving Victorville via Seventh St., you'll soon be forced to enter Interstate 15.

CAJON SUMMIT

At the Oak Hill exit is the Summit Inn, dating from 1952. Not only is this an authentic stop from the Route 66 era, there are also a number of relics on display outside, such as a 1930s tow truck and several items of antique gas station equipment.

It's here in the vicinity of Cajon Summit that Route 66 crosses the **Pacific Crest Trail**. This is a rugged hiking trail which runs all the way from the Mexican to the Canadian border, a distance of more than 2,600 miles. This trail was established at the same time as the more well-known Appalachian Trail in the east, and covers much more rugged terrain. It passes beneath I-15 along here.

A little past Cajon Summit is the junction with State Highway 138, a spot called Cajon Junction. There is a small obelisk-shaped marker a short distance to the south on the east service road. The inscription reads: "Santa Fe and Salt Lake Trail 1849. Erected in honor of the brave pioneers of California in 1917 by pioneers." If you drive Highway 138 about four miles west of I-15, you'll see there is another historical marker, this one

Cajon Summit, California.

commemorating the California branch of the Mormon Trail. This trail was established in 1851, and connected the Mormon capital at Salt Lake City to Los Angeles by way of Las Vegas. The marker states that it was erected in 1937 by Sons of Mormon Pioneers. In 1998, a cattle drive was held which retraced the path of the old Mormon Trail between California and Utah.

Cajon Summit, California.

You can leave the interstate at the Devore Road exit (Cajon Blvd.) for your approach to San Bernardino. Just prior to reaching San Bernardino you can see the remains of two old 66-era motels, the El Cajon and the Palms. The motels are in very bad shape, but the old neon signs are still legible. This road will become Mt. Vernon Avenue as you enter San Bernardino.

SAN BERNARDINO

The County of San Bernardino is the largest in the nation.

Once you reach San Bernardino, even though you are not traveling on the interstate, the pace of the road quickens measurably—there's a sea change, you might say. You are beginning to enter what might be called the Southern California Megalopolis, or what is euphemistically referred to as Greater L.A. From now on, you will be hard-pressed to observe everything you want to and still drive safely. This is a taste of what happened to Route 66

and the other major high-
ways like her, a development
which led to widespread public support for their replacement by limited-access
superhighways.

It was here in San
Bernardino in 1948 that the
McDonald brothers sounded
the first death knell for the
mom-and-pop hamburger
joints of the world. What
began as the very first
McDonald's restaurant is
today the **McDonald's/
Route 66 Museum**. Part of
the structure is dedicated to
displays pertaining to the history of the McDonald's fast-

San Bernardino, California.

food empire, and part of it is filled with photos, highway signs, and
other memorabilia associated with the Mother Road.

SAN BERNARDINO ATTRACTIONS

San Bernardino is home to the **California Theater**, a 1928
Spanish Colonial Revival showplace at 562 W. Fourth. It was at the
California that Will Rogers made his last public appearance—to benefit the Salvation Army—prior to his death in Alaska a couple of
months later. The California Theater was an early "soundie," having
been outfitted from the start for sound, even though *The Jazz Singer*
had only been released about one year before. Today, the restored
California Theater hosts live stage performances, including opera
and symphony.

The **Route 66 Rendezvous**—an enormous cruise and car show—is held each September right here in San Bernardino.

FURTHER AFIELD

Southeast of San Bernardino is the city of **Redlands**, California. Redlands is home to a mission dating from 1830, the **Asistencia Mision de San Gabriel**, at 26930 Barton Rd. Also in Redlands are:

Near San Bernardino, California.

the **Marmalade Mansions**, a group of Victorian homes from the era when "Citrus was King"; the **Historical Glass Museum** at 1157 Orange St., which features American glassware from the early 1800s; and the world's tallest water slide, at Pharaoh's Lost Kingdom.

East of San Bernardino is **Big Bear Lake**. Once known as Southern California's favorite mountain getaway, there are hiking trails, mountain biking slopes, and seasonal skiing in the surrounding San Bernardino National Forest. Big Bear Lake has also been called "Hollywood's Back Lot." Numerous films have been shot here, including such well-known classics as *Birth of a Nation*, *Kissin' Cousins*, *Parent Trap*, *Dr. Doolittle*, and *Creature from the Black Lagoon*. In May, Big Bear Lake hosts the Trout Classic, where some 400 contestants participate in trophy trout fishing. In summer, it's Old Miners' Days, with a chili cook-off, parade, and cowboy shootout. A motorcycle rally, the Ladies of the Harley Mountain Fun Run, takes place each August. To go to Big Bear Lake, take one of two very scenic highways: Route 18 (Rim of the World Drive) or Route 38. Each includes panoramic overlooks of the area.

RIALTO

You probably won't notice when you pass out of San Bernardino and into Rialto, since you're now in one of those "Greater Metropolitan" areas. On old Route 66 here in Rialto is the sister to the **Wigwam Village** we saw earlier in Holbrook, Arizona. This one was lovingly restored in 2004 after new owners took over and reversed years of neglect. In recognition of this enormous effort, the Cyrus Avery Preservation Award was presented in September 2005.

The Wigwam Motel in Rialto, California, has recently been beautifully restored and updated.

FONTANA

In Fontana, keep alert for Wheels, Etc., on Foothill Blvd. (old 66). **Carl the Hubcap Kid** has a wide selection of wheels and hubcaps for just about any car you can think of. His place is surrounded by a fence made up of hundreds of wheels welded together.

Also be on the lookout for an old orange stand outside the now-closed **Bono's Restaurant**. The inscription over the window reads "Bono's Historic Orange." You are in what was once the heart of citrus country.

This former fruit stand still sits beside the Mother Road in Fontana, California.

RANCHO CUCAMONGA

Cucamonga is thought to be a Shoshone word meaning "sandy place." This really was a large ranch at one time, and the area eventually found itself awash in vintners. At the corner of Foothill and Vineyard is an old wine barrel bearing an inscription letting

Rancho Cucamonga, California.

Rancho Cucamonga, California.

the traveler know that this was once the site of the oldest vineyard in California.

The **Sycamore Inn** (circa 1848) was once a stagecoach stop in the days before motorized travel. There is a small stone monument out front featuring a bear sculpture. Just a little further west is the **Magic Lamp Inn**. The neon sign out front, which is shaped like Aladdin's lamp, actually spouts a gas flame when the neon is illuminated each evening.

UPLAND

In Upland is the twelfth and final **Madonna of the Trail** monument, signifying the end of the National Old Trails Highway at Euclid. South of Upland, in **Chino**, is the **Planes of Fame Air Museum**, featuring WWII aircraft and memorabilia (7000 Merrill).

One of a series of monuments marking
the old National Trails Highway. Upland,
California. (See sidebar on page 276.)

CLAREMONT

This city is home to the Claremont Colleges, a collection of seven
colleges in a park-like setting. Also here are the Rancho Santa Ana
Botanic Gardens.

The old Claremont High School building has been converted into a small retail and office center called the Old School House,
and is right on Foothill Blvd. (old 66). There is some decorative
tiling around the main entrance in the Art Nouveau style. The PFF
Bank & Trust (at the corner of Indian Hill) sports a decorative mural
facing Route 66.

Left: Detail from the old high school. Right: Trailer park. Claremont, California.

LAVERNE-GLENDORA

Right about where LaVerne becomes Glendora is the Pinnacle Peak Steak House. There is a **covered wagon** out front to attract your attention. Sally Rand, whom we first met way back in Chicago, died here in Glendora in 1979.

Glendora has two Route 66 corridors. The later alignment (formerly Alosta but renamed "Route 66") is the better known of the two. To explore the earlier alignment, turn right at Amelia, which will then take you left onto old Foothill. Along this older route are lots of classic bungalows for the inner architect in you to enjoy.

Glendora, California.

SAN DIMAS

San Dimas, though not well-known as a Route 66 town, is the setting for the cult film classic *Bill & Ted's Excellent Adventure*, with comedian George Carlin in a key supporting role.

Sign for Roady's Café, downtown San Dimas, California.

The real San Dimas is a former citrus-growing region which today is quite equestrian-oriented, with a large equestrian center visible from the highway (note the yellow "horse crossing" warning signs marking the road). There is also a very nice old downtown that is worth visiting, with late-nineteenth-century commercial buildings and plank sidewalks. To find downtown, leave 66 at San Dimas Avenue and turn south several blocks to Bonita Avenue. There is also a small 1930s-era Santa Fe depot in the downtown area which now houses the local historical society. Out in front of the depot is a water fountain and trough built to serve "both man and beast."

This historic home started life as a hotel. San Dimas, California.

On San Dimas Avenue just north of Bonita is a very large residence with a sign out front identifying it as the **Walker House**. According to the San Dimas Historical Society, it is the last standing railroad hotel in California, and was later used as a residence by Mr. J. W. Walker, a prominent local citizen.

AZUSA

Azusa calls itself "Canyon City." How the name Azusa came about is a source of some debate. One explanation I've read (which I assume to be tongue-in-cheek) is that it came from a local general store which was said to provide "everything from A to Z in the USA." The **Azusa Foothill Drive-In** was still operating when I drove through here for the first time. Since then, however, the near-by Azusa Pacific University bought the property and gained permission to demolish the theater.

Azusa's business district is just north of Foothill on Azusa Avenue. Just north of the business district is a residential area lined with extremely tall, slender palm trees that remind me of the

Azusa, California.

introductory footage from the
Beverly Hillbillies television series.
See if you agree.

DUARTE-MONROVIA

The **Aztec Hotel**, at 311 N.
Foothill in Monrovia, was built in
1926—coinciding with the inaugu-
ration of the highway—and is on
the National Register. Take a stroll
into the Brass Elephant bar area
just off the lobby and look upward.
There is a wide-ranging system of
ceiling fans all run by one central
motor and driven by an array of
fan belts reaching hither and thither and yon. Restoration work has
begun on the hotel, so this place is
destined to become a real treat.

Duarte, California.

ARCADIA

In Arcadia, the **Santa Anita Racetrack** is widely regarded as an
architectural treasure, exhibiting design elements of Art Deco,
Spanish Revival, American Colonial, and New Orleans styles. It was
designed by Gordon Kaufmann, the same architect who designed
the massive Hoover Dam on the Colorado River. Out front is a
bronze statue of racehorse Seabiscuit, whose most famous comeback
race occurred here at this track. Santa Anita was also the setting for
the Marx Brothers' film classic, *A Day at the Races*. During WWII, it
was used as a detention center for Japanese-Americans, including

Disused doorway, Duarte, California.

George Takei of *Star Trek* fame.

Also in Arcadia is a **Denny's** restaurant which has a Dutch-style windmill dominating its roofline.

Enter Pasadena on Colorado Boulevard. From this point onward, following Route 66 becomes difficult for a number of reasons. First, there is the fact that traffic picks up exponentially because Route 66 early on was "improved" in this area so that it became more of the type of highway we are accustomed to today. Secondly, Route 66 was re-routed many, many times over the years, and so there are several true paths for you to choose from. I recommend lots of exploration here in Southern California, and lots of patience, too. As a byproduct of all this complexity, one of our road warrior brethren, Scott Piotrowski, has assembled a detailed guide to help clear up the confusion (see bibliography). One of the many paths you can follow from here to the coast is Colorado-Figueroa-Arroyo Seco Parkway-Sunset-Santa Monica Boulevard.

PASADENA

As early as 1890, "games" were held here in Pasadena which included foot races, tugs of war, and burro races. There were even what might be called "floats" in those early days. Later, these festivities became known as the Tournament of Roses, and in 1902 a football game was added to the program. The rest, as they say, is history.

The city of Pasadena is architecturally blessed, particularly for those of us with a weakness for Mission or Arts and Crafts style. The

Pasadena, California.

most outstanding example is the **Gamble House**, designed by Charles and Henry Greene and situated at 4 Westmoreland Place. For a tour of some fine architecture, drive along Oak Knoll and San Rafael and into the hills near the Rose Bowl. The **Colorado Boulevard Bridge**, which crosses the Arroyo Seco River, was built circa 1912.

In 1939, Pasadena managed to capture first place in Columbia University's Quality of Life Competition. In 1924, at Pasadena's Rite Spot Restaurant, grill chef Lionel Sternberger concocted the **world's first cheeseburger**, which at the time he dubbed the cheese hamburger.

One of the earliest transcontinental auto trips originated from Pasadena way back in 1908. Jacob Murdoch loaded his son, two daughters, and 1,200 pounds of supplies into his Packard for a 25-day expedition from Pasadena to New York City. Packard later published a publicity booklet about the adventure entitled *A Family Tour From Ocean to Ocean*.

PASADENA ATTRACTIONS

The **Tournament House**, at 391 S. Orange Grove Blvd., is a sort of museum of Rose Bowl memorabilia in a former home of millionaire William Wrigley, Jr. It also serves as the headquarters for the annual parade festivities.

The **Pasadena Historical Museum** is housed in the Feynes Mansion, constructed in 1905 in the Beaux-Arts style. Its rooms are furnished in authentic period pieces. Also on the grounds is the **Finnish Folk Art Museum**, with exhibits including handmade furniture, utensils, and sundry decorative arts.

Candace Frazee and Steve Lubanski invite you to tour their home, otherwise known as the **Bunny Museum**, at 1933 Jefferson Drive. These folks are crazy for bunnies; their collection (over 10,000 strong) includes celebrity bunnies such as Bugs Bunny, Peter Rabbit, Thumper, and the Trix Rabbit, along with more obscure cousins from the hare family. It all started years ago when Steve made Candace a present of a small plush rabbit. A tradition was started, and now they exchange bunny presents almost daily. Come tour the fruits of an obsession.

Pasadena hosts the **Absolut Chalk Street-Painting Festival** each year in June. Contestants used to descend on the town's Centennial Square to paint their little corner of town with chalk art, but the event has recently been held at Paseo Colorado mall while City Hall plaza is being remodeled. Prizes are awarded, and large crowds turn out to view the artwork.

FURTHER AFIELD

In nearby **Altadena** is the **International Banana Club and Museum**, at 2524 El Molino Ave. There are more than 17,000 banana-related items in the museum at last count.

LOS ANGELES

Entire books have been written about Los Angeles, and that's not what this book is about. Lots of major cities around the world consider themselves the center of the known universe, but L.A. probably more so than most. Say what you will about L.A., it is indeed true that western culture pushes its envelope here, takes chances here, and subsequently affects the rest of the modern world.

Depending on the air quality on the day of your visit, you can catch some excellent views of the city from the observation deck of Los Angeles City Hall. The city hall, built in 1928, might be familiar to you due to its countless appearances on television's *Dragnet*.

LOS ANGELES ATTRACTIONS

Los Angeles's **Union Station**, at 800 N. Alameda (at Cesar Chavez), is a combination of Art Deco, Streamline Moderne, and Spanish Revival styles which was completed in 1939. A 125-foot-tall clock tower is incorporated into the design. The interior appointments include mahogany and black marble.

The **Bradbury Building** is also on the National Register, and is located at 304 S. Broadway. Its modest-looking exterior masks an expansive inner Victorian-style courtyard featuring marble stairs, open-cage elevators, and copious amounts of ornamental metalwork. The Bradbury is the oldest commercial building remaining in Los Angeles's central business district.

Located in Wells Fargo Center, at 333 S. Grand, is the **Wells Fargo History Museum**. This museum recounts western history in general, and the development of the Wells Fargo Company in particular. Visitors can climb aboard an authentic stagecoach and hear a firsthand account of the journey west from St. Louis, Missouri, which took three weeks.

The **Museum of Neon Art** (MONA) is at 501 W. Olympic Blvd. in downtown Los Angeles. Both modern and vintage neon art is featured here. On permanent display is an animated sign which once stood in front of the Steele's Motel in Van Nuys. You can sign up for an eight-week neon art workshop at MONA, which also sponsors the highly regarded Neon Bus Cruises of Los Angeles.

Watts Towers is one of only nine works of "folk art" listed on the National Register of Historic Places. They were built by an Italian immigrant, Simon Rodia, over the course of more than 30 years, using steel, wire mesh, mortar, and embedded pieces of tile and glass. The towers are located at 1765 East 107th St.

The **African American Firefighter Museum** is housed in old Fire Station No. 30, parts of which were constructed in 1913. Number 30 served as one of two segregated fire stations in Los Angeles between 1924 and 1955. (Note that it was during this same 30-year period that the Watts Towers were constructed.) The museum is at 1401 S. Central Ave.

The **Autry Museum of the American West** pays homage to the Old West, both the historical, as in gold rush days, and the romantic, as in Hollywood's notions of the era. There are about 45,000 square feet of paintings, sculptures, prints, and artifacts to explore. At 4700 Western Heritage Way, Griffith Park, across from the Los Angeles Zoo. A stone's throw away is the **Autry Southwest Museum of the American Indian**, at 234 Museum Drive.

Forest Lawn Cemetery, at 6300 Forest Lawn Drive, has such stars as Buster Keaton, Stan Laurel, and George "Gabby" Hayes among its tenants. Forest Lawn is even evolving into a kind of odd theme park, with such attractions as "The Birth of Liberty"—the world's largest historical mosaic—and a reproduction of Boston's Old North Church.

Scheduled to reopen in 2006 following extensive renovations is the **Griffith Observatory**. You'll recognize the Observatory from its starring role in the film *Rebel Without a Cause*.

At 2800 E. Observatory Rd., on the slope of Mount Hollywood, in Griffith Park.

At 5801 Wilshire in Hancock Park is the world-famous **La Brea Tar Pits**. About 10,000 to 40,000 years ago, during the last Ice Age, extinct creatures such as saber-toothed tigers and mammoths roamed the Los Angeles area. There is a museum containing many of the fossils found in the vicinity, as well as a viewing area where you can see fresh excavations taking place.

The **Petersen Automotive Museum** is at 6060 Wilshire Blvd. (at Fairfax). Herbie the Love Bug lives here. The museum also features an ever-changing program of exhibits. A recent look at their website revealed an exhibition dedicated to car-decorating, including those festooned with such things as buttons, post cards, cameras, and mirrors. Over 300,000 square feet of exhibit space means there's something of interest for everyone.

The **Franklin D. Murphy Sculpture Garden**, on the campus of UCLA, covers about five acres with sculptures from such notables as Matisse and Rodin.

Near the UCLA campus is the very tony community of **Bel Air**. Several stars still live here, but one of the most interesting sites to most people is the mansion used in the *Beverly Hillbillies* television series, at 750 Bel Air Road.

FURTHER AFIELD

In **Glendale** is yet another **Forest Lawn Cemetery**. You can pick up a guide to the more notable gravesites at the office. These include Humphrey Bogart, Walt Disney, and W. C. Fields. There is also a marriage chapel called Wee Kirk o' th' Heather, where Ronald Reagan and Jane Wyman were wed in 1940. 1712 S. Glendale Ave.

Nearby **Anaheim** is home to the original **Disneyland**, which opened its gates on July 17, 1955. An employee who was there on opening day says it was a near disaster—someone had counterfeited tickets, so there were around three times the visitors in the park as there were tickets sold. Not only that, but the day was warm, and the new asphalt still soft, so ladies' heels were continually getting stuck in it.

Right next to Anaheim is **Buena Park**. This is the home of the world-famous **Knott's Berry Farm**. Knott's has the tallest and longest roller coaster west of the Mississippi, the Ghost Rider, and also the world's tallest water ride at its 113-acre water park, called Soak City, USA. Knott's Berry Farm had the country's first log flume ride way back in 1969.

Buena Park also has the **Ripley's Believe It or Not** at 7850 Beach Blvd.

In **Garden Grove** is Robert Schuller's famous **Crystal Cathedral**. Dr. Schuller is well-known for having come to Southern California in the 1950s, and soon thereafter conducting Sunday services from the roof of the snack bar at the local Orange Drive-In Theater.

The city of **Gardena** is the home of the **Ascot Speedway**. The Ascot was the starting point for the Great Transcontinental Footrace, also known as the Bunion Derby, on March 4, 1928. This was the promotional footrace from Los Angeles to New York City which was won by Andy Payne of Foyil, Oklahoma. Automobile races were being held at this track as early as the 1910s.

Long Beach is where the **Queen Mary** is berthed. The Queen Mary was one of the largest passenger liners ever built, and is now restored as a first-class hotel. Featured in over 200 films, the Queen Mary nowadays hosts the Annual New Year's Eve Shipwalk Party celebrations.

Also in Long Beach is the **Toyota Grand Prix**, held every April on city streets.

Nearby **Huntington Beach** is known as Surf City, USA, which makes it the natural home for the **International Surfing Museum**, at 411 Olive Avenue. Huntington Beach also features a

Surfing Walk of Fame, and is on the Pacific Coast Highway.

Catalina Island is a retreat that Angelenos have long treasured. Catch the ferry from either San Pedro, Long Beach, or Marina Del Rey and spend the day here. There are glass-bottomed boats to ride, and a herd of 400 buffalo roam the island. There is also a mansion on Catalina which was built by the Wrigley Gum fortune; author Zane Grey used to make his home here, too. What is now the Avalon Ballroom was originally a gambling casino built by Mr. Wrigley shortly after he first acquired the island way back in 1911.

HOLLYWOOD

Now a district of Los Angeles, Hollywood was plotted as an independent town as early as 1887. The name may have come from the native toyon trees (California Holly) which cover the local hillsides and bear bright red berries in the wintertime.

For decades now, the name "Hollywood" has been near-synonymous with the movie and television industries. Many a twentieth-century traveler with Southern California as his or her destination has made the trip with this in mind. Even today, Hollywood has a sizable entertainment presence, and the related tourism flourishes.

HOLLYWOOD ATTRACTIONS

Notable sites in Hollywood are extremely numerous. Most tourists make a pilgrimage to the Mecca of tinseltown, **Grauman's** (or Mann's) **Chinese Theater**. This is where they began collecting footprints (and later, other imprints) of Hollywood celebrities in the concrete out front. That tradition started in 1927 with Norma Talmadge, who was soon followed by Douglas Fairbanks and Mary Pickford. At 6925 Hollywood Blvd. Just across the street from Mann's is the **El Capitan Theater**, where the premiere of *Citizen*

Kane was held in 1941.

Over 2,500 bronze-inlaid stars stud the sidewalks in the **Hollywood Walk of Fame**, which runs along Hollywood Boulevard between Gower and Sycamore, and on Vine between Sunset and Yucca.

The **Hollywood Bowl** and the **Hollywood Bowl Museum** are at 2301 N. Highland Ave. The museum features exhibits on the many famous acts who have played here. Some of those include The Beatles, Elton John, Jimi Hendrix, and The Doors. The Bowl is the current home of the Los Angeles Philharmonic.

The **Hollywood Studio Museum** is across from the Bowl, at 2100 N. Highland, and is housed in the 1895 Lasky-DeMille Barn— the birthplace of Paramount Pictures, where Cecil B. DeMille filmed *The Squaw Man* way back in 1913. It features memorabilia from movies of all stripes.

The **Hollywood Entertainment Museum** specializes in television, and even includes some TV series sets, including those of *Cheers* and *Star Trek*. Also included is a studio backlot tour. 7021 Hollywood Blvd.

The **Hollywood History Museum** is housed in what was formerly the Max Factor Museum, and the original Max Factor salon. 1600 Highland Ave.

Frederick's of Hollywood, at 6608 Hollywood Blvd., includes a lingerie museum which features the undergarments of celebrities as diverse as Isabel Sanford (Weezy Jefferson), Madonna, and Milton Berle. The building is a former S. H. Kress five-and-dime store constructed in 1934.

Packed into the 6700 block of Hollywood Boulevard are the **Ripley's Believe It Or Not Museum**, the **Guinness World of Records**, and the **Hollywood Wax Museum**.

The **Hollywood Palladium** has seen just about everything. Opened in 1940, this music venue featured such acts as Frank Sinatra. In the 1960s, it hosted the Grateful Dead, Rolling Stones, and The Who, even though the owner at that time was none other than Lawrence Welk, who broadcast his show from here for a time. The *Blues Brothers* concert sequences were filmed here, too. 6215 Sunset Blvd.

The **Capitol Records** tower was constructed in 1954 based on a concept hatched by Nat King Cole and Johnny Mercer: it is designed to resemble a stack of records on a spindle (remember 45s?). There is a pulsing light atop the tower which is rumored to spell out HOLLYWOOD in Morse code. The lobby contains a huge array of gold records recorded by artists represented on the Capitol label. 1750 Vine Street.

Don't forget the famous **Hollywood Sign** on the hillside. It used to say "Hollywoodland" at one time, which was the name of a housing development. The letters are about 50 feet tall, and are as iconic to Southern California as the Eiffel Tower is to Paris. A caretaker used to live behind one of the L's in the old days. To get a close-up view of the sign, use Mulholland Drive. At 6342 Mulholland is a place known as Castillo de Lago, once a gambling den run by the infamous Bugsy Siegel.

Universal Studios offers movie-making tours. Next door to Universal Studios is the **Universal City Walk**, a sort of faux pedestrian community which has actually received high praise from some architectural critics. Parking costs six dollars at last count, but you can easily spend a day here, and it's a safe, family appropriate, and pedestrian-friendly area. Other movie studios in Hollywood/West Hollywood include Fox, Paramount, and Warner Brothers.

At 1822 Camino Palmero Drive in Hollywood is a house you may recognize from somewhere. This was the home of **Ozzie and Harriet Nelson**, both on and off the screen.

The **Sunset Strip** is a section of Sunset Boulevard known for its clubs, boutiques, and overall edginess. The Virgin Megastore occupies the same site as the old **Schwab's Drug Store**, which closed in 1986. It was at Schwab's that F. Scott Fitzgerald suffered a heart attack in 1940 while buying a pack of cigarettes. And it was there that songwriter Harold Arlin wrote "Over the Rainbow" by the light of Schwab's neon sign. You might also have heard that Lana Turner was "discovered" at Schwab's, but that romantic tale has since been discredited. The television series *77 Sunset Strip*, filmed from 1958 to 1964, featured shots of Dino's Lodge, which used to be at 8524 Sunset. There is now an office building at the location, but there is a plaque confirming the pop-culture significance of the site. The Sunset Strip runs from Crescent Heights Blvd. on the east to Doheny Drive on the west.

The **Whiskey**, at 8901 Sunset Blvd., has seen its share of rock-and-roll history. The Doors played here regularly on their way to stardom, and soon after this club began putting dancers in cages, the go-go girl craze of the sixties began.

Sadly, the **Dudley Do-Right Emporium**—located at 8200 W. Sunset Blvd. and housed in the former offices of Jay Ward Productions, creators of Rocky, Bullwinkle, and the rest of the gang—is now closed. The beloved giant statue of Rocky and Bullwinkle, however, remains on the site.

At **Henson Studios**, the front gates include a 12-foot statue of Kermit the Frog dressed as Charlie Chaplin's *Little Tramp*.

Barney's Beanery is at 8447 Santa Monica Blvd. in West Hollywood. Since 1920, this chili shack has been serving an eclectic blend of foods to an eclectic clientele, where international tourists and local pool sharks come together in rainbow-colored booths under a ceiling of mirrors. The menu is 12 pages long at last count, so if you can't find it here, maybe you shouldn't have it after all. Once a hangout for Jim Morrison, Barney's is reportedly where Janis Joplin did some partying the night she died.

At 7047 Franklin Ave. is the **Highland Gardens Hotel**. In October 1970, Janis Joplin died in Room 105 of a heroin overdose at what was then the Landmark Hotel.

In the Hollywood Hills is a street named **Blue Jay Way**.

You may have trouble finding it, because the signs keep getting stolen. This is the avenue made famous in George Harrison's song of the same name that began: "There's a fog upon L.A. . . . ." George wrote the song after renting a home here in 1968.

Hollywood Memorial Park, at 6000 Santa Monica Blvd., is one of the most famous "cemeteries of the stars." Hundreds of movie legends are interred here, such as Douglas Fairbanks, Sr., and Rudolph Valentino. There is also the grave of one Carl Morgan Bigsby, whose marker is a replica Atlas missile. Mel Blanc's simple granite headstone states flatly: "That's all, folks."

BEVERLY HILLS

Formerly called Morocco Junction, Beverly Hills is synonymous with movie stars and other rich-and-famous types. You can buy a "Map of the Stars' Homes" here, but you're more likely to spot a gardener than you are a celebrity using that strategy. If you're serious about star-spotting, buy a daily update as to where location filming is taking place in the area.

BEVERLY HILLS ATTRACTIONS

Trader Vic's is located at Wilshire and Santa Monica Blvd. at the Beverly Hilton.

Legend tells us that it was here in Beverly Hills, at the **Lawry's Prime Rib Restaurant,** that toppings were first added to a baked potato in 1938. 100 N. La Cienega Blvd.

At 810 Linden Drive is where gangster **Bugsy Siegel**, of Las Vegas fame, was gunned down at the home of his girlfriend, Virginia Hill, in 1947.

In 1969, 10050 Cielo Drive was the scene of the **Sharon Tate** murders. The killers then followed that grisly crime with the murders of the LaBiancas at 3301 Waverly in Los Angeles. Charles Manson is still behind bars for those horrors, having been refused parole several times over the years.

Don't fail to stop and see the famous **Spaden House** (or Witch's House) at the corner of Carmelita and Walden, just north of Wilshire. The house was built in 1921 as the administration building for Willat Studios in Culver City, and it subsequently appeared in several silent movies. In 1926, it was moved to this residential neighborhood. The house is designed with exaggerated features, such as crooked shutters, an extremely steep-pitched roof, and a small moat with bridge—as though it came straight out of a Brothers Grimm fairy tale. The house is a private residence, so you'll have to content yourself with viewing the exterior from the public street.

Just off the route near Beverly Hills and Bel Air is the **Westwood Village Mortuary**, at 1218 Glendon Avenue. The celebrity list here includes Marilyn Monroe, Daryl F. Zanuck, Natalie Wood, Frank Zappa, and Roy Orbison.

In Studio City's residential district, just north of Beverly Hills in the San Fernando Valley, is the house used in the *Brady Bunch* television series, at 11222 Dilling Street.

SANTA MONICA

As you cross Centinela Blvd. on Route 66 (Santa Monica Blvd.), you enter the city of Santa Monica. Santa Monica Boulevard—and your run to the coast—abruptly ends at Ocean Avenue. Across Ocean Ave. is Pacific Palisades Park, where you should stroll around and relax at the end of your journey. There is a small monument in the park, dedicated to Will Rogers, which reads in part: "Highway 66 was the first road he traveled in a career that led him straight to the hearts of his countrymen."

Popularly considered the symbolic end of Route 66, but technically blocks away, is the **Santa Monica Pier**, originally constructed in 1908. This may well be because the pier, with its large neon sign, is more photogenic than the true terminus on the nearby street corner. Today, the pier includes a nine-story ferris wheel, a five-story roller coaster, other rides, and midway-style games. Also here is the venerable Looff Hippodrome, named for carousel builder Charles Looff. The building has, since 1916, housed a hand-carved carousel. The one there currently is a 1922 model which was brought here in 1946. The carousel was featured prominently in the 1973 movie *The Sting*, starring Robert Redford and Paul Newman, and was refurbished in 1981. The pier, much like **Venice Beach** to the south, is always awash with colorful local characters.

On Adelaide Avenue, overlooking **Santa Monica Canyon**, lived the composer Ferde Grofé. It was here that he composed his most famous work, the *Grand Canyon Suite*. The piece was originally titled *Santa Monica Canyon Suite*, but, fearing a lack of recognition, Grofé renamed it after the far more famous landmark. Grofé is also the man who wrote the world-famous orchestral arrangement of Gershwin's *Rhapsody in Blue*. Gershwin had written the piece not for symphony, but for a small band, with blank spaces left in it for Gershwin's own piano improvisations. Grofé was at that time the chief arranger for the Paul Whiteman jazz ensemble, for whom the piece was originally written. Whiteman's famous band was also where a crooner named Bing Crosby spent his salad days as one of the "Rhythm Boys."

SANTA MONICA ATTRACTIONS

The **Museum of Flying** features more than 30 vintage aircraft, some of which are in flight-worthy condition, all maintained on the site where Mr. Donald Douglas built the very first DC-3. 2772 Donald Douglas Loop.

Bergamot Station is a collection of over 20 galleries housed in renovated warehouse spaces on approximately six acres in Santa Monica. Media include photography, paintings, sculpture, and more. 2525 Michigan Avenue.

The building at 1855 Main Street may look vaguely familiar. The **Santa Monica Civic Auditorium** was the regular site of the Academy Awards from 1961–68.

The **Galley** restaurant, at 2442 Main, was opened in 1934 and was popular with the likes of Errol Flynn. The restaurant features memorabilia from the 1935 film classic *Mutiny on the Bounty*.

Shirley Temple was Santa Monica-born, and once lived in a house at 924 Twenty-Fourth Street.

At the Miramar Sheraton Hotel stands an 80-foot-tall, 100-year-old **Moreton Bay** fig tree.

On Second Ave. between Broadway and Santa Monica Blvd. is the former **city hall**, which was constructed in 1873. This is the oldest building of masonry construction in the city, and was designated a historical landmark in 1975.

FURTHER AFIELD

Just to the northwest of Santa Monica is the **Santa Monica Mountains National Recreation Area**, bounded by the Pacific Ocean on the south and by U.S. 101 on the north. Included within this preserve is the **Will Rogers State Historic Park**, which includes the home in which Rogers lived from 1928 until his death seven years later. There is also a visitors' center, nature center, corral, stable, polo field, and hiking trails on the grounds. Adventurous hikers and bikers can take the Backbone Trail into the Santa Monica Mountains. The trail goes all the way to Point Mugu, some 70 miles away.

South of Santa Monica is **Venice Beach**, including the famous Muscle Beach. This area is prime habitat for surfers, down-and-outers, muscle builders, skateboarders, and an abundance of other species. Venice was the brainchild of one Abbot Kinney, who envisioned cloning Venice, Italy, right here in Southern California. Canals were dug throughout the area in 1904–05, and two dozen black, silver-prowed gondolas were imported from Italy to ply the waters here. A tourist in 1906 observed: "The architecture was the grandest, an intricate blend of Italian columns, porticoes, and balustrades, only slightly marred by the presence of guess-your-weight machines." At some point, the Board of Health declared the canals a health hazard and ordered many of them filled in. Today, there are a few canals remaining, all cleaned up and lined with million dollar-plus homes. You can also still see many columns with rather ornate capitals scattered in town, the venerable Venice Beach Hotel being an example. In the 1950s, Venice had deteriorated to the point that Orson Welles used the area as the backdrop for the film, *A Touch of Evil*.

 If you've now successfully completed a journey of the entire length of Route 66, then you've hope-fully just had an experience that— whether you realize it right away or not—will change your life.

Though technically a short distance away from the end of Route 66, this recreational pier nevertheless serves as the highway's western landmark. Santa Monica, California.

TRAVELERS' SERVICES

F ollowing is a listing of information which may be useful to you, the Route 66 traveler. Contact information is provided for state tourism departments, chambers of commerce, local visitors' bureaus, and other agencies which might assist you in gaining maximum enjoyment of your Route 66 Adventure.

These contacts are listed in roughly the order in which you encounter their home cities in an east-to-west tour of the route. One of the advantages of listing in this way is that if you do not find a contact for the exact town in which you are interested, the same information may be available from the next nearest city of large enough size to have a visitors' information center.

You may want to consult this listing:
- when seeking detailed information and directions to difficult-to-locate sites;
- to call ahead to check and see whether an annual event's dates may have been changed;
- to inquire as to the availability of lodging, etc.;
- to determine operating schedules, fees, etc. for local attractions which interest you.

ILLINOIS

- Chicago's Official Visitor Information Centers are at 163 E. Pearson St. (Water Works) and at 77 E. Randolph (at the Cultural Center); 877-710-0294.
- Chicago Office of Tourism—78 E. Washington St., Chicago, IL 60602; 312-744-2400.
- Chicago Chinatown Chamber of Commerce—2169B S. China Pl., Chicago, IL 60616; 312-326-5320.

- Chicago Lodging—there are several commercial services in Chicago which operate as clearinghouses for hotel/motel accommodations; among them is Accommodations Express, at 800-605-ROOM (800-605-7666).
- Heritage Corridor Convention & Visitors' Bureau—81 N. Chicago St., Joliet, IL 60432; 815-727-2323 or 800-926-2262.
- Bloomington–Normal Area Convention & Visitors' Bureau—210 S. East St., Bloomington, IL 61701; 800-433-8226.
- A. Lincoln Tourism Bureau of Logan County—303 S. Kickapoo, Lincoln, IL 62656; 217-732-8687.
- Central Illinois Tourism & Development Office—700 E. Adams St. (in the Springfield Hilton Hotel), Springfield, IL 62701; 217-525-7980.
- Springfield Convention & Visitors' Bureau—109 N. 7th St., Springfield, IL 62701; 800-545-7300.
- Route 66 Association of Illinois—2743 Veterans Parkway #166, Springfield, IL 61704; 708-392-0860.
- Decatur Convention & Visitors' Bureau—202 E. North St., Decatur, IL 62523-1129; 217-423-7000.
- Collinsville Convention & Visitors' Bureau—One Gateway Drive, Collinsville, IL 62234; 618-345-4999 or 800-289-2388.
- Tourism Bureau of Southwestern Illinois—10950 Lincoln Trail, Fairview Heights, IL 62208; 618-397-1488 or 800-442-1488.

MISSOURI

- Missouri Tourist Info at 800-877-1234.
- St. Louis Visitor Center, Inc.—308 Washington Ave, St. Louis, MO 63102; 314-241-1764.
- St. Louis Convention & Visitors' Bureau—1 Metropolitan Square, Saint Louis, MO 63102-2733; 314-421-1023 or 800-916-0092.
- Greater Saint Charles Convention & Visitors' Bureau—230 S. Main St., Saint Charles, MO 63301; 800-366-2427.

- Eureka Tourism Commission—100 City Hall Dr., P.O. Box 125, Eureka, MO 63025; 636-938-5233.

- Rolla Chamber of Commerce & Visitor Center—1301 Kings Highway, P.O. Box 823, Rolla, MO 65402; 573-364-3577 or 888-809-3817.

- Lebanon Convention & Visitors Association—500 E. Elm St., Lebanon, MO 65536; 417-532-4642.

- Missouri Route 66 Association—1602 East Dale St., Springfield, MO 65803; 417-865-1318.

- Springfield Chamber of Commerce—202 S. John Q. Hammons Parkway, P.O. Box 1687, Springfield, MO 65801-1687; 417-862-5567.

- Carthage Convention & Visitors' Bureau—402 S. Garrison, Carthage, MO 64836; 417-359-8181 or 866-357-8687.

- Joplin Convention & Visitors' Bureau—222 W. Third, Joplin, MO 64801; 417-625-4789.

- Joplin, Missouri Area Chamber of Commerce—320 E. 4th St., P.O. Box 1178, Joplin, MO 64802; 417-624-4150.

KANSAS

- Kansas Tourist Info at 800-252-6727.

- Kansas Department of Travel & Tourism at 785-296-2009.

- Kansas Department of Wildlife & Parks 785-296-2281.

- Kansas State Historical Society at 785-272-8681.

- Kansas road and weather conditions at 800-585-ROAD.

- Kansas Route 66 Association—P.O. Box 66, Riverton, KS 66770; 316-848-3330.

- Coffeyville Area Chamber of Commerce—807 Walnut, Coffeyville, KS 67337; 316-251-1194 or 800-626-3357.

OKLAHOMA

- Oklahoma Tourist Info at 800-652-6552.

- Miami Convention & Visitors' Bureau—111 N. Main St., P.O. Box 760, Miami, OK 74355; 981-542-4435.

- Claremore Convention & Visitors' Bureau—419 W. Will Rogers, Claremore, OK 74017; 918-341-8688 or 877-341-8688.

- Tulsa Convention & Visitors' Bureau—2 W. Second St., Tulsa, OK 74119-1298; 918-585-1201 or 800-558-3311.

- Bartlesville Tourism Information—800-364-8708.

- Sapulpa Chamber of Commerce—101 E. Dewey, Sapulpa, OK 74066; 918-224-0170.

- Bristow Chamber of Commerce—1 Railroad Place, P.O. Box 127, Bristow, OK 74010; 918-367-5151.

- Stroud Chamber of Commerce—216 W. Main Street, Stroud, OK 74079; 918-968-3321.

- Oklahoma Route 66 Association—1023 Manvel, Suite A, P.O. Box 446, Chandler, OK 74834; 405-258-0008.

- Guthrie Convention & Visitors' Bureau—212 W. Oklahoma Ave, Guthrie, OK 73044; 405-282-1947 or 800-299-1889.

- Edmond Convention & Visitors' Bureau—1030 S. Bryant, P.O. Box 2970, Edmond, OK 73083; 405-341-4344.

- Oklahoma City Convention & Visitors' Bureau—189 W. Sheridan, Oklahoma City, OK 73102; 405-297-8912 or 800-225-5652.

- Clinton Visitor Info at 800-759-1397.

- Clinton Chamber of Commerce—600 Avant, Clinton, OK 73601; 580-323-2222.

- Weatherford Area Chamber of Commerce—P.O. Box 729, Weatherford, OK 73096; 800-725-7744.

- Elk City Chamber of Commerce—P.O. Box 972, Elk City, OK 73648; 800-280-0207.

- Sayre Chamber of Commerce—111 N. 4th, Sayre, OK 74756; 580-928-3386.

- Erick Chamber of Commerce—P.O. Box 1232, Erick, OK 73645; 580-526-3505.

TEXAS

- Texas Tourist Info at 800-452-9292.

- Shamrock Chamber of Commerce—207 N. Main St., Shamrock, TX 79079-2227; 806-256-2224.

- Old Route 66 Association of Texas—P.O. Box 66, McLean, TX 79057; 806-779-2225.

- Amarillo Convention & Visitor Council—on the second floor of the Bivins Mansion, 1000 S. Polk St., Amarillo, TX 79101; 800-692-1338 (U.S. and Canada) or 806-374-1497 (local).

NEW MEXICO

- New Mexico Department of Tourism—800-545-2040.

- Tucumcari/Quay Co. Chamber of Commerce—404 West Route 66 Blvd., P.O. Drawer E, Tucumcari, 88401; 505-461-1694.

- Santa Rosa Visitor Information Center—486 Historic Route 66, Santa Rosa, NM 88435; 505-472-3763.

- Las Vegas/San Miguel Chamber of Commerce—701 Grand Ave, P.O. Box 128, Las Vegas, NM 87701; 505-425-8631 or 800-832-5947.

- Santa Fe Visitor Information—491 Old Santa Fe Trail, Santa Fe, NM 87501; 505-827-7336.

- Santa Fe Convention & Visitors' Bureau—201 W. Marcy St., P.O. Box 909, Santa Fe, NM 87504-0909; 800-777-2489.

- Taos Pueblo Visitor Information—505-758-1028.

- Sandoval Co. Visitor Center—P.O. Box 40, 243 Camino del Pueblo, Bernalillo, NM 87004; 505-867-8687 or 800-252-0191.

- Coronado State Monument—485 Kuaua Rd., Bernalillo, NM 87004; 505-867-5351.

- Jemez Mountain Trail/Jemez Pueblo Information—505-834-7235.

- Turquoise Trail Association – P.O. Box 303, Sandia Park, NM 87407; 505-281-5233 or 888-263-0003.

- Moriarty Chamber of Commerce—P.O. Box 96, Moriarty, NM 87035; 505-832-4087.

- Sandia Crest Area Information—505-243-0605.

- Sandia Peak Tramway—#10 Tramway Loop NE, Albuquerque, NM 87122; 505-856-7325.

- Salinas Pueblo Missions National Monument—P.O. Box 517, Mountainair, NM 87036; 505-847-2585.

- Albuquerque Convention & Visitors' Bureau—20 First Plaza Center NW, Ste. 601, Albuquerque, NM 87102; 505-842-9918 or 800-733-9918.

- New Mexico Route 66 Association—1415 Central Ave. NE, Albuquerque, NM 87106; 505-298-2809.

- Los Lunas Visitors Center—3447 Lambros, Los Lunas, NM 87031; 505-865-1581.

- Northwest New Mexico Visitor Center—1900 E. Santa Fe Ave., Grants, NM; 505-876-2783.

- Grants/Cibola County Chamber of Commerce, P.O. Box 297, Grants, NM 87020; 505-287-4802 or 800-748-2142.

- El Malpais Visitor Center—620 E. Santa Fe Ave., Grants, NM 87020; 505-285-5406.

- Gallup Convention & Visitors' Bureau—103 W. Highway 66, P.O. Box 600, Gallup, NM 87305; 505-863-3841 or 800-242-4282.

- Gallup Cultural Center—201 E. Historic Hwy. 66, (old Santa Fe depot), Gallup, NM 87301; 505-863-4131.

ARIZONA

- Arizona Office of Tourism—888-520-3434.

- Holbrook Chamber of Commerce—100 E. Arizona Street, Holbrook, AZ 86025; 520-524-6558 or 800-524-2459.

- Winslow Chamber of Commerce—P.O. Box 460, 300 W. North Rd., Winslow, AZ 86047; 520-289-2434.

- Flagstaff Visitor Services Center—1 E. Route 66 (in the train station), Flagstaff, AZ 86001; 520-774-9541 or 800-842-7293.

- Flagstaff Convention & Visitors Bureau—323 W. Aspen Ave, Flagstaff, AZ 86001; 520-556-1305.

- Flagstaff Chamber of Commerce—101 W. Route 66, Flagstaff, AZ 86001; 520-774-4505.

- Prescott Tourism Information Center—117 W. Goodwin Street, Prescott, AZ 86303 (SE corner of Montezuma and Goodwin); 520-445-2000 or 800-266-7534.

- Prescott Arizona Chamber of Commerce—101 S. Cortez, P.O. Box 1147, Prescott, AZ 86302-1147; 520-778-2193.

- Jerome Chamber of Commerce—P.O. Box K, Jerome, AZ 86331; 520-634-2900.

- Williams Visitor Information Center—200 W. Railroad Ave., Williams, AZ 86046; 520-635-4707.

- Kingman Chamber of Commerce—333 W. Andy Devine Ave., P.O. Box 1150, Kingman, AZ 86402; 520-753-6106.

- Historic Route 66 Association of Arizona—Powers Visitor Center, 120 W. Andy Devine Ave., P.O. Box 66, Kingman, AZ 86402; 520-753-5001.

- Oatman–Goldroad Chamber of Commerce—P.O. Box 423, Oatman, AZ 86433; 520-768-8070.

CALIFORNIA

- California Tourist Info at 800-862-2543.

- Needles Chamber of Commerce—100 "G" St., P.O. Box 705, Needles, CA 92363; 760-326-2050.

- California Welcome Center, Barstow—2796 Tanger Way, Suite 106, Barstow, CA 92311; 760-253-4782.

- Barstow Tourism Association—706-328-9256.

- Barstow Area Chamber of Commerce & Visitors' Bureau— 409 E. Fredricks Ave., Barstow, CA 92311; 760-256-8617 or 800-4-BARSTOW.

- Victorville, California Chamber of Commerce—14174 Greentree Blvd., P.O. Box 997, Victorville, CA 92392; 760-245-6506.

- California Route 66 Museum—16825 D Street, P.O. Box 2151, Victorville, CA 92393; 760-951-0436.

- San Bernardino Convention & Visitors' Bureau—201 N. E St., Suite 103, San Bernardino, CA 92401; 909-889-3980.

- Big Bear Lake Chamber of Commerce—P.O. Box 2860, Big Bear Lake, CA 92315; 909-866-4607.

- National Historic Route 66 Federation—P.O. Box 1848, Lake Arrowhead, CA 92352-1848; 909-336-6131.

- California Historic Route 66 Association—P.O. Box 1359, Rialto, CA 92377; 909-874-9448.

- Pasadena Convention & Visitors' Bureau—171 S. Los Robles Avenue, Pasadena, CA 91101; 626-805-4604 or 800-307-7977.

- Hollywood Visitors' Information—6541 Hollywood Blvd., Hollywood, CA 90028; 213-461-4213.

- West Hollywood Convention & Visitors' Bureau—310-289-2525 or 800-368-6020.

- Los Angeles Visitors' & Convention Bureau—633 W. 5th St., Los Angeles, CA 90071-2005; 213-624-7300.

- Santa Monica Convention & Visitors' Bureau—203 Santa Monica Place, Santa Monica, CA 90401; 310-393-7593 or 800-544-5319.

BIBLIOGRAPHY &
RECOMMENDED READING

Baker, T. Lindsay. *Ghost Towns of Texas*. Norman, OK: University of Oklahoma Press, 1986.

Barth, Jack. *Roadside Hollywood*. Chicago: Contemporary Books, 1991.

Basten, Fred E. *Santa Monica Bay*. Los Angeles: General Publishing Group, 1997.

Bradfield, Bill, and Clare. *Muleshoe & More*. Houston, TX: Gulf Publishing Co., 1999.

Cantor, George. *Pop Culture Landmarks: A Traveler's Guide*. Detroit: Gale Research, Inc., 1995.

Chicago Tribune Staff. *Chicago Days*. Lincolnwood, IL: Contemporary Books, 1997.

Cleaver, Joanne Y. *Twain, Plains, & Automobile*. Chicago: Chicago Review Press, 1994.

Debo, Angie. *The WPA Guide to 1930s Oklahoma*. Lawrence, KS: University Press of Kansas, 1986. Originally published by the University of Oklahoma Press, 1941, under the title *Oklahoma: A Guide to the Sooner State*.

Foreman, Julie, and Rod Fensom. *Illinois Off the Beaten Path*. Old Saybrook, CT: Globe Pequot Press, 1996.

Fugate, Francis L., and Roberta B. *Roadside History of Oklahoma*. Missoula, MT: Mountain Press Publishing Co., 1991.

Goddard, Connie, and Bruce Boyer. *The Great Chicago Trivia & Fact Book*. Nashville, TN: Cumberland House, 1996.

Howard, Rex. *Texas Guidebook, 4th Edition*. Grand Prairie, TX: The Lo-Ray Co., 1962.

Jenkins, Myra E., and Albert H. Schroeder. *A Brief History of New Mexico*. Albuquerque, NM: University of New Mexico Press, 1974.

Jensen, Jamie. *Road Trip USA*. Chica, CA: Moon Publications, Inc., 1996.

Kelso, John. *Texas Curiosities*. Guilford, CT: Globe Pequot Press, 2000.

Mangum, Richard, and Sherry. *Route 66 Across Arizona*. Flagstaff, AZ: Hexagon Press, 2001.

McClanahan, Jerry. *EZ 66 Guide for Travelers*. Lake Arrowhead, CA: National Historic Route 66 Federation, 2005.

Miller, Arthur P., and Marjorie L. *Trails Across America*. Golden, CO: Fulcrum Publishing, 1996.

Moore, Bob, et al. *Route 66: A Guidebook*. Del Mar, CA: USDC, Inc., 1994.

N.Y. Public Library. *Book of Popular Americana*. New York: MacMillan, 1994.

Piotrowski, Scott. *Finding the End of the Mother Road: Route 66 in Los Angeles County*. Pasadena, CA: 66 Productions, 2005 (Revised Second Printing).

Rittenhouse, Jack. *A Guide Book to Highway 66*. Albuquerque, NM: University of New Mexico Press, 1998. Facsimile of the 1946 First Edition.

Rubin, Saul. *Offbeat Museums*. Santa Monica, CA: Santa Monica Press, 1997.

Schneider, Jill. *Route 66 Across New Mexico: A Wanderer's Guide*. Albuquerque, NM: University of New Mexico Press, 1991.

Scott, David L., and Kay W. *Guide to the National Park Areas—Western States*. Old Saybrook, CT: Globe Pequot Press, 1999.

Scott, Quinta, and Susan Croce Kelly. *Route 66*. Norman, OK: University of Oklahoma Press, 1988.

Sharpe, Patricia, and Robert S. Weddle. *Texas* (Texas Monthly Guidebook). Austin, TX: The Texas Monthly Press, 1982.

Simmons, Marc, and Joan Myers. *Along the Santa Fe Trail*. Albuquerque, NM: University of New Mexico Press, 1986.

Snyder, Tom. *Route 66 Traveler's Guide and Roadside Companion*. New York: St. Martin's Griffin, 2000.

Taylor, Nelson. *America Bizarro*. New York: St. Martin's Griffin, 2000.

Tennyson, Jeffrey. *Hamburger Heaven*. New York: Hyperion, 1993.

Time-Life. *The Patriotic Tide, 1940-50*. Alexandria, VA: Time-Life Books, Inc., 1969.

Wallechinsky, David. *Twentieth Century History with the Boring Parts Left Out*. New York: Little, Brown & Co., 1995.

Wallis, Michael. *Route 66: The Mother Road*. New York: St. Martin's Press, 1990.

Wilkins, Mike, et al. *Roadside America*. New York: Simon & Schuster, 1992.

Witzel, Michael K. *Route 66 Remembered*. Osceola, WI: Motorbooks International, 1996.

Yonover, Neil S. *Crime Scene USA*. New York: Hyperion, 2000.

Young, Don, and Marge. *America's Southwest*. Edison, NJ: Hunter Publishing, 1998.

INDEX